JUST A GEEK

JUST A GEEK

*Unflinchingly honest tales of the
search for life, love, and fulfillment
beyond the Starship Enterprise*

Wil Wheaton

with a foreword by Neil Gaiman

O'REILLY®

BEIJING · CAMBRIDGE · FARNHAM · KÖLN · PARIS · SEBASTOPOL · TAIPEI · TOKYO

Just a Geek
by Wil Wheaton

Copyright © 2004 O'Reilly Media, Inc. All rights reserved.
Printed in the United States of America.

Published by O'Reilly Media, Inc., 1005 Gravenstein Highway North, Sebastopol, CA 95472.

O'Reilly Media books may be purchased for educational, business, or sales promotional use. Online editions are also available for most titles (*safari.oreilly.com*). For more information, contact our corporate/institutional sales department: (800) 998-9938 or *corporate@oreilly.com*.

Editor:	Brett McLaughlin
Production Editor:	Mary Brady
Cover Designer:	Ellie Volckhausen
Interior Designer:	David Futato

Printing History:

June 2004:	First Edition.

ISBN: 0-596-00768-X

[C]

for Anne
◇◇◇

Table of Contents

A C T   I V

Foreword

JUST AN INTRODUCTION

Q: *Who is Wil Wheaton?*

A: Wil Wheaton is an actor. He is also, as you'll realize once you've read this book, a writer. He was famously in *Star Trek: The Next Generation* and the Rob Reiner film *Stand By Me*, and much less famously in Roger Avary's wonderfully peculiar Frankenstein film *Mr. Stitch*.

Q: *Who are you and why are you writing this introduction? Do you know Wil? Were you in* Star Trek *too?*

A: I'm Neil Gaiman. I write stuff, comics—most famously a comic called *Sandman*—and screenplays and books.

And no, I've never met Wil. We were meant to be guests together at a Linux and sci-fi convention called Penguicon in April 2004, but he wound up missing it entirely because he was on call for a part in a movie. He stayed home and waited, and they didn't need him after all. This phenomenon will seem less surprising to you after you've read this book.

As to why I'm writing this foreword, well, Wil asked me (although that doesn't always work, and that isn't why I said yes). The nearest I came to being in *Star Trek* was once writing an episode of *Babylon 5,* which isn't really very near. And even though I pointed out that having an introduction by Patrick Stewart would sell more copies, Wil held firm in his belief that he wanted me to introduce his book. This is because Wil is a geek. If you're a true geek, I'm pretty much as cool as Patrick Stewart.

And I said yes, because...

I completely missed *Star Trek: The Next Generation.* Maybe I wasn't watching much TV when it was on, or maybe I was just looking in the wrong direction, and the names of the actors in *Stand By Me* never made it into my head. So I found out about Wil when I came to live in the U.S., a dozen years ago, and was told that I needed to sign up for GEnie (an online bulletin board) because that was where all the writers I knew hung out and conversed.

So I went to GEnie, and I noticed, in passing, that the *Sandman* discussion there had been started by one WIL WHEATON under, I believe, the alias of "Roq Lobster," but I could be wrong. It was long, long ago after all, back in the days when we knew how much faster a 14,400 modem was than the 300 down, 75 up ones we'd been using a few years earlier, back in the days when Spam was only a noxious pinkish-grey lunch meat, back when you could lose an entire afternoon tinkering with your *config.sys* file in a desperate attempt to make your computer do something the manual was convinced it already did.

Time passed, as it has a habit of doing. In early 2001, I started an online journal, ostensibly because I had a book releasing and I liked the idea of taking people backstage and showing them what happens between an author finishing a book and the book coming out. I'd keep the journal for a few months. That was the plan. Three years later, I'm still keeping it, pretty much daily, and I'm damned if I can tell you why.

I learned about Wil's journal back then, when I started: he began his around the same time, and he made the mistake of mentioning online that he'd always wanted to play Morpheus in a *Sandman* movie. Several dozen people helpfully sent me the link.

I started reading Wil's journal, checking up and checking in every month or so to see what he was doing and how he was doing. Not because he was famous, or semi-famous, or whatever, but because he was interesting, and what he was writing was interesting. The Internet is cruel and harshly Darwinian in that regard. People read what you write if they want to. If you don't interest them, they go away. Wil's life is interesting, and he communicates that well. Also, he's really likeable. He's having too much fun.

Which is, I suppose, why I said yes to writing this introduction. How could I refuse? I've never met him, and I like him. I worry about him—or at least, his career—too, a bit. You can't help it.

This is a book, as you'll discover, about honesty, about the erasure of image. In an era of people blogging as pseudo-celebrities, this is the story of a celebrity blogging as a person. In *Just a Geek*, Wil uses his online journal as a place to begin to tell his story—diaries as performance art. This is his account of himself and of growing up (at least partly) in public.

It's a lot of work, keeping a journal, inviting the world into your head. Sometimes you stay up much too late writing it, and you always reveal more than you planned. That's the way of it. (Although *Just a Geek* is a lot more than a fix-up or a "best-of" wilwheaton.net. The journal entries punctuate it, but the story he tells is bigger than that.)

As you read this you'll learn about life in the shadow of *Star Trek*; you'll learn about being an actor, and the jobs that come and the jobs that don't; you'll cheer and you'll care.

Somebody—probably F. Scott Fitzgerald, and a quick Google would confirm that, but I'm typing this late at night, on a plane home, in a thunderstorm, having spent the day in Hollywood, pitching a movie to a terribly literal studio boss and the first actual Hollywood Yes Man I've ever run into, so you're on your own on this one—said there are no second acts in American Lives. The joy of *Just a Geek* comes as we watch Wil begin by desperately trying to refute this, in transparent denial of the facts; but then, simply by writing and talking, he creates his own second act. And it's not the one he was expecting, or the one he was looking for. Much more interestingly and satisfyingly, it's the one he needed. And the one we need too.

You'll see.

Anyway, as we all discover, sooner or later, you're never *just* a geek.

—Neil Gaiman
Somewhere over America in a Thunderstorm, May 2004

"Not that it matters, but most of this is true."

—William Goldman
Butch Cassidy and the Sundance Kid

A Note to the Reader

MOST OF THE MATERIAL in this book was originally written for my weblog, (the cool kids call it a "blog") an almost daily diary that I publish at my website, wilwheaton.net.

As I went through my archives and pulled out entries to include here, I was strongly tempted to make massive changes to the material. I think I'm a much more competent writer now than I was when I started keeping the blog, and some of the earlier entries make me cringe.

However, I resisted. My evolution as a writer is a big part of this story, and cleaning up the older entries too much would rob you (and me) of some fun.

I *have* made small changes: hyperlinks have been removed, and I've filled in some details that would not be obvious "offline," but the fundamental meaning of each entry is unchanged.

It may help the reader to see the conventions I use in this book when I quote weblog entries:

THE DATE OF THE WEBLOG

The title of the entry

The body of the weblog.

All of the entries are still online at wilwheaton.net, organized by date, if you're the type of person who has to run a mental /usr/ bin/diff on everything you see. Just make sure you pipe the output into a text file. There's a lot of information in there.

This book chronicles a long journey. It has its peaks and valleys, but I promise it has a happy ending.

I hope you enjoy the ride.

—*Namaste.*
Wil Wheaton
Los Angeles, CA
April 14, 2004

INTRODUCTION

"If man is five, then the devil is six. If the devil is six, then god is
seven. This monkey's gone to heaven."

—The Pixies

This Monkey's Gone to Heaven

IN JULY OF 2003, I was invited to Portland, Oregon, by my friend and fellow O'Reilly Author, Randal Schwartz, to attend the release party for his newest book, *Learning Perl Objects, References & Modules.** While I was there, I also attended O'Reilly's Open Source Convention and did a signing of my own, at Powell's Technical Books in downtown Portland.

That's right. The artist formerly known as Wesley Crusher had written a book and published it himself. The book is called *Dancing Barefoot*, and it's five short-but-true essays about my life as a husband, stepfather, and former *Star Trek* actor.

I was about six steps through the door at Powell's when the store manager, Amber, approached me.

"We have completely sold out of your book!" She looked concerned.

I took a moment to digest this exceedingly good news. I'd just walked into my very first in-store book signing. I didn't know what would happen . . . but a sellout never entered my mind.

---

* This book is also called "The Alpaca," which is the animal on its cover. Randal also co-wrote "The Llama" (*Learning Perl*). I guess this book will be called "The Geek."

"That's the greatest thing I've ever heard," I said, as I took my iBook bag off my shoulder.

<><><>

Pasadena, 30 hours earlier

I'm packing my bags for the trip to OSCon. My dog, Ferris, lays on the bed, looking at me with her "I see the suitcase, so I know you're going to be gone" look.

I fold some pants and a few shirts. My wife, Anne, walks into our room.

"Are you taking any extra books?" she asks.

"No, I don't think so. Powell's already ordered a ton of them. I think I'll be okay." I put my folded shirts into my bag.

"You should really take some extras, Wil," she says.

Ferris sighs and rolls onto her side. The tip of her tail wags against my cat, Sketch.

"I really don't think there are going to be that many people there. I don't want to schlep a bunch of books up there and back," I tell her. "Besides, my bag is full."

She looks into my suitcase. Sketch meows at Ferris and jumps off the bed.

"You're taking two pair of shoes for a 36 hour trip?"

"Well . . . yeah."

"Why?"

I resist the urge to shout, "I learned it from you, okay?! I learned it by watching you!!" Instead, I say, "Dress shoes for my reading, and Converse for the rest of the time."

"If you take your dress shoes out, you can lose your dress pants, too. Just take your jeans and wear your Converse. You can put books in the extra space."

"But I think I should look nice for— "

"You're going to a computer convention, dork. You'd be better off wearing your Trogdor shirt."

I've already packed it, but I don't tell her. Ferris exhales loudly and stretches out on her back. Our other dog, Riley, walks into our room and sits at Anne's feet. She looks up, expectantly.

Anne pets her and says to me, "You're going to regret it if you get there and you don't have books for everyone. You'll feel bad, and you'll lose sales. Just take a few."

I've learned something in the seven-and-a-half years I've known and loved her: she's always right about this stuff.

"Okay," I say. Riley thinks I'm talking to her and jumps on the bed. Ferris flips over and snarls at her.

I end up packing an additional 47 books.

I put my bag on the counter. "It's a good thing I listened to my wife!" Amber was visibly relieved when I began pulling small stacks of books out of it.

"This is the biggest crowd we have ever had at this store," she said. "For anything."

"Really?!" I said.

"Yes! And we've never sold out of a book before. Usually, we'll sell about 10 or so."

"Oh my god. This is so cool!" I said.

"I'll take all the books you have in there, and we may even have to issue rain checks."

Rain checks?! Holy crap! This is so cool!!

I gave them to her, and she began putting stickers on them. There were two other authors there, too, so I snuck away to a back room to prepare while they talked about their books.

Even though I've read these stories countless times, and even though I lived them all, I feel a need to familiarize myself with them before I perform them. Even though my book was doing unbelievably well in terms of sales and audience response, I was nervous each time I took it before a crowd.

On this particular night, I had some giddy excitement to go along with the nerves. I felt good. I was marking a significant waypoint on my journey from actor to author. I was taking my work to an audience that was NOT at a *Star Trek* convention. There were lots of non-Trekkies in this crowd. This was a big test for me.

The other authors talked for about 30 minutes, and then it was my turn.

I read two pieces from *Dancing Barefoot*: "Inferno," and a selection from "The Saga of SpongeBob Vegas Pants." When I was finished reading, I looked up to thank the crowd for coming and saw that it had grown substantially since I began. I was elated.

All these people came and shared in this experience with me for almost an hour! I earned their time and attention. I earned it with my writing! I passed the test! I passed the test!

I sat down at a little table they'd set up for me, which had a laminated "Meet Wil Wheaton, author of *Dancing Barefoot*" sign on it. The crowd transformed itself from a mass to a line (like Optimus Prime, but without the cool sound effects), and I began to sign books.

I signed for people from just about every demographic you can imagine. Many of them had their own copies of my book, which they'd bought online or earlier in the day from Powell's. They complimented me on my website, on my performance, even on my cool shirt.

I signed a girl's celebrity bible, right there next to Dr. Demento, and I met the project lead for Quanta Plus, a web development application that I love and use regularly. Eric S. Raymond, author of *Cathedral and the Bazaar* (O'Reilly) and major force in the open source movement, also came and listened to me read. He even sat right in the front, and had several kind words for me when I was done. It was awesome.

When I was down to my last three books, a guy walked over to me, and extended his hand.

"Hi, Wil," he said, "I'm Tim O'Reilly."

HOLY MO— WIL! IT'S TIM O'REILLY!! HE CAME OUT TO SEE YOU!

Before I could scream out, "I KNOW! I KNOW! I KNOW! GREAT GOOGLY MOOGLY!" my brain said, *"Stay cool, Wil. Don't geek out."*

I heeded my brain's advice and was grateful for all those times I didn't stab it with a key.

"It's really nice to meet you," I said. I was very proud of myself . . . and kept my geeking out to a minimum. "Your books have made my life much easier and much more interesting."

Check me out. I totally behaved myself.

"Nicely done," said my brain. *"Have some serotonin."*

Oh . . . that feels good.

He said something about how he'd heard good things about my book and thanked me for coming to OSCon.

He thanked me for coming!

"Would you like a copy of my book?" I asked him, "I have an extra one that you can have if you want it."

"Sure," he said, "but I'd rather buy it."

So that's what he did. Tim O'Reilly bought my little book, and shortly after that, I sold my final copy.

That's right. I sold out all my books, including the additional books I brought with me.

It's a good thing I listened to my wife, eh?

I packed up my bag, and said good bye to Randal. He pointed at the little laminated "Meet Wil Wheaton, author of *Dancing Barefoot*" sign.

"You should take that, Wil. It's from your first signing. You're going to want that someday," he said.

I picked it up off the table, and when I held it in my hands, I knew that he was right. I didn't ever want to forget this very significant moment in my life. Signing my first book, in a book store, and selling it out . . . it's better than the first time I got to sit at the helm of the *Enterprise* . . .

. . . because it was *real*.

ACT I

"No one knows what it's like
To be hated, to be fated
To telling only lies

No one bites back as hard on their anger
None of my pain and woe
Can show through"

—The Who
Behind Blue Eyes

"Tell me is something eluding you, sunshine?
Is this not what you expected to see?
If you wanna find out what's behind these cold eyes
You'll just have to claw your way through this disguise."

—Pink Floyd
In The Flesh?

ONE

Where's My Burrito?

ON A HOT JUNE AFTERNOON IN 2000, I joined my best friend Darin for lunch at one of our teenage haunts, Old Town Pasadena. An afternoon in Old Town is a trip to a time when we were free of responsibility, and the world was filled with possibility and opportunity.

The changes in Old Town reflect the changes within ourselves. Thanks to the efforts of the Pasadena preservationists, the historical building façades haven't changed, but they are the only thing that remain the same. The empty doorway where a punk rocker once sneered at passing businessmen is now a Pottery Barn, occupied by a San Marino yuppie who screams into her cell phone. The eclectic record store where we'd buy imported Smiths singles is now a Sam Goody, its windows plastered with posters announcing the latest release from Justin Timberlake. Tourists stand uncomfortably at crosswalks, trying to ignore the homeless who have come to enjoy the trickle down economics of a prospering shopping thoroughfare.

All of this progress is not without its benefits, though. Old Town is safe, if sanitized, and several good restaurants have moved into the area.

On this particular afternoon, Darin and I walked down Colorado Boulevard, following the same route as Pasadena's claim to annual fame, the Tournament of Roses Parade. We passed The Cheesecake Factory, several trendy Japanese noodle houses, and walked straight into Hooters.

Hey, Darin was engaged, and I'm married. Sometimes a guy's gotta know if he still has it.

We walked in ahead of the lunchtime rush, so we could sit wherever we liked. Through a speaker above us, Bob Seger rhetorically asked, "ain't it funny how the night moves?" We looked around the mostly empty restaurant and chose the section with the hottest waitress in the joint.

As we took our seats, our waitress came over to our table: a cute-but-not-beautiful girl in her early 20s. Bleached-blonde, fake tan, long legs. Hooters. Her name tag said "Destiny."

She flirted with us as she took our order, all smiles and giggles. We ordered wings. Super Fire Hot, baby.

She stood up and left to put in our order. Darin and I stared at each other, grinned, and exchanged a mental high five. We still had it, and it felt *good.*

She'd only walked a few steps, when she stopped suddenly, turned around, and came back to our table.

She looked at me, lustily. "Can I ask you something?"

"Oh, hell, yeah, Willie," I thought to myself, *"The ladies still want your sweet action!"*

My face flushed and my pulse quickened.

"Sure," I said.

She screwed up her courage and leaned close to me, her full, pouting lips just inches from mine. Her perfume embraced me. Her ample cleavage seductively longed to bust out from beneath her thin cotton T-shirt. She drew a nervous breath, bit down on the corner of her mouth, and asked, breathlessly, "Didn't you used to be an actor?"

"WHAT?! USED TO BE?! I STILL AM!" I hollered, as mental images of a hot Hooters threesome were replaced with the cold reality of appearing on *Celebrity Boxing.*

She immediately knew that she had made a mistake. She thought quickly, licked her lips, self-consciously fussed with her over-processed hair and tried again: "Oh, I mean, weren't you an actor when you were a kid?"

All I could do was numbly answer, "Yeah, when I was a kid," as I hung my head and ordered the first of many pints of Guinness.

Funny story, right? Yeah, funny like when you watch another guy get kicked in the nuts. In the days that followed, I tried to write it off. Tried to bolster my wounded self-esteem by telling myself that she was just a Hooters waitress, so she didn't matter. But the truth was, that simple, scantily clad waitress had driven home with painful acuity my deepest fear: I was a has-been. I "used to be" an actor, when I was a kid.

If I "used to be" an actor, it wasn't for lack of trying, but it *was* the result of a series of choices I'd made, starting all the way back in 1989, when I was just 16 years old, and in Florida for a *Star Trek* cruise . . .

Even though it was early in the morning, it was already hot and humid in Miami. My brother and I stood together in front of the hotel and waited to get on a bus that would take us to the port. There were hundreds of Trekkies swarming around us, and a ripple of excitement went through the crowd when the hotel doors opened and the entire cast of the original *Star Trek*, minus Shatner and Nimoy, walked out. Most of them looked a little drunk, and some of them looked a lot unhappy.

Marina Sirtis, who played Counselor Troi on *Next Generation* and was the object of a very large teenage crush, came out of different door and approached us.

"How are you doing, Teen Idol?" she said.

"I'm okay, I guess," I said. "What's up with them?" I pointed at the original series cast, who were now posing for pictures and signing autographs.

"Oh, they're just having a good time," she said.

"Oh," I said.

"Okay. I'll see you on the bus. We are going to have so much fun on this cruise!" She hugged me and walked away.

My brother pointed at one of them and said, "Dude! He is *fucked up!*" and began to laugh, but I couldn't join him. In 1989, *Star Trek* was my life. At 16 years old, I was a veteran actor—I worked on the series for 50 hours a week—but I was also a veteran of the *Star Trek* convention circuit. Three weekends out of the month I entertained audiences at Holiday Inns all over the country. When I looked at these original series actors, I saw The Ghosts of My Career Yet To Come.

I had no idea at the time that it was probably not that big a deal to have a few drinks early in the morning while you were on vacation. I had no idea that some of the *Star Trek* alumni were quite happy traveling around the country and performing for Trekkies at conventions. It also didn't occur to me that some of those actors, who had only done three or four episodes, had willingly chosen to live out their lives recalling their time on the *Enterprise.*

I spoke with the arrogant surety of a 16-year-old. "Look at that," I said. "That's my future, if I don't get out of *Star Trek* and do movies. There is no fucking way I'm going to spend the rest of my life talking about what I did when I was a kid. I'm going to prove to everyone that I can do more with my life than just be on *Star Trek.*"

"Dude," was all he could say. It was a multipurpose word in our vernacular. "Dude" could stand in for several words and phrases, such as "Check out that hottie," or "Stop talking now because Mom's standing right behind you," or "This is seriously fucked up."

"Exactly," I said.

A couple of hours later, we were on the ship, and today, after 15 years, all I can recall about the entire 3-day cruise is that conversation, because at that moment, I made a choice that would drive my life and haunt me for years: I would get out of my *Star Trek* contract, and I would go on to a huge career in movies. I would prove to everyone that I was a great actor and that *Star Trek* was just a small part of my resume.

Yeah. It didn't quite work out that way, and it's probably my karma for having such a negative impression of those original series actors, who I have come to know as kind and wonderful people. Actually, I have such regard for them now, I almost hate to open this book showcasing such a negative view of them, but that moment in 1989 was the foundation upon which the last 15 years of my life have been built.

I thought about that moment often, especially over the next few years, when the writers reduced my role on *The Next Generation* to little more than saying, "Aye, Sir. Course laid in," and the producers of *Next Generation* prevented me from taking a major roll in Milos Forman's *Valmont*.*

As an adult, getting paid thousands of dollars a week to say, "Aye, Sir. Course laid in" is a seriously sweet gig, but when I was a teenager, it sucked. I felt like I had to prove to everyone† that *Stand By Me* wasn't a fluke, that I *deserved* all the attention that I got from that movie. I never considered that most actors go their entire careers without one film like *Stand By Me* to their credit. I never considered that I could have stuck around on *Star Trek* until the end, and then stepped off into a film career, like, say,

---

* This is detailed in Appendix A.

† As you'll see, having something to prove to people was a major motivating factor in my life right up until about a year ago.

Patrick Stewart. Because of that moment on the dock in Miami in 1989, I was convinced that if I stuck around until the end, I'd be stepping off onto a dock in Miami in 1999.

I have often wondered how different my life would have been if my brother's "Dude" had meant, "Hey, why don't you relax? You're young, and you have your entire life ahead of you. You have an opportunity to work on a great series for a few more years, build up a nice bank account, and then parlay the success of *Star Trek* into a film career. But don't quit now, or you'll regret it for the rest of your life. And stop staring at Marina's ass. That's just rude." Maybe that sentiment was a little too deep for a couple of teenagers.

Of course, I'm still talking about what I did when I was a kid, and I never got that big film career I was hoping for. When I was released from my *Star Trek* contract, I was 18, and like most 18-year-olds, I knew everything. I realized that I had never had a childhood, and I'd never really just gone off and done things that I wanted to do. I also realized that when I looked in the mirror, I saw the reflection of everything I hated about Hollywood and humanity staring back at me from behind angry and unhappy eyes.

How the fuck did I let this happen to me? I have to get out of here.

In the early 1990s, I vanished from Hollywood and moved to Topeka, Kansas. I spent a little over a year there, working on computers during the day, and on my incredibly screwed up psyche at night. When I felt like I'd put myself back together, I returned to Los Angeles, and enrolled in a five-year acting program. I remember thinking that I'd gotten all the way to *Star Trek* on instinct alone, and if I wanted to move beyond it, I'd need some technique.

When I was in drama school, I passed on several film opportunities, among them, *Primal Fear*. You may know it as the movie that started Ed Norton's career. I know it as The Huge Opportunity That I Completely Fucked Up. When my agent told me that I was making a huge mistake, I told him, "Look, man. I'm in drama school now, and I can't leave until I finish. It's like when Luke was on Dagobah, and he wanted to go to Bespin to save his friends. Yoda told him not to quit in the middle of his training, but Luke didn't listen, and he was never able to be as great a Jedi as his father."

I foolishly thought that Hollywood would wait for me. When I graduated from drama school five years later, I had a rude awakening. Not only had Hollywood forgotten me, they'd completely forgotten my type of actor. The everyman was out, and a new type, called "edgy," had taken my place.

Think about that for a second. *Edgy*. What does that conjure up in your mind? Now ask the person next to you what their description of *edgy* is. Your descriptions didn't match, did they? They weren't even close, right? Now talk about it for a minute and see if you can reach an agreement on exactly what it means. Can't do it, can you? Don't worry, it's not your fault. I'll let you in on a dirty industry secret: nobody knew what *edgy* meant, beyond "unwashed" and . . . uh . . . "unwashed" and . . . er . . . well, that's it. I've just spent several unproductive minutes staring at a blinking cursor, trying to come up with another word besides "not Wil Wheaton," which is really three words and more of a descriptive phrase than a synonym.

While Hollywood didn't quite know what *edgy* was, they were certain that I wasn't it. I am passionate, too smart for my own good, unfulfilled, caring . . . but not *edgy*. So I spent several years struggling, unable even to book a commercial. I wasn't well known enough for product endorsements, but I was too well known to be some random guy extolling the virtues of floor wax. The flood of opportunities I enjoyed when I was a child and teenager slowed to a trickle, then stopped. I "used to be an actor, when I was a kid."

It was so hard to get work, I often contemplated giving up life as an actor and going back to college.

"You have to love the work more than you hate the rejection, and the unemployment," my mom said.

I *did* love the work, and I believed in my abilities as an actor. I felt that I could take direction well, and understood the vagaries of storytelling: those ephemeral things that make an actor's performance greater than the words on the page. I was compelled to act.

That compulsion became obsession. Success as an actor had always come my way without any real effort when I was a kid (resulting in that feeling of undeserved success). After I graduated from drama school, I felt like my acting chops were better than ever, and spent several years being just one big part away from making that elusive comeback. That drove me crazy. I was in my twenties, but I looked like I was in my teens, so I often auditioned to play a teenager. Since I didn't have the same energy or mentality as the *real* teenagers around me, I never got cast. When I walked into auditions, I was rejected before I opened my mouth, and I felt like I was wasting everyone's time—including my own. It didn't take long for the word to spread around Hollywood: Wil Wheaton may *look* young, but he can't *play* young. After countless failed auditions where I was 10 years older than everyone else, I became cynical and pessimistic.

On the very few projects where I was reading for an older character, I would often be one of the final two or three actors to be considered. But consistently coming in second or third was actually worse than not making it past the first round of meetings. It was like scaling Mount Everest, only to die within sight of the summit . . . over and over again.

I couldn't understand why I kept getting so close to booking jobs without anything to show for it, so I asked my agents to pursue feedback from casting directors. The answers provided more questions: "Wil was absolutely the best actor for this job, but he just wasn't handsome enough, or *edgy* enough, for the part." I suppose telling me I was "absolutely the best actor" was intended to make me feel better, but it only made me feel frustrated and depressed. Each time I heard the word *edgy*, I seriously wondered whether I would ever be able to support my family by being an actor.

Family? That's right. I was 27 years old and I had a family. Shortly before I graduated from drama school, I had fallen in love with a wonderful woman. Five years later, we were married. I had taken on the responsibility of helping to raise her two children, with little financial and no emotional support from their father, who actively worked to disrupt not only our marriage, but our relationship with the kids as well. I'd taken everything I had saved from *Star Trek* and *Stand By Me* and invested it in our home and our wedding.

My life as a husband and stepfather was very rewarding, but a desire to regain the success I'd enjoyed as a child and teenager pulled at me constantly. It kept me awake at night and was a constant distraction. Like the Not Me ghost from Family Circus, Prove To Everyone That Quitting *Star Trek* Wasn't A Mistake slept between my wife and me in our bed and ate with us at every meal. When I could have been playing with my stepkids, Prove To Everyone That Quitting *Star Trek* Wasn't A Mistake and I would sit and stare vacantly at the TV, wondering what could have been.

⟨⟨⟩⟩

The weekend after the Hooters Incident (as it came to be known), my wife was out of town and Prove To Everyone That Quitting *Star Trek* Wasn't A Mistake and I found ourselves in front of my computer. I surfed the Internet, played Diablo II, created WinAmp play lists . . . I did everything I could to get that Hooters waitress out of my mind.

Yes, that's how badly it hurt me: I was actively trying to get a Hooters waitress *out* of my mind. While my wife was out of town.

Somewhere in that day, while I was battling the forces of polygonal evil on Battle.Net, Prove To Everyone tapped me on the shoulder, and said, *"Dude. You should make a website and let the world know that you are still alive and still acting."*

I paused the game and looked back at him. I had wanted a presence on the Web for a long time, but I didn't have the skills to build a website. I'd been given the names of several designers, but wanted to do the whole thing myself, for better or for worse.

"Oh my god. That's a fantastic idea! Maybe we'll even get noticed by Hollywood again!"

"Just make sure you make the website edgy,*"* he said.

"If you were real, I'd cock-punch you for that," I said.

I quit the game and went to Yahoo! Geocities, where I created an account called "tvswilwheaton." (Get it? "TV's Wil Wheaton!" Because I'm still on TV, except I'm not.) Because I had absolutely no idea how to write HTML, and I knew nothing about tables, CSS, RSS feeds, or the W3C, I spent the next few hours clumsily learning my way around the Yahoo! Pagebuilder. I used their WYSIWYG editor to—ahem—"design" my very first web page. The result was incredibly lame, but it was mine. I named it *Where's My Burrito?* after one of my favorite episodes of *The Simpsons*.

When it was done, Prove To Everyone That Quitting *Star Trek* Wasn't A Mistake and I shared a high five. I was proud of what I'd created. I posted a link to it in a small Wil Wheaton online fan club and wondered if anyone would care.

Boy, *did* they care! I had over 700 visitors in a couple weeks, without being listed in a single search engine. The response excited me, and I started updating the site quite frequently by hand-coding "news updates" into the main page. Here's the very first "news update" I did, way back before I had even heard of a weblog:

22 JULY, 2001

Hey party people.

I've just come home from the San Diego ComiCon, where it's very possible I gave you a lame flyer for this very lame website.

So you actually came, eh? Suh-weet. I feel just slightly less lame than I did last night.

Want to know some cool stuff that's happened in the recent past?

Tough. I'm telling you anyway.

Here we go:

See, TNN is re-branding themselves. Re-branding is when a network changes its image and programming and goes after a new audience. Well, that's what TNN is doing. I guess someone decided that there were more Gen-X-ers than rednecks out there (thank god) and they've changed The Nashville Network (home of *NASCAR* and *Hee-Haw*) into The National Network (home of *Miami Vice*, *Starsky and Hutch*, *NASCAR* and *Hee-Haw* and *Star Trek: The Next Generation*).

So this is quite cool, if you ask me. I've been doing lots of stuff with the TNN folks in the last few days and they are really some of the coolest people on earth. And I'm not just saying that because they gave me a free trip to New York. Okay, well, maybe a little.

But check this out: There is this big thing called "The Television Critics Association." I think there are TV critics in it, or something. Anyway, they get together every year to run up huge tabs on their corporate credit accounts and see what's coming up on TV in the next quarter. That's where I come in. TNN asked me to go to the "TCA" (when you're a hip, edgy, media-savvy person, you use lots of acronyms, FYI) to be part of this *TNG* launch-thing. So I went and it was sooo cool! I got to see some of the old *TNG* kids, who I don't ever see anymore since they're millionaires and I'm living in a refrigerator box and the coolest thing of all . . . I got to take a pee right next to BILLY FREAKIN' IDOL!!!

Yes, you read that right. Here's how it happened: I went into the bathroom and I'm doing my business and I notice the guy next to me is rather dressed up, like in serious rocker clothes. So I try to just glance at him, without getting all gay and weird and he looks right at me, sneer and all. That's when I realize that it's HIM! HOLY CRAP! So I say, "My wife and I just saw you on *Storytellers*. You really rocked, man!" (tap, tap). And he looks at me and from behind his cool-guy sunglasses says, "Cheers, mate." And he's gone.

YES! How cool was that?

So after that, I'm off to New York to do a cool show called *Lifegame*, which will be on TNN in a month or so. It's an improv show where they asked me to tell stories about my life and then they have improvisers act out scenes based on my so-called life, in different styles. Like the time my parents cornered me in the bathroom and gave me "The Talk" . . . when I was 20, done as a reggae musical. Very funny. And I got to play the Devil in a scene. YES!

While I was there, I got a tour of MTV networks, met Carson Daly (!) and was given a CHIA MISTER T! That's right. Let me tell you, everything after that was just Jibba Jabba.

So after NYC, I came home to LA, my wife picked me up at the airport and I got on a train to San Diego for the Comic-Con, where I signed autographs and promoted *TNG* on TNN

(I like that. It sounds like NBA on NBC) and this lame website. Honestly, it was mostly lame. I didn't sell many pictures, so I barely even covered my costs for the trip and there weren't as many people there as last year. HOWEVER! There were a few cool things, which I will relate now:

I met Oscar Gonzalez. He's an artist for Bongo Comics, who make "The Simpsons" comic. He drew, for me, a picture of me signing autographs for THE COMIC BOOK GUY! It's totally cool. I'll scan it at my brother's house and post it this week sometime. Two other cool guys, Jason Ho and Mike Rote, also Bongo artists, did cool Simpson's caricatures of Ryan and Nolan (my stepkids). Thank you Bongo guys!

I also met Spike, of Spike and Mike's Sick and Twisted Festival of Animation, (the first guys to recognize Mike Judge's brilliance in the pre-Beavis days), and did a little sound bite for their 25th anniversary special, so Spike gave me an autographed DVD of their greatest sick and twisted hits. Cool!

My buddies at TROMA, home of the Toxic Avenger and distributor of *Fag Hag* also gave me some DVDs, including *Terror Firmer*. Very cool.

Finally, I traded an autographed picture of yours truly for a copy of "College Girls Gone Wild." You know the one you see on TV? Trading things is cool.

That's it, kiddies. I'm back in LA now and getting ready for my Big Birthday Bash next weekend. I'm turning 29 on the 29th! YES!

Your punching bag,

Littlest Giant

I am so embarrassed when I read that and compare it to the way I write now. It's a horrible mangling of the English language, I change from present to past tense and back again, and use an annoying passive voice throughout the whole thing. Oh, and all the ComicCon stuff is bullshit. I may have been at the keyboard, but Prove To Everyone That Quitting *Star Trek* Wasn't A Mistake was definitely in the driver's seat, so I projected my idealized self: I was a devil-may-care Gatsby, funny and irreverent, and living the celebrity dream.

ComiCon was nothing like I had expected, and the truth is, it was a horrible experience. I went there expecting to sell hundreds of autographed pictures to hundreds of adoring fans, but hardly anyone was interested. I sat in a cavernous and undecorated area far away from the main convention floor, surrounded by people who were definitely on the downside of their careers. The hundreds of adoring fans I'd hoped to see did show up . . . when people like Kevin Smith and the cast of the short-lived *Witchblade* took up temporary residence at tables near mine. When they left, so did the fans, who glanced dismissively at me, if they noticed me at all. I was humiliated and depressed. *"This is what my life has come to,"* I thought, *"I am a has-been."* Prove To Everyone made sure I left those details out, and encouraged me to play up the success of the TCA event and the subsequent trip to New York for *Lifegame.* So that's what I did. (By the way, it *was* pretty cool to take a pee next to Billy Idol. If you get a chance to pee next to a rock star, make sure you do it.)

Though the dishonesty bothered me, Prove To Everyone spoke with a silver tongue, and I convinced myself that if I projected a successful image, it would somehow become a reality. It was a lot of work to fictionalize my own life, though, so I wrote about things that were safe and mundane. I posted links to other websites and talked about my experiences building my self-described "incredibly lame website." I issued pathetic pleas for e-mail and comments, but I avoided talking about myself or revealing anything too personal. That all changed when my dad came home from a surfing trip in Indonesia. He was so sick I thought he was going to die.

27 JULY, 2001
Surfer Rosa

I just got back from the hospital. My dad is really sick and the scary thing is nobody knows what the hell is wrong with him.

I can talk to someone, in real time, who is on the other side of the world.

Spacecraft are taking pictures of Mars.

My Palm Pilot has more memory than my first desktop computer.

But not one doctor can tell me what the %^$#@ is wrong with my dad.

I've been on the verge of tears all day.

Sorry, kids. I know you've come to expect a certain irreverence from your Sweet Uncle Willie, but I am scared shitless.

I love my dad. I've never known my dad as much as I wanted to, because he works all the time and I work all the time. Then there's the whole "You don't understand me!" thing, which basically adds up to a bunch of wasted years from 14 to about 22. **Pay attention, young 'uns: your parents are not as bad as you think and someday they'll be gone and you'll regret every single moment you wasted being mad at them because they wouldn't let you go to your fuck-up friend's house because they knew you'd get drunk there.**

I remember, when I was a little kid, like 7 or 8, my great-grandfather died. I was in the kitchen of my house and my dad was sitting on this high-chair stool thing we have and he started to cry. Like really a lot. He cried hard. I was freaked. I didn't know what to do. At all. So I ran into the laundry room and I said, "Mom. Dad needs you." My mom came into the kitchen and she did what I just didn't know how to do at 7 or 8: she hugged my dad and let him cry on her. I can see the two of them, my dad in his ultra-groovy 1979 perm and my mom in her pantsuit, holding each other in the beautifully wallpapered kitchen in Sunland.

Later, I asked my dad why he was crying so hard. I had hardly known my great-grandfather and he was cool and all, but I just figured that if I didn't know him that well, nobody else did, either. (Yes, the world did revolve around me, apparently.) My dad told me that he was thinking about his own dad, my grandfather and how my grandfather was so sad, because his own father had just died. My dad then told me that he realized then, for the first time in his life, that someday his dad would die. Even at 7 years old that really struck me and I think about it all the time.

A number of years ago, when I was working on *Mr. Stitch* in France I awoke with a start one night. I thought "something horrible has just happened" and I couldn't go back to sleep. So I called my friend Dave and told him what had happened and asked if there had been an earthquake, or something. He told me I was just being lame (I am) and that everything was fine. So I went back to sleep. Later that night, as I was going out the door of my apartment to dinner, my phone rang. It was my mom. She made some small talk, then told me that my dad wanted to talk to me. He got on the phone and told me that his dad, my grandfather, had suffered a massive heart attack and died. I didn't know what to say. I asked him how he was doing and he choked back a sob and said, "sometimes okay and sometimes not." I had no comfort to offer my dad and that really bothered me.

Months later, we had a funeral and scattered my grandfather's ashes out to sea. It was really cool and I cried really hard, but not for myself. I cried for my dad, remembering what he had told me 15 years earlier.

So tonight, I spent as long as I could at the hospital, talking with my dad, reading my lame HTML book and watching *Blind Date* and *Letterman*. I kept taking his temperature, which started out at 103 today (scary, since my dad's 53), then went back to normal and started a slow climb back up to 100.6 when I left.

I don't know what to do now. I know I won't sleep well, not knowing what's happening with my dad. The doctor will be calling in someone from the CDC in the morning if my dad's not better, since he was just in Indonesia on a surfing trip and they think he may have brought something back.

But it's the not knowing that is the worst.

That and replaying in my head every wasted moment with my dad. Every time I wouldn't play catch with him, or go surfing, or acted embarrassed when he told a lame joke around some girl I was trying to impress.

Go call your mom. She's worrying about you.

And for god's sakes, play catch with your dad.

For the longest 48 hours of my life, I was terrified that I was going to lose my father. After two days, the doctor from the CDC determined that my dad had contracted a blood infection when he stubbed his toe on a boat anchor during his trip. If he hadn't been in the United States when he'd gotten sick, he would have died. Thankfully, he managed to fight off the infection and made a full recovery.

I still don't know why I chose to write about my dad, and my very real and unprotected feelings, but when I was face to face with my father's mortality, Prove To Everyone was silenced and releasing my fears and doubts was liberating.

The few people who were reading my website appreciated the raw honesty. In the days after I wrote that entry, I got several e-mails and comments from people who shared similar experiences with their own fathers, and while I read them, I thought that it might be okay to talk about some of my real feelings.

"As long as you don't let on about how much you're struggling in your career," Prove To Everyone said.

"Oh, you're still here," I said. *"I thought you'd found something else to do."*

"I think I'll be sticking around for quite some time," he said. *"With The Voice of Self Doubt to keep us company."*

He was right. After that brief moment of honesty, Prove To Everyone regained control over everything I wrote and I was back to attention whoring and posting links to other websites. About two weeks later, Prove To Everyone and I sort of collaborated on a weblog post. He got to talk about Auditions, and I got to talk about my family.

02 AUGUST, 2001
Beach-o-rama

Tuesday was my stepson's 12th birthday. It was also the first time in 3 months that I'd had an audition. (Apparently, a bunch of jackass producers, working for vertically integrated, multinational media conglomerates were afraid that the Writer's Guild and the Screen Actor's Guild may want to stop work, so that we can all make a living wage, so they didn't "green light" any new projects. Go figure.)

Things have been tough the past few months. Money has been tight and I've been super bored. If I didn't have my kick-ass sketch comedy show at ACME to look forward to, I probably would have ended up on the sidewalk in front of the Viper Room.

Just kidding. Jeeze, lighten up.

The first call is at 11:15 a.m., to be a regular on this WB show called *The Young Person's Guide To Being A Rockstar*. It's to play a gay drummer. (Why does everyone think I'm gay?). The second call is at 4:45 p.m., for a movie called *Waiting* . . .

that is just about the funniest ^%$#ing script I've read in over a year.

I'm completely excited, since I have way too much free time right now and I would like to work. (You know, actors are the only people who are unhappy when they're not working. Unlike most "normal" people, who can't wait for a break from work . . .) The only problem was, Tuesday was Ryan's birthday and I was really torn about what to do. I need to work and I really like both of these projects, but I really wanted to be part of Ryan's 12th birthday party, which was a trip to the beach with some of his friends.

I went over and over it and made the tough choice to take the auditions and see Ryan that evening.

Well, on my way to the first audition, I got a call from my agent and she told me that the afternoon session was canceled! So I went from my first audition (where I kicked ass, thank you very much . . . I'm told that I'm "in the mix" which is Hollywood-speak for "we're considering you") to the beach. I must have been quite the vision in my jeans, Sketchers and black socks, walking down the sand.

Long story short, it was awesome. We skim-boarded, played football and wiffleball and barbecued hot dogs in the parking lot, which was majorly against the beach parking lot rules (yes! breakin' the law! breakin' the law!).

When we got back, I had e-mail waiting for me from my friend Roger Avary. Roger is one of the coolest people on earth and a fucking rad writer and director.

Roger won an Academy Award for writing *Pulp Fiction* and is pretty much responsible for everything good that Tarantino has ever taken credit for. Roger also wrote and directed my absolute favorite movie that I've ever worked on, *Mr. Stitch*. To get back to my point: I e-mailed Roger, because he's doing a new movie and I asked him if I could be in it, because he is the most fun director EVER and always makes good movies. He e-mails me back and tells me, "of course," and sends me the script (which ^%$@*ing ROCKS, by the way) and we're hooking up this week.

So I've got that going for me, which is nice.

That's all for right now, kids. I'm going back to work on the new, improved, easy-to-remember website!

How about some e-mail for your uncle willy?

How about that pathetic plea for attention? Yeah, that's nice. Prove To Everyone said I was bored, which was partially true, but he stopped me before I could continue with, "I'm scared, and I'm horribly depressed. I am a husband and stepfather who can't provide for his family. I 'used to be' an actor when I was a kid."

The total absence of acting work was hard on my ego, but it was also a terrible financial strain on my family. My wife and I often borrowed money from my parents, and she was working over 40 hours a week just so we could have food on our table. I felt guilty that I didn't go with them to the beach for Ryan's birthday, and I told myself that if we hadn't been getting calls from bill collectors every day, I would have blown the auditions off to spend the entire day with him. But the insistent voice of the collectors was nothing compared to the Voice of Self Doubt and my good friend Prove To Everyone That Quitting *Star Trek* Wasn't A Mistake. They were the real reason I went on the auditions, which didn't result in any work, because the part I was "in the mix" for went to someone who was—wait for it—*edgy*, and the other was already cast when I got there.

When I e-mailed Roger Avary and I told him that I wanted to work with him again, I meant it. *Mr. Stitch* was an amazing experience and Roger is a talented writer/director, as well as a great person to be around. However, Prove To Everyone knew that this movie, called *The Rules of Attraction*, would be noticed by Hollywood when it was released. If Roger gave me a part in his movie, I would silence Prove To Everyone, The Voice of Self Doubt, and the Voice of Bill Collectors.

For the first time in years, I had some hope that my stalled acting career would begin to climb again. I relaxed a little bit, and when I wrote in my weblog, Prove To Everyone took a break, and I was able to talk some more about my stepkids.

14 AUGUST, 2001
Kids Are Cool

Tonight, while I was sitting here, cursing up a storm while I tried to get the new site closer to operation, my stepkids decided that they wanted to watch *The Mummy* on DVD.

I told them that they could, but Ryan had to shower before he could start it and Nolan would have to wait for him.

Ryan runs off to his room, (kids have two speeds at 12: the excited run and the sullen stalk) and shouts back to Nolan, "Make some popcorn!"

Nolan looks at me and says, "I'm really burnt out on popcorn, Wil."

"So just make some for Ryan," I replied, "that would be a really cool thing to do."

He goes into the kitchen, (he hasn't hit the two-speed phase yet) and gets out the popcorn (I can't endorse *Newman's Own* enough . . . it rules and the profits go to charity, so we all win).

I sit back at the computer, trying to make the new site look less lame (it's not coming along as well as I'd like, dammit) and Nolan calls to me from the kitchen.

"Wil! There's a lot of smoke coming out of the microwave!"

I get up and as I get closer to the kitchen, I recognize that smell that is so familiar to college dorms . . . no, not weed, jackass. The smell of burnt microwave popcorn.

Nolan is standing there, looking perplexed, like he can't figure out what is wrong with the microwave. So I stop it and asked him how long it's been in there and he tells me 4 minutes, because that's what it says on the bag. Now, whenever I make it, it's 2 minutes 25 seconds. I've gotten it figured out. But I somehow didn't pass that knowledge on to the next generation; even now, at 2:50 a.m., my house STILL smells like burning popcorn!

Well, Ryan comes out of his room and Nolan looks crestfallen.

"Ryan, I ruined the popcorn and it was the last one," he says, looking like a puppy who's just been caught chewing up your Boba Fett that was still in the blister pack.

Ryan looks at me and back to his upset little brother and he totally says, "That's okay, Nolan, I'll eat it anyway."

So we open the bag and take out a black ball of burning popcorn, toss it into the sink and Ryan pours the rest of the popcorn into our popcorn bowl. (You see, when you're married, all of a sudden you get all this stuff that only has one use. Like The Popcorn Bowl, or The Water Glasses. I don't know about you, but when I was a bachelor, I only had two bowls and about five glasses and they pulled serious double and triple duty.)

Sorry. Tangent.

So Ryan ends up sitting on the couch, eating the totally burnt popcorn and all was right with the world.

See what I mean about kids being cool? Nolan made the effort to do something for his brother and Ryan made the effort to appreciate it, even at his own peril.

I wish adults were more like that.

When I wrote about my family I felt like I was showing school pictures or vacation slides, and even though it was personal, it wasn't about my struggles in Hollywood. I liked writing about my wife and stepkids, because I knew that I was a good husband and stepfather. I didn't feel like I had anything to prove to anyone—a dramatic difference from the way I felt when I wrote about auditions and my (lack of) acting work.

I was "blogging" almost every day, and even though Prove To Everyone spoke more often than I did, more and more people were stopping by to read what I wrote. *Where's My Burrito?* was a fine place to start, but I was outgrowing Geocities. I was ready for a real website, so I bought the domain name www.wilwheaton.net and spent the next several weeks teaching myself how to build a website from scratch.

I thought *Where's My Burrito?* had a certain unpolished charm, but Prove To Everyone knew that if we were going to rejuvenate the acting career, we needed to have a more professional-looking presence on the Internet. The problem was, I couldn't afford to hire a designer, and I was afraid that even if I did, I would end up with a "celebrity" site that would be just be a marketing tool.

Prove To Everyone thought this was a fine idea, but I wanted to do something more than that. I compared the entries *I* wrote to the entries Prove To Everyone wrote, and saw a remarkable difference in the responses and the way I felt about them. I locked Prove To Everyone in a shed in my back yard and spent several weeks learning HTML and PHP. I bought a copy of Macromedia Dreamweaver, and surfed around the web for design ideas. I looked at "celebrity" sites, and "personal" sites. All the "celebrity" sites were exactly what I expected: marketing tools, controlled by publicists and professional image-meisters. But the "personal" sites felt like there was some dude sitting at a computer, putting up stuff that he thought was cool. The "personal" weblog sites gave me a window into the writer's world, and I decided that I would do the same thing.

TWO

WIL WHEATON dot NET

I OFFICIALLY LAUNCHED **WIL WHEATON** DOT **NET** on August 23, 2001. It didn't occur to me at the time, but that would have been River Phoenix's 30th birthday.

Word of its existence spread quickly around the Internet, and I was asked to give interviews to several popular websites, including Salon, Wired, Slashdot and BBspot. Prove To Everyone did most of the talking, but I managed to get a few words in myself. I began to get e-mails from people I . . . uh . . . admired, like Asia Carrera. Friends who I hadn't talked to in years heard about it around the water cooler, or in the chatroom, or via the prison grapevine, and got back in touch.

Here is an early review of WWdN from Chris Pirillo's *Lockergnome*, a very popular and respected technology and Internet culture newsletter:

Wil Wheaton

http://www.wilwheaton.net/

{Stand by him} He was the scrawny writer in Stand By Me, *and then he became Wesley Crusher of the* Starship Enterprise. *If you mention the name "Wil Wheaton" to anyone in my generation, they'll know exactly who you're talking about. But what has this actor been up to*

lately? You can find out at his official Website—written, designed and maintained by Wil (himself). And ya wanna know what makes it cool? He isn't afraid to kick back and let his hair down. He's actually a pretty funny guy. Just goes to show you that who you see on screen isn't always who that person is in real life. Dude, he always seemed so mellow . . . walking along those railroad tracks.

Chris Pirillo was one of the first people to "get" that I was just a geek, and when I saw myself reviewed favorably by him, I was euphoric. Yahoo's Net Buzz for August 31, 2001 mentioned *"The triumphant return of Wil Wheaton!"* That made me *and* Prove To Everyone happy.

The interviews created a lot of buzz around the Internet, and thousands of people came to my site to see what the big deal was. Ironically, many people praised the honesty and humor, and admired the insights into my personal life.

Unfortunately, the reaction wasn't entirely positive. Several people viciously attacked me for all sorts of reasons, mostly related to my work on *Star Trek*. Sentiments like, "You ruined *Star Trek*, and your blog is stupid! Shut up, Wesley!" were very popular. Many people e-mailed me, in great detail, about what a washed-up, has-been loser I was.

These personal attacks hurt. A lot. They hurt so much, I almost abandoned the website before it really got going. In retrospect, I should have ignored them, but it's hard to drink in praise and discard criticism. The opinions of anonymous strangers shouldn't have mattered to me, but their comments struck at the heart of my own insecurities: my deep-seated fears that leaving *Star Trek* had been a huge mistake and that I'd never be able to leave Wesley behind.

"Why am I doing this?" I wondered one morning while I read the hate mail.

"Because we're going to show them all," Prove To Everyone said. *"We're going to prove to everyone that you didn't make a mistake*

by quitting Star Trek*! You're going to get that part in Roger's movie, then you're going to get more parts in other movies! Producers will read your site and see how popular you are. This time next year, we'll be drinking Pina Coladas in Cancun."*

"*I don't think I want to do this,"* I said. "*I'm pretty sure I put up with enough personal attacks when I was on* Star Trek.*"*

"*Here, let me write for a while,"* Prove To Everyone said.

24 AUGUST 2001
Audition Update

If you've read the old weblog, you may remember an entry I made about some auditions. Here is the status of those auditions:

The Young Person's Guide To Being A Rockstar: I was "in the mix," which is Hollywoodspeak for "we're considering you until someone bigger comes along." Apparently, someone bigger came along.

Waiting . . .: I had the audition for this last week and the casting director told me that the director has someone in mind, but she thought I did such a great job, she was going to send the director my tape and try to change his mind.

Since it's been a week, I guess he was pretty committed. However, this is one of the funniest movies I've ever read. Ever. I really hope the guy they cast gets gangrene (and recovers, of course), so that they call me and put me in it.

Rules of Attraction: This is my friend Roger Avary's movie, based on Brett Easton Ellis' novel. Roger and I have been friends since I worked on *Mr. Stitch* with him. We talked about three weeks ago and Roger offered me the COOLEST ROLE EVER in the film, "A Junkie Named Marc."

So Tuesday, I went in to read the part. I guess the producers of the film are making everyone read (or, more likely, Roger wanted to be sure that I didn't suck and is too nice a guy to say that to me).

Anyway, I went in a read and I still haven't heard anything back . . . so . . . I dunno . . . guess I shouldn't be shopping for that PS2 just yet.

I Just got off the phone with my agent, who called while I was making this entry. The casting director for *Rules Of Attraction* called this morning and told us that "It's between Wil and another guy."

What the fuck? I wonder how I went from, "I want you in my movie" to "It's between you and another guy."

Wow, the Universe sure does like balance, doesn't it?

Talk about understatement. I felt betrayed by my friend, and I was despondent, but Prove To Everyone wouldn't let me reveal just how unhappy I was.

"If you let them see how upset you are," he counseled, *"you're just going to prove all those people right who are attacking you. You just keep showing the world that the kid who once had it all still does, and that will shut them up."*

"I don't know if that's the best idea. All these people think they're getting this inside look at my life, and we're not exactly telling them the truth."

"Do you want to be a famous actor again or not?" he hissed.

"I just want to be happy again," I said. *"I can't keep lying like this."*

I took the keyboard out of his hands, and I gave the Internet a look inside my mind.

25 AUGUST, 2001

A look inside my mind

I just got this e-mail:

"You're funny, you're smart, you have experiences that are go from ordinary to out-of and back and again and yet . . .

. . . most of what you talk about is your friggin' website!

Talk about your day, what you ate for breakfast, rant and rave. But pretty please, make a separate section for the site updates, HTML and greymatter coups and the linking excitement. All of that is certainly worth keeping track of, but it doesn't communicate much about you."

So, I think that's a point well taken . . . here's some insight into my mind, because you asked for it:

I am fighting tears today, with each passing second. Why? Because the defining characteristic of my work as an actor the past few years has been, "It came down to you and another guy and they went the other way." Translated, that means, "You didn't get the job." If I had a dollar for every time that's happened in the past two years, I could retire. It always seems to come down to me and one other guy, usually some flavor of the month, and they always hire the other guy. And you know what I hate? I always hear, "You are the best actor we've seen" or something similar . . . yet I always seem to lose to the guy with the perfect hair and the Kirk Douglas jaw. Let this be a lesson to you aspiring actors out there: being the best actor is NEVER enough.

I took some classes a long time ago and the teacher always admonished us to not let our jobs become our life— because when we don't work, and there are times when we won't, we'll freak out, because we don't know what to do with ourselves. It's advice I was unable to heed.

Here's something you may not know about me: I love acting. I love working and creating, more than anything. I love it so much, I'm willing to suffer the extended periods of unemployment and the constant rejection, as well as the constant attacks from people who really should either try this themselves or shut the fuck up.

Sorry, I digress. Back to point: since yesterday, when I got the "It's you or another guy" phone call, I've been sliding deeper and deeper into depression, because if I can't get hired by MY FUCKING FRIEND, who practically promised me the part, I don't know what to do. I'm sorry, but I am getting so sick and tired of having a project dangled in front of me for weeks and then having it yanked out from under me at the last second. It hurts. It hurts a LOT and I don't know if you can understand the depth of the hurt, unless you're an artist or some sort, because I think that type of rejection is really a personal one, regardless of what they say.

Put in typical, irreverent "Wilspeak," it's like this: you get hooked up with the hottest girl (or guy, if that's your thing), EVER. You're all naked and ready to go. She's dancing around, telling you all the crazy shit she's gonna do to you and how she's calling her sorority sisters over later, so you'd better stay ready. She's just about to jump you and she tells you to close your eyes and get ready. The next thing you hear is the slamming of the door and the squealing of the tires as she drives away.

(You know what I'm thinking right now? Those morons who have some primal need to hate me are going to have a field day with this one and I almost deleted it. Well, fuck them. You wanted to know what goes on in my head and I want to share . . . I think I'll feel better when I'm done with this. I hope.)

So I feel like I was punched in the stomach. I feel hurt. This movie is going to be AMAZING. It is going to do AMAZING THINGS for the people who are in it, because Roger is an AMAZING writer and director. And I am *this close* to having a complete rebirth in my career and it will only take one part to do that.

This movie would do that for me. Roger asked me to play a junkie in this movie . . . if that doesn't shatter the image people seem to have of me and gets people to stop seeing me as 12 years old or in outer space, I don't know what will.

There was a movie that I recently did, which may have helped the career. The script was great, the cast was great, but the director was the biggest flaming asshole I've ever worked with in my life. As a matter of fact, calling him a director isn't right. He couldn't direct traffic on a one-way street, and I have absolutely zero confidence in his ability to properly edit this film.

And if that wasn't bad enough, I worked on the film for 3 weeks, and earned less than 500 dollars, because the producers promised me a role in a film that has never materialized. These producers have jerked me around for 4 months with empty promises of a project that will most likely never happen now. Thank Bob I have sketch comedy shows and late-night comedy talk shows to perform in, or I'd go crazy.

There's a chance that Roger will still cast me and this whole entry and the awful way I've been feeling will be for nothing and I'll look back at this and laugh and I can get back to the normal me, who is too busy making jokes to feel sad.

But you wanted to know how I was feeling and what was going on in my mind . . . well, there it is.

(And I *will* talk about my website, because I worked hard on it and I knew nothing about HTML or CSS or ANYTHING six weeks ago when I started it, so I'm proud of it, such as it is.)

The business of acting puts great importance on the appearance of success, even if the reality is very different. Actors spend thousands of dollars a month on publicists and image doctors to ensure that they look good to the public. Prove To Everyone knew that was risky to be so bold and honest with my pain and frustration, but those words came straight from my heart, and he didn't get a chance to edit them before I posted.

The reaction to my entry was amazing. I was flooded with e-mails and comments from people all over the world who had experienced the same frustrations—the same unfairness—in their jobs. In fact, a theme emerged: I wasn't alone in my struggles, and many people took comfort in knowing that *they* were not alone either.

I felt validated, and the clouds of depression began to lift. I had made myself vulnerable to the world and the world hadn't kicked me in the nuts. I was certain that this revelation of my inner demons would humanize me in the eyes of my critics.

"See?" I told Prove To Everyone, *"Now they know that I'm just a regular guy, trying to make it to the end of the day the same way they are!"*

It turned out that I was wrong. The very real honesty and vulnerability I had shown just fed their cruelty.

26 AUGUST, 2001
My Velouria

First, I have been overwhelmed with the support, the kindness and the sheer volume of comments and e-mails regarding my last entry.

I have to say "Thank you" to everyone. It's simply amazing, how many different people, separated by distance, culture, career and whatever, are feeling the same things I'm feeling. People said things to me that I've thought at one time or another and forgotten . . . about "risk" and about "giving up." I thank you, all of you, from the bottom of my heart, for opening yourselves to me and sharing with me your advice and experiences. I'd like to post them all in the future, and share your wisdom with the masses.

Mixed in among the e-mails was one from my mom. My mom told me that she'd read my weblog and that she was "proud to have given birth to a person like me." She told me that she could feel my hurt and that I should "be sure to cry all the tears, because the joy is waiting in the last tear."

So that's what I did. I went into my bedroom, sat on my bed and this 29-year-old man sobbed like an 8-year-old child. Big sobs. The kind that hurt your throat. The kind that shake your body and soak your face with tears. I cried so long and so hard, I don't even know what I cried about. I cried for the hurt of losing the job and for the hurt of being attacked by idiots who don't even know me. I cried for all the times I picked on my little brother when we were kids and all the times I've sat here at my computer and let my wife go to bed alone while I worked on this site. I cried for every bad choice I've ever made, but mostly, I cried for myself. I cried and when I thought I was done, I cried some more. Then, just as quickly as it started, it stopped. And I felt better.

Then I made the enormous mistake of checking my logs, so I could see where people are coming from and thank them for linking to me, and I found that some guy uses my site as "hell." Thanks, fucker. Some dude at metafilter says "I'm too good" to join them. Yeah, I can't wait to get into that shit. Please, can I join your little club, so you can hold me up to further vilification, without ever getting to know me? Can I PLEASE spend even LESS time with my family, sitting here at this computer, so I can try to change the minds of people who are going to judge me no matter what, without EVER walking an inch in my shoes?

So you didn't like my fucking character on a fucking TV show I haven't even worked on in 10. Fucking. Years. Thank you for blaming ME for the writing of a fictional character, on a fictional TV show. That makes complete sense, considering all the input the writers would take from a 15-year-old kid. Have you ever bothered to ask? Did it ever occur to you that I just said the lines I was given? I'm sorry Wesley messed up your precious television show.

Fortunately, there were whole seasons without me after I quit. Watch them and feel better. But don't take it out on me. I'm just an actor, doing the best job he could with what he was given. So I worked on a TV show. So I have made a living as an actor. Big deal. I'm no better than anyone else and I have never said I was, or thought I was. I am just a geek, looking for validation from his fellow geeks.

Congratulations, sir. I'm glad that your empty, pathetic existence is made whole by shitting on a person you've never even met.

You know, I promised myself that I wouldn't get into this. I promised myself that I wouldn't get sucked in to the mire with the lowest common denominators. Well, guess what, guys? I don't care if you're "The Guy From TV" or if you're "the kid from math class." Being personally attacked hurts. It sucks. I wonder, do you spend a fifth of the time you spend dumping on me doing something constructive with your life? I certainly hope so. You people are just like the people in high school who never took the time to get to know me, who judged me before I even showed up.

Aren't we mostly geeks here, online? Didn't we all, at one time or another, get bullied by "the cool kids"? Don't any of you remember what that felt like?

My mom said to me that she was amazed at how honestly I revealed my feelings.

She said that I've always reacted in anger when I am hurt and she didn't think I was angry. Well, I wasn't, but I am now.

So here's the deal, people: you can read this or not, and you can see the stuff at my site or not. But if you are going to judge me—me, the person, Wil, who gets up in the middle of the night when his kids are sick and worries about making the bills this month and tries to find time in the day to spend with his wife and works his ass off for auditions that are going to go to the flavor of the month, anyway, well, you can fuck all the way off. Zip up your spacesuit and hurry to the comic shop. Your weekly supply of Magic cards has just come in.

I will never understand why the Internet seems to take away the basic humanity of most people, and allows—no, *enables*—them to say things that they'd never say to another person face to face. I couldn't believe that after I bared myself naked before them, people could still be so cruel and inhuman. In retrospect, my reactions were very extreme, almost as if they came from the defensive teenager I once was. I had been away from *Star Trek* for almost 15 years, but when I read those websites, I saw the same people say the same things that they had when I was a teenager. Clearly there were unresolved feelings left over from that time, and they all came violently back to the surface.

I felt a little bit better because I stood up for myself, but I regretted the emotional and manic way that I'd done it.

"Way to go, Wil. You played right into their hands," The Voice of Self Doubt said.

"See what happens when you let people into your life like that? They cock-punch you," said Prove To Everyone.

"You should write some more jokes," The Voice of Self Doubt said.

"Maybe I'll talk about Anne," I said.

"Oh, that's nice. Things get rough and you bring out your wife to silence the critics," said The Voice of Self Doubt. *"What are you, some kind of politician?"*

"Shut up, you guys. I'm writing about her and Ferris. Maybe when they hear that I have a cool wife, they'll see that I'm just a geek."

27 AUGUST, 2002
Save Ferris

My wife is the coolest, ever. You know that stupid corny Hall-mark-card thing about someone making you want to be a better person? Well, sorry, I like to be anti and all Emo and shit, but it's true. I love my wife more than anything and she really does make me want to be a better person. I could gush about her for pages here, but I'm not gonna. I am going to exercise restraint.

Oh, fuck that. I knew from the moment that I saw Anne that I would marry her. Isn't that weird? Has that ever happened to someone who wasn't in some godawful Nora Ephron movie? And the way we met . . . it was all timing. My best girlfriend, Stephanie, worked with Anne for YEARS, but she never introduced us . . . I mean, she even baby-sat Anne's kids, at MY PARENT'S HOUSE, when we were younger and she never introduced me to Anne . . . because, when we look back at stuff, the timing was just all wrong. We weren't ready to meet each other. But when we did, it was bootylicious.

Anne is beautiful. I mean, she is fucking hella rad.

Hella.

Hella.

Hella.

I always joke that when we are out, people look at us and complain that there's another hot babe with a geek. I say that I am Bob Goldthwait to her Nikki Cox, David Copperfield to her Claudia Schiffer, Siegfried to her Roy . . . I truly adore my wife.

One of the things I adore about her is how she has what Soul Coughing called "Boundless Love." Anne works every day, takes her kids to school, picks them up, deals with their dad and still has time to make me feel like I'm important in her life.

We have this fake dog poop that someone gave us a long time ago and we have the game that we play where we try to put the poop in each other's stuff. Recently, I stuck it in the toe of her shoe, which was in her suitcase. She found it when she put her shoe on in Vegas. She put it in the exact middle of my bed, under the sheets and it scared the hell out of me when I jumped into bed around 2:30 or something last week. My point is, my wife is cool, okay?

Yesterday, when I was sobbing like a little bitch in our bedroom, she came in, sat next to me, put her arm around me and just sat there, loving me. I could feel it. Then she gave me Kleenex and told me that she'd leave me alone until I felt better.

You need to know that to understand the story of Ferris.

Anne is a sucker for hard-luck cases, especially animals. One time a few years ago, she almost got hit on the freeway, because she saw a kitten running in the slow lane . . . so she stopped her car right there and got out to save the kitten, but it got hit by a car just before Anne could get to it and Anne sat on the freeway, holding the kitten while it died in her hands.

She was fucked up about it for months.

So about 18 months ago, she and I were on our patio and we heard this meowing coming from our garage. We both thought it was one of my cats, Biko or Sketch (who are both inside cats, but occasionally get out), so we went to look . . . and out came this skinny black cat with no tail. Anne immediately fell in love with him and took him to the vet, to get him healthy again, while I made the "Found Cat" posters. (Long story short: we thought he was going to die, the vet said he was just dehydrated, we got him shots and Anne named him "Felix." He has lived with us ever since and he is one of the coolest cats, ever.)

Cut to Memorial Day this year. We have no dog. Anne took the kids to Home Depot, so they can buy the materials to make a grind rail. (They're all about the short boards. I'm all about the long boards. It makes for an interesting dynamic when we skate.)

Funny aside: Ryan (12) and Nolan (10) were talking about how excited they were to get a grind rail, which they kept calling a "pole." Nolan says to Ryan, "We TOTALLY have to get some grinding wax, Ryan!" Ryan replies, "Yeah, so we can wax our pole!"

Okay, so they're leaving the Home Depot. Instead of going to the left, to get back to the freeway like we always do, Anne went right and passed this bus stop, where this tiny little dog was chewing on a T-shirt. Anne says that she felt compelled to stop and save her . . . so she did. As soon as Anne got out of the car, the dog ran into some oleander bushes and Anne spent close to 30 minutes getting her out. Then Anne took her to an emergency vet for some shots and to get the ticks out of her ears.

So Anne brought home this skinny, 27-pound, depressed little dog and, I must be totally honest, I was pissed. I was so mad that she had made this huge decision, to take on the responsibility of a dog, without consulting me. I mean, we have enough responsibilities already, you know? We really had it out. There was much gnashing of teeth and Sir Robin soiled his armor. We finally agreed to keep her for a few days and see how she was and if she wasn't any better, we'd take her to a shelter where they don't euthanize the animals.

Well, the dog was terrified of me. She had CLEARLY been abused by a man and she was terrified of men. "Great," I thought, "I'm going to be responsible for a dog who never lets me pet her. Terrific."

For the first 12 hours, she sat by the side door: never moving, never eating, just looking depressed. But somehow, my amazing wife loved this dog enough and totally turned her around. Within just 12 hours she was wagging her entire body, eating, chasing a tennis ball and generally acting like a dog. *And* she let me pet her and started following me everywhere around our house.

So we decided to keep her. But she needed a name . . . and that was very important. I wanted to give her a name from Mythology . . . "Athena" or "Psyche" or something. I know, lame. Deal. The kids wanted to name her "Haley," which didn't work for me at ALL, because in high school I had the most painful crush on a girl named Haley . . . so we decided that we'd try different names for a few days and the right one would reveal itself to us.

Anne came home from work the next day, walked in the door, looked at me and said, "Ferris."

"Bueller?"

"Sort of. Save Ferris!"

There is this band that we LOVE from OC called Save Ferris. They play with our friends fairview (another band) a lot. They rule.

Anne says, "Get it? Save Ferris. I totally saved Ferris!"

I looked at the dog, looked at her sweet, marble eyes and soft little puppy-fuzzy-head and it was perfect. Not surprising, considering that it came from my wife.

So her name is "Ferris."

Isn't that a cool story?

Anyone?

Anyone?

Bueller?

Bueller?

Our friends joke that my wife and I have had an eight-year honeymoon. It was very easy to write about the love I feel for her, because I didn't have to put on a brave face or risk revealing how frustrated and tormented I was in my career.

THREE

SpongeBobVega$ Pants

I SPENT THE FIRST WEEK of September 2001 in Las Vegas, at a *Star Trek* convention which celebrated the 35th anniversary of the original series.

In addition to the things we *Star Trek* people usually do at conventions (signing autographs, posing for pictures, answering questions, and saying *"Engage!"*), I took a group of people from the ACME Comedy Theatre with me to perform a sketch comedy show. The entire convention experience is chronicled in "The Saga of SpongeBob Vegas Pants," which is the centerpiece of my first collection of essays, *Dancing Barefoot*.

Here's a primer for readers who aren't familiar with *Star Trek* conventions: conventions (or "cons," as they are known among people who are too busy to say "conventions") are part trade show, part collectible show, and part geek fest. It all adds up to a celebration of everything related to *Star Trek*, and the atmosphere is always festive and excited.

Promoters hire actors, writers, producers and others from the show to give lectures, answer questions, and sign autographs for the fans. There are also people who sell collectibles and bootlegs and other sci-fi- and fantasy-oriented merchandise. The organizers usually run episodes of *Star Trek* on a big screen, and there are always costume contests. Oh, the costume contests. Think *Rocky Horror Picture Show*, with less drag, but strangely, more singing. In Klingon. Seriously.

When I was invited to participate in this show, Prove To Everyone That Quitting *Star Trek* Wasn't a Mistake grabbed the phone out of my hand and said, *"I'd love to come to the convention, but I'm in this sketch comedy group that performs at the ACME Comedy Theatre in Hollywood, and I'd like to bring some of it to Vegas, and prove—I mean, show the fans that I can do something different and unexpected."*

The promoter thought it was a great idea, so I approached some of the funniest and smartest ACME writers and performers about doing a sci-fi-oriented comedy show for some sci-fi fans. The ones who didn't ask me for money or run away screaming came with me to Vegas.

The Q&A Talk that I gave to the fans was a complete failure, but my sketch comedy show was a resounding success.

Prove To Everyone and I were very proud of ourselves, and The Voice of Self Doubt was temporarily silenced . . . but that was nothing compared to the experience I had at the Las Vegas Hilton's Star Trek: The Experience.

The following excerpts are from "The Saga Of SpongeBob Vegas Pants or How I Learned to Stop Worrying and Love Star Trek," which was first published in *Dancing Barefoot*.*

◇◇◇

OCCASIONALLY GLANCING UP THROUGH THE RAIN

I check my watch: 4:55 p.m. I'm supposed to go on at 5 p.m. and talk for about 50 minutes. I usually talk for 90 minutes, which gives me time to let the audience warm up to me, tell

---

* What I've reprinted here is just part of the story. All the stuff I couldn't put in because of space limitations is in *Dancing Barefoot*.

some involved stories, take lots of questions, and make some jokes. With just 50 minutes, I can't waste any time: I have to go out there and nail 'em with a good joke right away, so the audience is on my side.

Well, I've got three things working against me before I even walk into the room:

1. I'm the last speaker of the day. The fans are tired and a little burned out.

2. I'm following Michael Dorn and Marina Sirtis. They do conventions together all the time, have a set routine that never fails, and the fans *adore* them.

3. I was Wesley Crusher.

Performing well at a convention is extremely important to me. I care about what the fans think. I don't write them off or take them for granted. I know that they've spent a large portion of their disposable income on this show, and I want to make sure they get their money's worth.

I remember how I felt when WILLIAM FUCKING SHATNER dismissed me on the set of *Star Trek V*. That feeling of humiliation and disenchantment is easy for me to recall, and I do everything I can to ensure that I don't inflict it on another person.

When I am on stage, the only real difference between me and the people I'm talking to is that I got paid to wear the spacesuit. I'm a huge science fiction geek. I've been attending conventions since I was in the fifth grade, and I know what it's like when a guest is only there to take the fans' money.

I pace backstage, checking my watch every 40 seconds. Michael and Marina are really working this crowd, and the fans don't want to let them get off stage. At 5:15, they finish.

My mouth and throat get dry. My hands sweat and tremble. I've got the *Mind Meld* cast, my parents, and my wife in the audience. The last thing I want is to have a whole room of Trekkies hate me in front of them.

Michael and Marina come off stage, and smile at me. Marina gives me a warm hug and kisses my cheek.

"You look great, Teen Idol." She turns to Michael. "Doesn't he look great?"

"If you say so," Michael teases me.

I love these two. I'm terrified about going on stage, but a smile that starts in my feet spreads across my face.

"The fans loved you guys," I say. "I have a lot to live up to."

"You're going to be great, Wil." It's the promoter, Dave Scott. "Are you ready?"

I take a deep breath. "Yeah. Let's do it."

Michael and Marina wish me luck and leave. I wonder if any of us have ever stayed around to watch each other on stage. I've watched Patrick a few times, hoping that he'll break into some spontaneous Shakespeare, but nobody's ever watched me, as far as I know.

Dave pats my shoulder and takes the stage.

"Oh, ladies and gentlemen! Our next speaker is going to really surprise you!" The crowd begins to applaud.

That was nice. Surprising people is cool.

"He did a show for me in Waterbury, Connecticut, and he was the funniest, most entertaining, and charming guest I've ever had!" The applause is joined by some whistling.

Woah, Dave! Let's not build me up too much.

"You are going to have the time of your life in the next 50 minutes!"

I can hear some screams of "WESLEY!" join the cacophony.

Oh Christ. "The time of your life?!" Stop now, please.

"Please welcome to the stage, all the way from Los Angeles, the man, the myth, the legend, Wesley Crusher himself, WIL WHEATON!"

The crowd explodes. They cheer. They stomp their feet. They whistle. The stage is littered with panties.

Well, maybe not the panties part, but everything else is true. I swear. I take a deep breath, and walk through the curtain.

◇◇◇

I burst out onto the stage, and they jump to their feet. In this moment, I understand the appeal of living a rock-and-roll lifestyle.

I walk around the stage, waving, throwing the goat, and enjoying the positive response.

When the crowd settles down, I hit them with my funny.

It's hot in Vegas. Tenth Circle of Hell hot. Fortunately, TNN has shown up and, in a humanitarian and self-promotional effort, have handed out bottles of "Altair Water." It's plain old bottled water, but it's in a nifty green bottle with some *Star Trek* graphics on it and a friendly reminder to "Watch *TNG* on The New TNN!" They were handing them out by the hundreds, because those spacesuits really make you sweat, if I remember correctly.

So I hold up the bottle of water and I say, "I've been drinking this 'Altair Water' all morning . . . and you know what I'm thinking? This isn't actually from the planet Altair. It's just regular water! So if you paid for it, I think you got ripped off."

Oh yeah, baby. It's comedy gold.

The applause and cheering of moments before is replaced by the hum of fluorescent lights, as the first surly heckler shouts, (with the appropriate mix of condescension and contempt), "It's free, Wil!"

Self Preservation speaks up. *"Get off the stage, Wil. You had your chance and you blew it."*

He's right. I've been on stage for 15 seconds, and they already hate me.

I try to shake it off, and move right into the Q&A. "Okay . . . uh, I only have 50 minutes here and I want to maximize our time together today, so here's the deal: I have some stories that I like to tell, but I also like to take questions from the audience, so you can direct the discussion. Since we only have a short time today, I'll answer the most frequently asked questions first: No, yes, umbrellas, I can't remember, and they were real."

Bingo, baby! "They were real!" How can they not love that?!

Silence. I see a teenager in a "Sexy women of Star Trek" T-shirt roll his eyes, as four Klingons sigh heavily and walk out.

Oh shit. They are walking out. I'm dead.

I panic. *"What's wrong?"* I ask Self Preservation.

"Hey, I told you to get off the stage. You're on your own, jackass," he says.

An experienced performer has a few jokes or stories that always get a good response. We call them "back pocket" material, and they are held in our minds for occasions like this. I decide to bring one of them out . . . but my mind draws a complete blank.

I have nothing, so I say, "Uh. Does anyone have any questions?"

I honestly expect someone to shout out, "How come you suck?" But nobody says anything.

I look at the crowd for a second, and I say with a smile, "Well then, I guess we're done here! Thanks a lot for coming, and have a great rest of the weekend!" I start to walk off stage, with every intention of continuing down the hall and into the bar.

After a couple of steps, though, they all laugh. Hard.

What? *That was funny?* Well, I guess after the water crack, pretty much anything is funny. Okay, I'll take what I can get at this point. I relax a bit and we get going. I begin to share my *Star Trek* memories, and the crowd gets involved.

A woman dressed as Doctor Crusher stands up and says, "Say hello to your mother!"

"Okay . . ." I say, and turn to my real mom, Debbie, who is sitting on the opposite side of the theater. "Hey mom! Thanks for coming! Do I still suck?"

The whole room turns to find her.

"No. You're doing great, honey," she says.

"Thanks, mom," I say.

I call on a cute girl who wears a babydoll "Social Distortion" shirt.

"What was it like to kiss Ashley Judd?" she asks.

I smile broadly. "Come on up here, and I'll show you!"

Huge laugh. She stands up!

"Oh! No! I'm just kidding!" I hold up my hand, and point into my palm, "my ifeway isay inay the eatherthay!"

I glance at my wife. She's laughing and shaking her head, and she winks at me.

I feel good. They're laughing with me and having a good time.

I call on an older man, who sits near the front, several bags of collectibles at his feet.

"Do you have a favorite episode of *Voyager*?" he asks.

"Well, The truth is, I've only watched *Voyager* a couple of times, and I really don't like it."

There is a little bit of a gasp. *Did Wesley just say he doesn't like Voyager?*

I try to explain. "The episode was called "Scorpion," and I watched it because my friend designed the monster that terrorized the crew for the entire episode."

I hear angry sighs. People turn to talk to each other. Some of them leave.

What happened? All I said was that I don't like *Voyager!* What's the big deal? Lots of Trekkies don't like *Voyager*. Maybe I should have called it "V'ger."

A guy waves his hand rather urgently, fingers spread in the Vulcan "Live long and prosper" salute. I point to him.

"What was your favorite episode of *Deep Space Nine?*"

"Well, the truth is, *DS9* and *Voyager* just never appealed to me. The stories didn't interest me as much as the stories on *Next Generation* or Classic *Trek,*" I say.

Big mistake. This is not what the fans want to hear. They want to hear how I love and care about these shows as much as they do, because that's exactly what they hear from the other actors. They get up on stage, and they give the fans exactly what they want.

Well, I don't do that. I tell them what it's truly like for me, warts and all. The truth is, sometimes being on *Star Trek* was the greatest thing in the world. Other times, it completely sucked. And, as blasphemous as this sounds, at the end of the day it was just a job.

But when all is said and done, I am still a fan at heart. I loved the original series. I am proud of the work I did on *Next Generation.* I cried when Spock died, and I saw *Star Trek IV* in theaters six times.

I failed to mention all that, however. Without that information, it can piss people off that I don't have the same unconditional love for *Star Trek* that they do.

I look at my watch, and I have 10 minutes left to fill. I have nothing to lose, so I reach into my back pocket . . . and find it filled with material.

"I have the limited edition *Star Trek Monopoly* game." I say.

"Of course, it's a limited edition of *65 million.* But it's extremely valuable, because I got a number under 21 million."

They laugh. It's funny, because it's true.

I go one better. "Plus, it's got a certificate of authenticity signed by Captain Picard!

"Yes, that's right, my *Star Trek Monopoly* game, which I've rendered worthless by opening, comes with a certificate of authenticity signed in ink by a fictional character."

I see a guy in the front row say something to his buddy, and they both nod their heads and laugh.

"Cool thing about the game, though, is that there is a Wesley Crusher game piece in it, and the first time we sat down to play it as a family, Ryan grabbed Wesley and proclaimed, as only an 11-year-old can, 'I'm Wil!! I'm Wil!! Nolan!! I'm all-time Wil!! I call it!!'"

I see some people smile. I start to pace the stage. I'm hitting my stride, and the stories flow out of me.

"One time, when we were renegotiating our contracts, we were all asking for raises.

"We all felt a salary increase was appropriate, because *The Next Generation* was a hit. It was making gobs of money for Paramount," (I like that word—*gobs*) "and we felt that we should share in that bounty.

"Of course, Paramount felt otherwise, so a long and annoying negotiation process began.

"During that process, the producers' first counter offer was that, in lieu of a raise, they would give my *character* a promotion, to lieutenant."

I pause, and look around. I wrinkle my brow and gaze upward.

"What? Were they serious?"

A fan hollers, "Yeah! Lieutenant Crusher! Woo!"

I smile back at him.

"My agent asked me what I wanted to do. I told him to call them back and remind them that *Star Trek* is just a television show."

Okay, that was risky to say. It's pretty much the opposite of just a television show to these people, but I've gotten the audience back, and they giggle.

"I imagined this phone call to the bank," I mime a phone, and hold it to my ear. "Hi . . . uh, I'm not going to be able to make my house payment this month, but don't worry! I am a *lieutenant* now." I pause, listening to the voice on the other end.

"Where? Oh, on the *Starship Enterprise*."

I pause.

"*Enterprise D*, yeah, the new one. Feel free to drop by Ten Forward for lunch someday. We'll put it on my officer's tab!"

Laughter, and applause. My time is up, and Dave Scott stands at the foot of the stage, politely letting me know that it's time for me to go.

The fans see this, and I pretend to not notice him.

"In 2001, startrek.com set up a poll to find out what fans thought the best *Star Trek* episode of all time was. The competition encompassed all the series. The nominated episode from Classic *Trek* was "City On The Edge Of Forever." The entry for *The Next Generation* was "Best of Both Worlds, Part II." *DS9* offered "Trials and Tribble-ations," and *Voyager* weighed in with "Scorpion II.""

As I name each show, various groups of people applaud and whistle, erasing any doubt as to what their favorite show is.

"Now, look. I know that *Star Trek* is just a TV show. Matter of fact, I'm pretty sure I just said that five minutes ago, but there was no way I was going to let my show lose. It just wasn't going to happen. Especially not to *Voyager*—er, V'ger, I mean."

I pause, and look out at the crowd.

"So I went into my office, sat at my computer for 72 straight hours, and voted for *TNG* over and over again.

"I didn't eat, and I didn't sleep. I just sat there, stinky in my own filth, clicking and hitting F5, a Howard Hughes for *The Next Generation*.

"Some time around the 71st hour, my wife realized that she hadn't seen me in awhile and started knocking on the door to see what I was doing.

"'Nothing! I'm, uh, working!' I shouted through the door. Click, Click, Click . . .

"'I don't believe you! Tell me what you've been doing at the computer for so long!'

"I didn't want her to know what I was doing—I mean, it was terribly embarrassing . . . I had been sitting there, in crusty pajamas, voting in the *Star Trek* poll for three days."

Some people make gagging noises, some people "Eeww!" But it's all in good fun. They are really along for the ride now. This is cool.

"She jiggled the handle, kicked at the bottom of the door, and it popped open!"

The audience gasps.

"I hurriedly shut down Mozilla and spun around in my chair.

"'What have you been doing on this computer for three days, Wil?' she said."

I look out across the audience, and pause dramatically. I lower my voice and confidentially say, "I was not about to admit the embarrassing truth, so I quickly said, 'I've been downloading porn, honey! Gigabytes of porn!'"

I have to stop, because the ballroom rocks with laughter. It's a genuine applause break!

"She was not amused. 'Tell me the truth,' she said.

"I sighed, and told her that I'd been stuffing the ballot box in an online *Star Trek* poll.

"'You are such a dork. I'd have been happier with the porn.'

"I brightened. 'Really?'

"'No,' she said. She set a plate of cold food on the desk and walked out, muttering something about nerds.

"I stayed in that office for another 10 hours, just to be sure. When my eyes began to bleed, I finally walked away. It took several weeks of physical therapy before I could walk correctly again, but it was all worth it. "Best of Both Worlds, Part II" won by a landslide."

I pause dramatically, and the theater is silent.

"And it had *nothing* to do with my stuffing the box. It's because *Next Generation* FUCKING RULES!"

I throw my hand into the air, making the "devil horns" salute that adorns my satanic T-shirt, and the audience leaps to their feet, roaring with applause and laughter.

I can't believe it. I got them back. I say thank you, give the microphone to Dave Scott, who is now sitting on the stage pointedly checking his watch, and exit, stage left.

◇◇◇

IF YOU LIVED HERE, YOU'D BE HOME NOW.

Star Trek: The Experience is split up into three main areas: a restaurant that features Quark's Bar, a replica of the *DS9* Promenade that is filled with memorabilia and souvenirs, and the actual Star Trek "Experience" itself, which features an amazing trip right onto the bridge of the *Enterprise D*.

The whole thing is built beneath a huge model of the *Enterprise D* that hangs from the ceiling in midflight.

This is my first trip to Star Trek: The Experience, and I gasp involuntarily when I see my spaceship hanging there.

Staring at this giant model now, which must be 20 feet across the saucer section, I recall the first time I saw the *Enterprise D* in flight, when Paramount screened "Encounter At Farpoint" for us back in 1987. I sat in a darkened theater, and when Patrick Stewart intoned, "Space . . . the final frontier . . ." I got goosebumps. The seats began to rumble, and there was my spaceship, cruising by. She was beautiful. When she went to warp speed, my mouth hung open, and tears sprung into my eyes. I knew that I was part of something wonderful.

I point at it and say to Anne, "Hey! Look! I can see my house from here!" I giggle, and she has no idea what I'm talking about, which is one of the reasons I married her.

Anne and I are a little overwhelmed by how large and detailed everything is, but we don't have any time to take it in, because as soon as we arrive, the fans begin to approach. They're all very cool and friendly. Most of them have seen my sketch show and want to compliment me on it.

"It's one of the funniest things I've ever seen," says one man.

"I haven't laughed that hard at anything, ever, in my entire life. You guys rocked!" says another.

A woman recounts an entire sketch called "What Dreams May Come," where I play a 12-year-old kid who is supposed to have his first wet dream. His "nice dream angel," played by Travis (at 280 pounds, wrapped in a sheet, Travis got laughs just walking on stage) has a battle with his "naughty dream angel," played by Maz, who wore leather pants and a vest. During the sketch, all I do is lay in bed and occasionally hump the mattress. The sketch always kills, and this show was no exception.

"I'll never be able to see you as just Wesley Crusher again," she says.

"That's the idea, ma'am," I say.

"Are you ever embarrassed to perform that sketch in front of your wife?" she asks.

"It's nothing she doesn't see at home several times a week," I say. Anne punches my arm, and we all laugh.

Another man tells me that he had planned to see the other show that night, which was a performance of *Love Letters* that Rene Auberjonois did with Nana Visitor.

"I stayed in it for about 15 minutes, but I kept hearing laughter from your theater, so I left and bought a ticket to your show. I'm so glad that I did!" he tells me and claps me on the back.

Everyone wants to know when they can see the show again, and if they can buy audio or video versions.

"Sorry, but there aren't any recordings of the show. It's a once-in-a-lifetime deal," I say.

"Why didn't you tape it? It was great!" a woman asks.

"I don't know," I say, and that's the truth. We just didn't think to record it. I know that we all regret this fact. There will never be another *Mind Meld* performance like it.

I pose for pictures, visit with some friends who I only get to see at conventions, and decide to take Anne on the ride.

The line takes us down a long and winding path, flanked by props and costumes dating all the way back to the original series, in what they call "the museum of the future." It's the largest collection of *Star Trek* props in the world, and it's a Trekkie's wet dream. For me, it is the first stop on a trip through time. Behind thick panes of glass, I see tricorders and PADDS that I may have held one or more times during my years on the show. I see costumes that I remember being worn by guest stars or my fellow cast members. It's a very surreal experience to see these relics of my youth on display in a museum.

We take our time, looking at all the props, reading all the plaques. Every item we see sparks a memory and Anne patiently listens to all of the stories that go along with them. Imagine sitting through your crazy Aunt Dorothy's vacation slides. It's like that.

We finally make our way to the end of a short line of people waiting to get into the ride. We are in a passageway, standing right next to a large display about the Klingon Empire. A visual record of Klingon history plays on a monitor, next to a display featuring weapons and costumes worn by Michael Dorn. I look at them, and I can hear Michael's deep voice as he whines about how uncomfortable his makeup is. I smile to myself.

The Experience is closed to the public, so all the people in this line are hardcore Trekkies, most of them in costume. The people ahead of us are wearing *Next Generation Starfleet* uniforms.

We exchange greetings, as a group of Trekkies dressed as Klingons arrive behind us.

My Trekkie sense begins to tingle again.

There is a certain psychology that inhabits the minds of people who dress up like Klingons . . . they tend to be very extroverted and a little obnoxious from time to time. These Klingons fit that description completely. Before long, they've begun an argument with the people in front of us. Something about Klingon honor versus the Federation's Prime Directive. The whole thing is amusing to me, but it's beginning to scare my wife. I forget that she hasn't been around this type of thing for years, like I have.

The argument escalates, and both groups try to get me on their side.

"Wil! You were *in Starfleet!*" the "Federation" fans say. "Surely you're with us!"

The "Klingon" fans grunt and snarl at me in what I imagine is the Klingon tongue. One of them shows off a dangerous looking Klingon *batleth*.

Of course, I side with my now completely freaked-out wife: "I gotta go, you guys."

Anne and I step out of line and head down to Quark's for a drink. We end up talking with Garret Wang (an actor from *Voyager*) for a while. He's a super nice guy, very funny and friendly. Even though we've never met before, we get along instantly. He asks me if I've ever been on the ride before and I tell him about the Klingons. He sympathizes and suggests that we ride it together. He's been on it before, and he is certain I'm going to love it. We run into Stephen Furst (an actor from *Babylon 5* who I worked with on *St. Elsewhere* before I started *Star Trek*), and he joins us.

We work our way back through the museum and make our way to the entrance.

◇◇◇

The ride starts out like Star Tours. We're all in a line, watching some monitors. An actor is describing to us how the safety belts work, or something, when all the lights go out. The monitors flicker, lights strobe, there are some special effects and a gust of air. When the lights come back up, we're standing in the transporter room on the *Enterprise.*

I didn't expect this. I am stunned and stare at my surroundings. It's amazing.

The Transporter Chief says, "Welcome to the 24th century. You are aboard the *Starship Enterprise.*"

She could have said to me, "Welcome to 1987, Wil. You are on Stage 9."

She touches her communicator and says, "I have them, Commander."

Jonathan Frakes's voice booms over the comm, "Good work, Lieutenant. Please take them to the bridge."

We leave the transporter room and walk down a long corridor, which is identical to the ones I walked down every day. I realize as we walk that, in my mind, I'm filling in the rest of the sound stage. I'm surprised when we don't end up in engineering at the end of the corridor. Instead, we are herded into a turbolift, where we enjoy some more special effects. The turbolift shakes and hums . . . it's infinitely cooler than the real ones we would stand in for the show.

When the turbolift doors open and reveal the bridge of the *Enterprise,* I gasp.

The bridge is a nearly perfect replica of ours, with a few minor differences that are probably imperceptible to anyone who didn't spend the better part of five years on it. The hum of the engines, which had only existed in my imagination on Stage 8, is now real. I stare at the view screen, where a beautiful starfield gives the appearance of motion. I remember how much I hated doing blue screen shots on the bridge and how much I loved it when they'd lower the starfield. When I looked at those thousands of tiny mirrors, glued onto a screen of black velvet, I could lose myself in the wonderful fantasy that this spaceship was as real as the view.

I am consumed by hypernostalgia.

I am 14-years-old, walking out of the turbolift during "Encounter at Farpoint." Corey Allen, the director, excitedly tells me, "Picard controls the sky, man! *He controls the sky!*"

I am 15-years-old, sitting in my ugly grey spacesuit at the CONN. My fake muscle suit bunches up around my arms. I feel awkward and unsure, a child who desperately wants to be a man.

I am 16-years-old, working on an episode where I say little more than, "Aye, sir." I want to be anywhere but here.

I am 17-years-old, wearing a security uniform for "Yesterday's Enterprise." I am excited to stand in a different place on the bridge, wear a different uniform, and push different imaginary buttons.

I hear the voices of our crew, recall the cool fog that hung around our trailers each morning from Autumn until Spring.

I recall walking to the Paramount commissary with the cast, on our way to have lunch meetings with Gene before he died.

I have an epiphany.

Until this moment, all I have been able to remember is the pain that came with *Star Trek*. I'd forgotten the joy.

Star Trek was about sitting next to Brent Spiner, who always made me laugh. It wasn't about the people who made me cry when they booed me off stage at conventions. It was about the awe I felt listening to Patrick Stewart debate the subtle nuances of The Prime Directive with Gene Roddenberry between scenes. It wasn't about the writers who couldn't figure out how to write a believable teenage character. It was about the wonder of walking down those corridors and pretending that I was on a real spaceship. It was about the pride I felt when I got to wear my first real uniform, go on my first away mission, fire my first phaser, play poker with the other officers in Riker's quarters.

Oh my god. Star Trek was wonderful, and I'd forgotten. I have wasted 10 years trying to escape something that I love, for all the wrong reasons.

I am filled with regret. I miss it. I miss my surrogate family, and I will give anything to have those 10 years back. Like Scrooge, I want a second chance, will do anything for a second chance. But Christmas day came and went 10 years ago.

The stars blink out, and I'm looking into the smiling face of Jonathan Frakes on the view screen. I'm smiling back at him and I notice that everyone is staring at me. I become aware of wetness on my cheeks. I am embarrassed and make a joke. I say to the actors walking around the bridge, "If you need any help flying this thing, I've totally got your back!" The group laughs. Garrett says something about helping out the security guys if they get into trouble and we laugh over that too.

Jonny tells us that we have to leave the ship now and board a shuttlecraft so that we may safely return to Las Vegas.

I don't want to leave. I've just gotten here. I want to cry out "No! Don't make me leave! It's not fair! I want to stay! I *need* to stay! Please let me stay!"

Instead, I am silent and I stare hard at the bridge, trying to catch a glimpse of a dolly track, or a mark, or maybe my costumer waiting for me to come off stage so she can hand me my fleece jacket.

The group I'm with herds me into the turbolift, and the doors close. I remember all the times the FX guy didn't pull the doors open in time, and we'd walk into them.

The turbolift takes us to the shuttle bay, where we board a flight simulator that looks like one of our shuttlecraft. I don't pay any attention to the voyage home—I am deep in my own memories, consumed by thoughts of days gone by and time forever lost.

The ride comes to an end and we walk back to Quark's. Everyone we pass wants to know what I thought of the ride, if I enjoyed my Star Trek Experience. I tell them, truthfully, that it was just like being back on the set. I tell them that it's reminded me how cool *Star Trek* was. I keep the rest to myself. I don't think I can even give voice to the incredible series of emotions I have felt in the past 15 minutes. I don't even know if, in recalling that experience and writing these thoughts down, I have been able to convey how it affected me.

But it did. It *changed* me.

Being inside those walls, even though it was in a casino in Las Vegas, I was safe. I was protected from the bullshit that had been the focus of my life since I quit the show. When that bullshit was washed away, I saw *Trek* for what it is: a huge part of my life. I will probably never be bigger than *Trek*, so why try to avoid it? Why not love it, embrace it, and be proud of it? It was cool. Gene was cool. The cast *is* cool. *Star Trek* may never be what it once was . . . but I got to be there when it was great.

We stay at the party for another hour. We talk with friends, and I pose for pictures, sign a few autographs, and shake some hands. We watch Armin and Max perform a very funny sketch, and I have my picture taken with a cardboard stand up of WILLIAM FUCKING SHATNER, circa 1967.

Finally, the five days in Vegas catch up with us, and Anne and I need to leave. I seek out Dave and Jackie Scott and thank them for a great convention. I tell them that I'll see them in a few weeks, never thinking that in just two days I will never want to board an airplane again.

We take a cab back to our hotel. Anne puts her head on my shoulder and is asleep before we're even out of the driveway.

We drive up a wide and empty street, about a quarter mile off the strip. This part of Vegas seems lonely, desolate. The carnival glare of lights along The Strip robs the rest of the world of any light, and the whole desert is black, like outer space . . . I stare out the window into the darkness and imagine a starfield that's 15 years away.

I had forgotten how cool *Star Trek* was and how much I missed it. I feel a little sad.

The cabbie keeps looking at me in the rear view mirror, giving me that 'I think I know you but I'm not sure why' look. He says, "What brings you to Vegas?"

"*Star Trek*," I tell him.

"Oh yeah? You a big fan or something?"

"Yes I am," I tell him. "I love *Star Trek*."

When I left Las Vegas, I felt like I'd taken first place in the World Series of Poker. My sketch comedy show was an unqualified success,* and I'd found a way to temporarily silence the relentless Voice of Self Doubt, *and* Prove To Everyone That Quitting *Star Trek* Wasn't A Mistake. For the first time in almost a decade, I was able to watch *Star Trek* without much regret, enjoy the stories, and welcome the memories that came with each episode.

6 OCTOBER, 2001
Life in the so-called space age

Tonight I watched "All Good Things . . ." on TNN, as I wrapped up a week of watching the best of *TNG*.

God dammit all to hell if it didn't reduce me to tears, at the end, seeing all my friends seated around that poker table. I thought, as I watched them, about how much I wished *I* was at that table . . . and I can admit something here, to myself and to fandom: I miss *Star Trek*. I miss working with that

---

* Three years later, it's taken on a a life of its own in fandom. I *still* get e-mails from people who were there, and people who have heard about it. Whenever I attend a *Star Trek* event, someone asks me if I've brought my comedy group with me.

amazing cast. I miss being part of that amazing show. Watching *TNG* all this week has been the closest I will ever get to watching lots of home movies, or reading a high school yearbook over and over and over again.

So many memories came flooding back over the past few days. Here are some of them, in list form:

- In the first season, when LeVar was driving the ship (before a certain strapping young ensign took over), the chairs we had were really reclined. More suited for sleeping, than sitting . . . and that's what LeVar would do, all the time! When he was in a scene without any dialogue, he would sit in that recliner, VISOR securely in place and just doze off. More than once, he got busted for snoring.

- In one episode and I can't remember the title, so you'll have to excuse me, Patrick was strolling around the bridge, saying something about how we all needed to "consider the source" of something. Thing is, he was saying "consider the sauce." I didn't catch it the first few times, but Brent did and he turned to me, at the beginning of a take and just as they were about to roll, he said, "Patrick wants more sauce." I asked him what the hell that meant, because Brent was always fucking with me and he said, "Just listen." So they roll, and Patrick says that we should "consider the sauce." I cracked up. Out loud. I couldn't help it. They cut, everyone looked at me, all pissed off, because it was okay for the adults to crack, but if The Kid did it, it was another thing completely. I pointed to Brent, stammered that he made me laugh and Brent just looked angelic (in gold, mind you; I think that helped him pull it off). Nobody believed me, until later, when someone else heard Patrick saying something else, in his, er . . . unique . . . accent and Marina said, "I'm British and I know that's not how we talk." So I took the opportunity to point out "the sauce."

- I remember the first time Wesley got to play in one of those poker games that they had on the show. I remember how genuinely thrilled I was to be in that scene, because I felt like I was finally accepted as something other than The Kid.

- It's weird to watch *TNG* now, because when I watch *Enterprise*, my imagination fills in the ship around what the camera is currently showing . . . but when I watch *TNG*, my memory fills in the stage around the set . . . instead of picturing the rest of the corridors, or the Battle Bridge (my personal favorite set), I remember our chairs and the craft service table . . .

I remembered, as I was watching "All Good Things . . ." tonight, something that happened a very long time ago. Two things, actually, which, at the time, seemed to validate my reasons for leaving.

There was a big deal made about the screening of the final episode of *TNG* over at Paramount and I was asked to attend. I agreed, mostly because I wanted to see my friends, but also because I was curious to see how they had ended it.

They did the screening in a theater at Paramount and they sat all of us from the cast together in the theater. I sat between Marina and Brent, if memory serves. Some of our more high-profile guest stars had been invited and there were some empty seats on the other side of our row where they would have sat if they'd shown—somehow I'm not surprised that Mick Fleetwood didn't show—but John DeLancie was sitting behind me. That's important, as you'll see in a second.

Some stuffed shirt from Viacom got up, made some stupid speech that nobody wanted to hear about how great *Star Trek* was and he introduced Rick Berman, who came up to the podium and made another speech, about how great the last seven years had been and how it was through the work of some people, some people who are here tonight, that *TNG* was possible. Would those people please stand up? Patrick

Stewart. Jonathan Frakes. Brent Spiner. Marina Sirtis. Gates McFadden. LeVar Burton. Michael Dorn. Denise Crosby. John DeLancie.

They all stood up. The entire theater was now on its feet, applauding their hard work and commitment to the show. Berman was beaming as he applauded them.

They were all standing up, except for me. Berman looked right at me and didn't call out my name. The son of a bitch knew that I was there and didn't call on me to stand. Later, I asked him why he'd left me out and he said he didn't know I was there. I told him that I was the one person who was sitting with the cast who wasn't standing up. Maybe he remembered making eye contact with me, after he called Denise and before he called on John DeLancie? It sucked, it was petty, and it hurt.

Another time, I was invited to a big party for the 25th anniversary of *Star Trek*, also at Paramount. Again, I can't remember if this was before, or after the aforementioned snubbing. Again, they sat us all together and again, there was a "stand up and be counted" thing. Only this time, it was with all three casts. Maybe you've seen the picture? All three casts are on stage, holding these miniature American flags, which were given to them by astronauts who flew them on various space shuttle missions. Again, I was left sitting, surrounded by empty chairs. I was so embarrassed, as I sat there, feeling genuinely happy for my friends, from all the casts, who were standing on stage and at the same time, I felt so tiny and so lame . . . afterward, I told Berman that I thought that was really shitty and he said he hadn't known that I was coming. Well, the thing is, when you're the executive producer of *Star Trek*, you approve *everything* that goes on. Even guest lists.

I recall all this publicly, to maybe give some context to my remarks over the years and to help you, my dear monkey, appreciate what I will say next: I am filled with regret that I left. Now, I know some asshole out there will say that I feel that way because I didn't work as much after I left, but the truth is, that was by my choice. As soon as I was off the show, I realized that I could do whatever I wanted with my life and I quit. Ran away to Topeka, joined a computer company and discovered that I hated myself. I was truly disgusted with the person I looked at in the mirror each day and getting away from the environment I had always lived in was the only way to ensure that I changed all that.

You know who I would be if I had never left? Say it with me, my people: WILLIAM FUCKING SHATNER.

So, regrets? I have a few . . . but then again, I wouldn't be the person I am now, if I'd stuck around and I like who I've become.

That's an interesting entry for a couple of reasons. I genuinely enjoyed sharing those "on the set" memories with WWdN readers as much as I enjoyed recalling them . . . but I'm also trying to clarify—for myself, as much as for anyone else—why I had spent so much time and effort distancing myself from the franchise. I still miss the cast and my time spent with them, but I can't deny how awful Rick Berman made me feel, and it's pretty clear to me now that Prove To Everyone That Quitting *Star Trek* Wasn't A Mistake was born largely because of those events.

BREAKING NEWS

"Life is what happens while you're making other plans."

—*John Lennon*

The World Has Turned

WE WERE IN LAS VEGAS from September 4th until September 10th. The day after we came home, the joy I'd felt just 24 hours before was replaced by shock, horror, and confusion.

13 SEPTEMBER, 2001

He didn't know what to do. But he'd think of something.

I wasn't going to talk about this, because it's all anyone is talking about. I mean, I turn on TLC to get away from it and they're just running a feed of FOX News. Same for Discovery. Even ESPN has a ticker with updates scrolling across the bottom of the screen.

So since I can't get away from it, I give in. I will write about it. Because I am scared. I am distraught. I am upset. I am depressed. I am angry. Mostly, I don't know what to do and I'm not quite sure how to feel. It reminds me of when my friend hanged himself. How helpless I felt, how angry, sad, and scared.

My wife woke me up Tuesday, much earlier than we normally get up, because my mom had called and told her about the attack on the WTC. So I sat up, turned on the TV and watched in horror as that plane crashed into the tower, over and over and over and over.

I felt like I was watching a bad Steven Segal movie. I mean, this just doesn't happen in real life, right?

But here's the deal: I can't cry. I really want to. I feel it well up in my chest, but the tears won't come. And that is the hardest thing, so far. That and the fear.

I was walking Ferris last night and I kept getting this completely irrational fear that something awful was going to happen while I was away from the house. Didn't help that she kept stopping and looking behind us, like there was something there.

Here I find myself, at an uncommon loss for words. I don't think I really have much to add, so that's it for tonight.

Hrm. Worst. Entry. Ever.

Like much of the world, I spent the rest of September in a daze. I've never been a big fan of flying, and my thoughts often drifted to the passengers on those planes. I wondered what they did, how they felt, when they knew they were going to die. I had grown accustomed to feeling depressed about Hollywood, but 9/11 made my frustrations about work feel petty, and proving to everyone that quitting *Star Trek* wasn't a mistake seemed pretty goddamned unimportant.

ACT II

"You're out of control—and you want the world to love you
Or maybe you just want a chance to let them know
That you live and breathe and suffer
And your back is in the corner and you've got nowhere to go"

—Oingo Boingo
Out of Control

"You've got to cry without weeping,
talk without speaking,
scream without raising your voice."

—U2
Running To Stand Still

FOUR

Stop Me if You Think That You've Heard This One Before

IT WAS EARLY OCTOBER, and a thick blanket of gold and orange maple leaves covered the grass outside my office window. I looked up when I heard the phone ring, and saw Anne playing catch with Ferris, who seemed to have as much fun bounding through the piles of leaves as she did chasing the ball.

From the kitchen, Nolan shouted, "I've got it!"

"Hello?" he said. "No, this is Nolan. Do you want to talk to my mom?"

I laughed, and remembered all the times when I was his age that I was mistaken for my mom on the phone.

"Okay. I'll get him." A moment later, he stood in my office doorway.

"Wil, it's your manager and he wants to talk to you . . . and he thought I was *mom!*" He laughed, and ran back out of my office.

"I love how he's still got two speeds: running and sleeping," I thought as I walked out to the kitchen and picked up the phone.

"Hey, Chris. What's up?"

"Well, please apologize to Nolan for me. I should know better, but he sounded just like Anne."

"I'll tell him," I said with a grin.

"Have you ever heard of a show called *Win Ben Stein's Money*?"

"Of course I have. It's hilarious! Do I get to be a contestant?"

"Better than that. Their cohost, Jimmy Kimmel, is leaving the show, and the executive producer wants to meet with you. If he thinks you're funny, you'll do a dry run of the show with him and some other executives, then a test for the network."

Prove To Everyone, who had been quietly slumbering for over a month since I came back from Las Vegas, woke with a start.

"Oh my god, Chris! If I get this, I'll be on TV every single day!"

"Yeah, and you'll get to show people how funny you are, and you'll get to write."

"Chris, I can totally do this! I've got all that experience from writing sketch comedy for ACME, and I know how to be a good cohost from working on *The J.Keith vanStraaten Show!*"★

"This is a huge opportunity for us, Wil. Your meeting is at 2 tomorrow afternoon. I'm faxing the details right now."

I hung up the phone, and raced to the backyard to tell my wife about the meeting.

"Oh Puss!" she said. "I'm so happy for you!"

She turned to Ferris. "Your dad is going to be on TV again!"

Thump thump thump thump thump. I picked up the ball and threw it across the yard.

"This could turn everything around," I said.

"When's the meeting?" Ferris came racing back, and dropped the ball at my feet.

"Tomorrow at 2!"

★ I'm Ed McMahon to Keith's Johnny Carson on a *Tonight Show*–style late night comedy talk show that he and I do together for live audiences at the ACME Comedy Theatre.

We may have done a stupid little dance because we were so excited, but I'd never admit to that in public. Or in a book, for that matter.

I knew that I was a perfect match for this show, and for the first time in years I felt supremely confident that I could book a job. While I waited for the fax to arrive, Prove To Everyone said, *"You're going to blog about this, right?"*

Before I could answer, the Voice of Self Doubt convinced me to keep the specifics to myself: *"You're going to look like a big stupid asshole if you talk all about this and don't book the job, Wil. Talk about the opportunity, but don't give any specifics."*

05 OCTOBER, 2001
Tree Huggin' Hippie Crap

I can't go into the details, but I have a HUGE opportunity sitting in front of me and tomorrow is do-or-die time . . . if this thing happens, I am back baby! We're talking career rebirth, a new computer and nice things for Mrs. Wheaton.

So here's the deal: if you don't mind, would you take 60 seconds or so and send some good thoughts my way? I would be especially grateful if you were doing this between 2 and 3 p.m. Pacific Time tomorrow (Thursday).

If this works, I will have the coolest story, EVER, to post.

In less than an hour, my weblog was filled with over one hundred comments of support and "mojo." Many people promised to hold a good thought for me during my meeting, and as crazy as it seems, I swear it worked. Thanks to the positive energy and support I felt, I was able to leave Prove To Everyone and the Voice of Self Doubt in the car (with the window cracked, of course) when I had my meeting. I was relaxed, confident, and focused. I had fun, and I left the building certain that I'd get called back for a proper audition.

09 OCTOBER 2001

More Tree Huggin' Hippie Crap

Last week, I put out a plea for some vibes, mojo, good thoughts, tantric chanting, or whatever anyone felt they could throw my way, because I had an extremely important audition.

I said that if it worked, I would have the coolest story, ever, to tell.

I am the most skeptical person you could ever meet, but I swear, I felt mojo coming my way when I needed it most and I was relaxed, funny, charming and all the things I needed to be on my audition.

I don't let myself get too high or too low about auditions. As I've said before, being the best actor usually isn't what gets an actor the job. There are so many factors that I can't control that I just focus on doing my best read or having my best possible meeting. For me, a successful audition isn't necessarily one where I get the job. It's one where I leave the room knowing that I was the best I can be.

So, having said all that, I can tell you that your mojo and vibes and all that *worked*, because I was walking on air when I left that room and every time the phone rang, I was excited that it would be my agent telling me that I'd been hired.

But the phone call that came did not tell me that I'd been hired, but that they were bringing me back one more time, to perform again. This time it was between me and one other person.

So here I am, putting out yet another plea for mojo, vibes, good thoughts, voodoo dances, or whatever you'd care to send my way.

My final, final, final callback is today, at 3 p.m.

So, if you can, please send mojo between 3 and 4:30 p.m. PDT
and I will give up all the details of the project, the audition process and all that, later on today.

Later that afternoon, I wrote about my meeting.

Got my mojo risin', there's a poodle in my strudel!

. . . Minky Boodle!!

Wow. What a day.

Short story: I killed. I felt the mojo and it was good. I won't
know anything until sometime tomorrow, at the earliest.

It was a great audition. Everyone, including me, knew it. I was
funny, I was smart, I was having a blast, and I was entertaining as
hell. When I left the studio, I excitedly told Prove To Everyone,
"In just a few weeks, we will be BACK, BABY!"

When I got home, I anxiously waited by the phone.

And waited.

And waited.

When it didn't ring for three days, my spirits darkened. I've
worked in Hollywood long enough to know that when days go
by with no word from the studio, I'm not getting the job.

12 OCTOBER 2001

MojoJojo

Well, at last the phone call has come and I can tell my story.
Now, you can know where all your mojo has been going the
last two weeks.

Before I get into the details, I have to say that, whether it is
placebo or not, I felt more confident than I have ever felt, as I
went through this audition process and I know that it helped
me relax and do my best work.

One of the coolest things, ever, came from Susie, who takes care of kids in a day-care here in SoCal. On the day of Mojo-needing, Susie had her kids draw me good luck pictures. She said to me, "Is there any better mojo than the mojo of a child?"

I think not.

She scanned and e-mailed the drawings to me. I was going to put them all up, but I've decided that I'm going to keep them just for me. I'm giving too damn much of myself away on this site as it is, anyway.

So here's the shortened version of the story: I was auditioning to be the new cohost of the Comedy Central show, *Win Ben Stein's Money*. It was a long process and it was the most fun I have ever had, ever, auditioning for any show. The producers and everyone who works on that show are so fucking cool, I can't even begin to describe it.

Oh, if you haven't figured it out by now, I didn't get it. It came down to me and one other guy and, everyone say it with me, "They took the other guy."

Something that is really shitty for me right now, as an actor, is that I have don't have enough of a "name" and enough recognizability to put me "over the top" for shows, but I do have enough to take me out of shows. I can't even do commercials, because I'm not a big enough celebrity to be an endorsement guy and I'm too well known to be an average Joe. I wonder if that came into play on this job? I don't know.

The challenge for me right now is to get producers to see me in a different way. To see past their preconception of me and let me show them something that they weren't expecting.

Like this website. How many people came here expecting some jackass celebrity site, where the celebrity has nothing to do with it? How many people came here expecting me to be a complete ass?

Did I give them what they expected? I certainly hope not.

So this news has devastated me. I really wanted to work with the crew over there, because they are all so cool.

Get this: the producer of the show, the EXECUTIVE FUCKING PRODUCER, actually called me, to tell me how sorry he was that I didn't make it and how he really liked me and how he called other producers to let them know about me. That just doesn't happen and I am floored by that. He is, truly, one of the coolest people I have ever met.

A sincere "thank you" to everyone who sent me mojo and kept me in their thoughts. That was very cool and I think I'll be calling on you all again. I didn't get this one, but I'll get one soon, I can feel it.

I almost made it to the end before Prove To Everyone asserted his voice and said, *"I didn't get this one, but I'll get one soon, I can feel it."*

The only thing I could feel was overwhelming, nearly suicidal depression, pretty much the opposite of what I portrayed. The rejection could not have come at a worse time. Anne's ex-husband continued to find new and exciting ways to disrupt our marriage and our relationship with her children. For the second time in two years, he took us to court, in an attempt to get full custody of Ryan and Nolan. He was costing us thousands of dollars in attorney fees, and every parenting choice I made was heavily scrutinized. I was portrayed to the kids and the court as "The Evil Stepfather," and I felt like my life was under siege.

The second-place finish (out of hundreds of actors) was nothing to be ashamed of, but finishing second paid the bills as much as finishing last. I was utterly, completely, and totally destroyed by that phone call. I *knew* that I had given the performance of my life in that final callback—the executive producer of the show told me that on my way out of the studio, but as I said in my weblog, being the best is never enough. The job that

I'd fought so hard for, the job that I'd *earned*, had been given to Jimmy Kimmel's cousin, Sal. The pain and frustration I felt when I faced the reality of continued financial and professional struggles was compounded by a feeling of injustice. It was so unfair! Nepotism was something we joked about in audition waiting rooms. It wasn't something that actually *happened*. As usual, it didn't matter that I was smart, or funny, or talented, or capable. This time, I wasn't "related to the outgoing actor" enough for the job.

I told my wife, "I suppose it's not as bad as 'You're not *edgy* enough,' but not by much."

FIVE

Last Place You Look

I SPENT NEARLY THREE WEEKS wallowing in misery and self-pity. The Voice of Self Doubt and I spent long hours together replaying the auditions for *Win Ben Stein's Money*, but even with 20/20 hindsight, I couldn't find a single thing that I would have done differently.

"You know what the worst thing about being an actor is?" I rhetorically asked my wife. "The not working. You know what the second worst thing is? Knowing that my entire career—hell, my entire life—can turn around with just one phone call."

I'm not making this up, but at that moment, the phone rang.

Okay, maybe I am making it up, but it certainly makes for good drama, doesn't it?

It was my manager.

"I just got a call from TNN," he said. "They want to check your availability to play on an all-*Star Trek* edition of *Weakest Link*."

Weakest Link was a trivia game show hosted by a woman named Anne Robinson, who had a reputation for being very nasty to the contestants.

"Really?! When?" I said.

"Tomorrow afternoon," he said. "They're paying 10 grand to you, and giving 10 grand to the charity of your choice."

"Are you sure you want to do this? You'll just be resting on your Star Trek laurels," The Voice of Self Doubt said.

"Are you kidding me? They're going to pay me 10 thousand dollars. That's more than I've made all year, and we really need the money." I said.

"Not only that, but you can show millions of people—in prime time—that you're smart, funny, and not a kid anymore," Prove To Everyone added. *"If there are producers and casting people watching, it could make a big difference . . ."*

I accepted the offer immediately, and tried to not let it bother me when I found out that I had only gotten the offer after they'd gone through their "A" list.

For my charity, I chose the Electronic Frontier Foundation, an organization that lobbies for and raises awareness of privacy and free speech rights on the Internet—rights that were squarely in John Ashcroft's post-9/11 cross hairs.

I had a wonderful time, and in front of a national prime time television audience, I held my own with my peers. I didn't win, but I made the Ice Queen Anne Robinson laugh three separate times (which, strangely, didn't make it onto TV).

30 OCTOBER 2001
Who was the Weakest Link*?*

I just got back from my taping of *Weakest Link*.

I'm bound by contract to not say a single word about the show, like who did what, or who won, or anything like that . . .

BUT!

I can say something that is going to rock everyone's world. It certainly rocked mine.

I sat in the green room (a place where actors hang out while they get stuff ready—there's food, drinks and TV, usually) and watched the World Series.

Not a big deal, right?

Well, I watched The World Series with WILLIAM FUCKING SHATNER.

It was so goddamn cool. I was sitting there, talking about baseball with him, discussing Randy Johnson versus Curt Shilling (who was better), the various strategies employed by the teams during the few innings that we were watching . . . and he was so cool to me, I didn't even know what to do. He was nice. He was funny. He was warm, genuine and basically just a 100% cool-ass guy.

Matter of fact, I can say this one thing about the show: William Shatner was the funniest I have ever seen him, or anyone who was in *Star Trek*, ever.

William Shatner has earned 50,000 cool points with me, after tonight. One for each monkey at this site.

In retrospect, it was probably just a strategy move, so I wouldn't vote him off in the early rounds. I've seen him once since and he didn't seem to remember me.

. . . but I didn't care. When Captain Freakin' Kirk is cool to you, you don't take it with a grain of salt, man. You take it with a double shot of whiskey and leave a fiver on the bar.

Hanging out with Captain Kirk and bonding over baseball felt too good to be true, so over a year later, when Bill (yeah, I get to call him Bill now) did an interview with the website Slashdot. org, I asked him . . .

◇◇◇

Seriously . . . are we cool?_by CleverNickName

Hey Bill,

Are we cool, or what? I mean, I always thought you didn't like me, but I had a good time with you at Weakest Link *watching the World Series.*

So are we cool, or was that just pre-game strategy?

Wil

Bill:

Dear Wil,

We are so cool, we're beyond cool. We are in orbit man. I don't do pre-game strategy.

I look forward to some personal time with you.

◇◇◇

Right there, in front of every geek in the world, WILLIAM FUCKING SHATNER told me we were "cool." Of course, the "personal time" he's talking about could be in a Turkish prison, but I'm not going to read into this one too much.

Bill was voted off early in the game, but not before he'd done some incredibly funny stuff, including "making out" with Anne Robinson, Captain Kirk-style. I made it all the way to the final three before I froze up on some really easy questions and was voted off.

When we were finished, the producers informed us that we were the smartest group of celebrities they'd ever had, so they didn't give us the typical "Who is buried in Grant's Tomb" questions that they usually give celebrities to make them look good. They gave us the same questions that they gave *real* contestants.

On my way out of the studio, I literally ran into Anne Robinson in a backstage hallway. Seriously, I almost knocked her down.

"Oh god. I am so sorry!" I said.

She gave me the biggest smile I've ever seen. "Oh my dear! It was my fault. I wasn't watching. Are you okay?"

"Yeah, I'm fine," I said. "Listen, I know we're not supposed to talk to you and stuff, but I wanted to let you know that I had a great time on the show. Thanks for playing with me."

"I had a lovely time with you all. You were very good contestants," she said. A girl from the network rounded the corner and approached.

"I'd better go," she said. "It ruins my image when I'm seen fraternizing with the contestants. I'm supposed to be a horrible person, you know." She winked.

"Understood. It was nice talking with you," I said. She was out of the hallway by the time the girl reached me.

"Wil," she said.

Oh shit. I'm busted for talking to Anne Robinson. Perfect.

I cleared my throat. "Yeah?"

"I'm from NBC publicity . . ."

Uh-oh.

". . . and we all thought you were really funny. Would you be interested in doing some national media to promote your appearance on the show?"

What? National media?!

"Uhh . . ."

"If you'd rather not, we can—"

"No! No! I was just . . . making sure I understood you correctly," I said. "Of *course* I'd be happy to do publicity for this show! Anything you want; all you have to do is ask and I am there."

"Great! We'll be in touch." She shook my hand, and walked back down the hallway.

I stood there alone, next to photos of Johnny Carson and Ed McMahon. "You know, this is weird, weird, wacky stuff," I said, in my best Johnny voice. "Things are really looking up."

"Yes they are, sir!!" I said, in my best Ed voice. "Looking up sir! Hiiii-oooh!"

SIX

Balance

I AM NOT A RELIGIOUS PERSON. I'm not quite an atheist, but I'm certainly not a theist, either. Friends describe me as an agnostic Taoist, whatever that means. I prefer to apply philosophies, rather than follow a leader, and I'm always coming back to the Tao Te Ching and the teachings of The Buddha. If I had the patience, I suppose I'd be a Buddhist.

Though I'm a bit of a skeptic, I do believe that The Universe (whatever that means to you) seeks something that I call The Balance. Each time I suffer a setback, or think I can't sink any lower, I remind myself, *"The Universe seeks Balance, Wil. For whatever low you're feeling now, there will be an equal high. Just wait for it."* This belief sustained me throughout the years of struggling and the very difficult trials I faced throughout 2001.

As I was flying high on the resurgence of popularity and visibility *Weakest Link* and my website brought me, The Balance struck: my 84-year-old great aunt, who has always been the foundation of our family, who loved more unconditionally than anyone I've ever known, suffered a stroke and slipped into a coma. She never regained consciousness, and four days later she died, on November 9th, just two days after my wedding anniversary. Her loss sent shock waves through my family. I was devastated.

09 NOVEMBER 2001

Loss

My Aunt Val had a stroke on Monday, and she died around 10:30 this morning.

I was just going to keep this to myself, but I want everyone in the world to know what an amazing, wonderful, loving, kind, thoughtful, selfless person she was. No person, anywhere, at any time in my life ever loved me as unconditionally as she did. She was truly the matriarch in my family and, as the initial shock of her loss is wearing off, the growing sadness and emptiness is consuming me.

While she was struggling to survive on Tuesday and was mostly unconscious, I held her hand and Anne told her that it was our anniversary on Wednesday . . . she squeezed my hand and when I told her that I loved her and that I'd miss her if she had to go, she turned her head to me and she smiled and squeezed my hand, hard. It was the first time she'd been really responsive to us. I felt like she knew we were there and I felt like she was telling me goodbye and that she loved me. For that, I am eternally grateful.

Do not ever take anyone for granted, for even one minute. If there's someone in your family who you love, pick up the phone and call them, right now, to tell them.

I love you, Aunt Val.

A few days before her memorial service, my mom called me.

"I just spoke with Ray [Aunt Val's son]," she said. "We'll be having a small memorial at his house for Aunt Val, and he wanted me to tell you that you're welcome to speak at it if you'd like."

"What would I say?" I asked.

"Whatever you want to, honey," she said, "Do you feel like saying anything?"

"Yeah, I do," I told her, "but I don't want to just say, 'Me too.'"

"I know how you feel . . ." she trailed off.

"Mom?"

"Sorry. Hold on." Her voice caught, and I could hear her put the phone down while she cried. Alone in my living room, I cried with her.

"Sorry," she said. "I keep thinking I can talk about her, but I just miss her so much."

I nodded my head, as tears streamed down my face.

"Me too, mom," I said. "I'll think of something."

"I know you will. I'll see you Saturday. I love you."

"I love you too, mom."

I hung up the phone and just sat there, unable to move, and thought about Aunt Val. I remembered all the cool things we did together and what an amazing woman she was. I remembered how tangible her love was, how forgiving and patient and tolerant she was, and I couldn't help but feel happiness. Those two opposing emotions, the joy and sorrow I felt at once, made it impossible for me to write anything for her service. All my words felt like trite cliches, and I gave up.

The morning for the service came, and I had nothing to say. I didn't want to miss an opportunity to remember Aunt Val, so in a last-ditch effort to find inspiration, I looked through one of my many bookshelves, where I hoped I would find something to break the mental logjam.

On the third shelf from the bottom, tucked in between *The Tao Te Ching* and *Zen and the Art of Motorcycle Maintenance,* I saw *The Prophet* by Kahlil Gibran. Aunt Val had given it to me about two years earlier. I remembered how much she loved it, and I looked though it to see if I could find something that was appropriate.

At her service, I crammed into a room that was filled with family members and other loved ones. I laughed and cried with several generations of family, as they recalled what exactly she'd meant to them.

When it was my turn to speak, I said, "About a week ago, I told my mom that I wanted to remember Aunt Val today, but I didn't want to just say, 'me, too.'

"It's been really hard for me to come up with something to say, because even though I miss her terribly, all my memories of her are joyful, so when I think of her, I feel profoundly saddened by her loss, but overjoyed at her memory.

"As recently as this morning, I didn't have anything to say, until I happened upon this."

I held up the book. Its paper jacket was falling apart, and it was barely bigger than my hand.

"This is *The Prophet*, and Aunt Val gave it to me a few years ago, when I was struggling with something or other. I have to admit, I never took the time to read it until this morning, but within this tiny little book, I found the perfect words to express how I feel about Aunt Val, and what I've learned from her loss. This is titled, 'Joy and Sorrow:'

> *Then a woman said, 'Speak to us of Joy and Sorrow.'*
>
> *And he answered:*
>
> *Your joy is your sorrow unmasked.*
>
> *And the selfsame well from which your laughter rises was often-times filled with your tears.*
>
> *And how else can it be?*
>
> *The deeper that sorrow carves into your being, the more joy you can contain.*
>
> *Is not the cup that holds your wine the very cup that was burned in the potter's oven?*

And is not the lute that soothes your spirit, the very wood that was hollowed with knives?

When you are joyous, look deep into your heart and you shall find it is only that which has given you sorrow that is giving you joy.

When you are sorrowful look again in your heart and you shall see that in truth you are weeping for that which has been your delight.

Aunt Val was my delight. *Dancing Barefoot* is dedicated to her memory.

ACT III

"Blackbird singing in the dead of night
Take these broken wings and learn to fly
All your life
You were only waiting for this moment to arise."

—The Beatles
Blackbird

"And then one day you find ten years have got behind you.
No one told you when to run, you missed the starting gun. "

—Pink Floyd
Time

SEVEN

A Sort of Homecoming

WHEN I WORKED on *Star Trek*, I always struggled to fit in with the adults around me. It was easy to relate to them professionally, but on a personal level, no matter how hard I tried, I was still a kid and they were still adults. I often thought that Wesley Crusher could have been a much richer and more interesting character if the writers had taken advantage of that very real turmoil that existed within me, and used it to add some humanity to Wesley in between the Nanite making and polarity reversing . . . but I guess it was more fun (and easier) to write for the android. I can't say that I blame them.

For whatever reason, I was never able to entirely lose that teenage angst, and whenever I attended a *Star Trek* event, or saw one of the cast members, I immediately felt like I was 16 again. Because of that feeling—and, if I was willing to be truly, fearlessly honest with myself, the fact that I hadn't done very much with my career since leaving the show—I avoided *Star Trek* events (and that inevitable feeling of shame and angst that accompanied them) for years. Of course there were exceptions, but they were few and far between.

A couple of days after *Weakest Link*, I was presented with an opportunity to share the stage with the Big Three of *The Next Generation*: Brent Spiner, Patrick Stewart and Jonathan Frakes. The event was called "The Galaxy Ball." Robert Beltran, the actor who played Chakotay on *Voyager*, hosts it each year to benefit the Down Syndrome Association of Los Angeles, Doctors Without Borders, the Pediatric AIDS Foundation, and some other worthwhile charities. When I received the invitation, that familiar anxiety and apprehension sprung up immediately.

"What will I talk about? What have I done? How can I face them?" The Voice of Self Doubt was relentless.

"Easy," Prove To Everyone said. *"You've got your website. You've got the shows you do at ACME. You've got a wife and step-kids. You're not a kid anymore. You kicked ass in Vegas, and you can kick ass again. Besides, when will you have a chance to be on stage with these guys again?"*

"You're right," I said. *"But if you keep talking to yourself like this, they're going to throw you out of Starbucks."*

I looked up and offered a smile to the Girl Scouts who were staring at me. I bought several hundred dollars worth of Thin Mints to solidify my reputation as an eccentric millionaire playboy who hangs out at Starbucks in his Bermuda shorts.

When the day came to go to the ball, I dressed in my finest gown, and bid my wicked stepsisters goodbye as I got into my carri—

Wait. Sorry. That's not my story. That's Cinderella's story. I often get us confused.

The morning of the ball, I had a major fashion crisis. I was going to wear a suit, but I felt like I was playing dress up. I put on an ironic hipster T-shirt and black jeans, but then I felt like a child. I settled on this cool black cowboy shirt with eagles on the front and jeans. I looked at myself in the mirror that hangs on the back of my bedroom door and thought I looked kind of cool.

"You guys stay here," I said to Prove To Everyone and The Voice of Self Doubt. *"I'm doing this on my own today."* I ignored the explosion of discarded clothes that littered the rest of my room, and left the drawers open when I left.

The whole drive to the ball, I went over material in my head. I prepared jokes and did improv warm up exercises. By the time I got there, I felt like I'd been on stage for three hours.

I parked my car in the self-park garage. I convinced myself that it was stupid to cough up 7 bucks for a valet to drive it 40 feet, but the truth was all the other guys have luxury cars, and my VW seemed a little . . . unimpressive.

I made my way to the green room and discovered Jonathan Frakes, who had arrived ahead of me.

"Hi, Jonny," I said. I felt my face get warm.

A huge smile spread across his face as he stood up. "W!" he said, "You look great, man!"

I love it when he calls me "W" (pronounced "double-you")— my whole life I wanted a cool poker nickname, and it's the closest I've ever come.

He closed the distance between us in two strides and wrapped his arms around me in a big, fatherly bear hug.

"You too," I said.

"Have you eaten?" he said.

"Some coffee and toast this morning," I said. I didn't mention anything about my nervous stomach and the barely touched omelette I left on the table.

"Help yourself," he said, and pointed to a table where some food was set out. "They always give us too much food, you know?"

I laughed. I haven't spent nearly enough time in green rooms to know, but I took his word for it.

I opened a ginger ale and picked up a handful of veggies. As I munched on a carrot, he said, "How have you been?"

It was the question that I always dreaded. I would always smile bravely, ignore the knot in my chest, and say something like, "Oh, you know . . . things are slow, but I have an audition next week."

I spoke before that familiar knot could tighten.

"Not too bad. I haven't worked in ages, but I'm doing a really good sketch comedy show at ACME in Hollywood." I lifted my ginger ale with a mostly steady hand and took a long drink.

"And I made myself a website where I write a lot of stuff. It's pretty fun."

"Have you been doing any cons?" he asked.

"A few," I said. "I did one in Vegas last month."

"Slanted Fedora?"

"Yeah," I said.

"How did it go?"

"I took my sketch group out there and we did a show. It was really fun."

"Oh! I heard about that. I hear you're really funny."

"Yeah, I try to entertain the kids," I said. The knot tightened so violently in my chest, it felt like a heart attack. I felt intensely uncomfortable and embarrassed. The feeling surprised me; here was the one thing that I'd been doing, and doing well—I was very proud of my sketch work, yet I didn't want to talk about it.

"I may be funny in some sketch comedy shows that hardly anyone ever sees," I thought, *"but I'm struggling to pay my bills, I can't get hired for anything in Hollywood, and all of you guys have gone on to be rich and famous. I may be funny, but I sure fucked up the biggest opportunity of my career when I quit* Star Trek."

I shoved several carrots in my mouth and changed the subject. "Have you been watching *TNG* on TNN?"

"Yeah," he said, "it's amazing how those old shows hold up."

"Except 'Angel One,'" I said.

"And 'Code of Honor,'" he said.

"No vaccine!" we said in unison, quoting one of the actors in that show and laughed. The knot loosened.

"It's so weird for me to watch them," I said, "because I was so young. It's like my high school yearbook has come to life."

"That's because you've actually grown up since then," he said. "The rest of us have just gotten fatter."

"Don't let Marina hear you say that," I said.

He thought for a moment, and added, "Okay, all of us except Marina."

He winked. I smiled. The knot untied itself.

"Seriously, though," he said, "we've just gotten older. You're the only one of us who's actually *changed*."

"I guess you're right," I said. "Did you know that I just turned 30?"

"You're 30?!" If he'd been eating, he would have choked on his food. "Do you know how old that makes me?"

"Uh . . . 35?" I offered with a smile. I heard the elevator bell ring out in the hallway and a familiar voice echoed down the hall.

"Man, I can't believe you're 30," he said, shaking his head in disbelief, "and you're *married*."

"With children," I said.

"Goddamn! Children? Plural?" he said. "How many do you have?"

Before I could answer, Brent Spiner entered the room like an actor taking the stage.

"Hello, boys!" he said.

"Data!" Jonathan said with a smile. "Do you know how old Wheaton here is?"

Brent didn't miss a beat.

"Of course, I do. He's 37!" he said. "But he doesn't look it."

I stifled a laugh, but I couldn't deny the huge smile that spread across my face. I was overjoyed to be there with them.

"Brent!" I said. "How did you know?! I've worked so hard to keep it a secret!"

"Wil, you were 22 when we started," he deadpanned. "Do the math."

We all laughed.

Jonathan pointed at Brent's enormous goatee. "You know what I just realized, Brent?"

"What's that, Jonny?"

"For the first time in history, you look more like Robert Goulet than I do."

"Oh my god," I said. "You're right!"

Brent laughed. "It's for a character I'm playing called 'The Evil Devlin Bowman' in Dana Carvey's new movie, *Master of Disguise*."

"Are you *really* evil or just sort of evil?" I asked. I always admired Brent's ability to create and portray diverse characters. I was especially impressed with his comedic ability. I could just imagine him stroking that goatee and stealing the spotlight from everyone else on the set.

"I'm *really* evil. It's a lot of fun," he said. "But the hours are long. I'm really tired."

"As long as *Late Night With Les*?" I asked. I referred to a director we used to work with on *TNG* who would always turn in good shows, but took forever to shoot them. It was common for us to be at Paramount until midnight when he directed us. It felt good to recall our *Star Trek* days together, and I didn't realize it then, but I can see now that I was looking for commonality, familiarity. I wanted to reconnect with a happier time as much as I wanted to reconnect with the two of them.

"*Nothing* is as late as *Late Night With Les*," he said with mock gravity.

We laughed together, and it was like I never left. I felt a new knot beginning to form in my chest. This time, it wasn't regret, though, or embarrassment. It was sadness. I missed Jonathan. I missed Brent. I missed *this.*

"Did you get the latest draft of the script?" Jonathan said to Brent.

"Oh my god, they're talking about Nemesis!" my inner fanboy said.

"Shut up!" I said back. *"You're not a fanboy here. You're a peer. Be cool."*

I took my own advice and stood there, silent, and listened to them talk about the movie. Production hadn't started yet, but I could tell that they were excited about putting on their uniforms and getting back into character.

While they talked, I felt like a grounded kid, sitting at the living room window, watching his friends play kickball in the street.

"They want to make some substantial changes to the wedding," Brent said.

"I like it the way it is," Jonathan said.

"Well, I'm talking with Stuart and Logan about it," Brent said. "We'll see what happens."

"Is this really the last one?" I asked, in spite of myself.

"Yeah," Brent said.

"I think so," Jonathan said.

That made me incredibly sad. In the hallway, the elevator bell rang again.

"That's really sad," I said. "It's like the end of an era."

"We've done it for so long," Brent said. "I think it's time for me to do something new. I'm getting too old to play Data."

"I'm the only one who's changed. They've just gotten older." Jonathan's words echoed in my mind.

A deep, commanding voice bounced off the marble floor of the hallway and filled the room before its creator crossed the threshold.

"Are there *Star Trek* people in this room?" it boomed. "I just love those *Star Trek* people!"

We all turned to the door as Patrick Stewart walked in.

Patrick is one of the most disarming people I've ever met. If you only know him as Captain Picard or Professor Xavier, his mirthful exuberance is shocking. Patrick is one of the most professional and talented actors I've ever known, but he's also one of the most fun.

"Bob Goulet? I haven't seen you in *ages*, man! You look great!" he said to Brent and hugged him.

"Jonathan Frakes! I am a big fan," he smiled at Jonny and hugged him to.

He turned to me. "Who are you? You look familiar, but . . . I can't place you."

"Wil Wheaton, Mr. Stewart," I said.

He looked thoughtful for a moment and shook his head. "I'm sorry, but it doesn't ring a bell."

"I was Wesley on *Next Generation*," I said.

"Get out! You were never that young!" he said.

"Oh, but I was, sir," I replied, solemnly. "I believe we spent some time in a shuttlecraft together."

He nodded slowly, but remained unconvinced. "Go on . . ."

"That's all I've got, man," I laughed.

"Wil, darling, you look wonderful." he said with a huge smile. He held his arms wide and pulled me into a warm embrace. "I am so happy to see you!"

He held me at arm's length, and looked at me. Even though Patrick and I are the same height, I felt, like always, that he towered above me.

"You too," I said.

"I like that shirt, Wil. It's very cool."

He looked at Jonathan, then at Brent. We all wore black shirts. Brent and Jonathan wore black pants. Patrick wore a blue shirt and khaki pants.

"I guess I didn't get the memo about wardrobe," he said.

"It's okay," I said. "I don't think anyone will notice."

"Gentlemen, we're ready for you downstairs," one of the convention volunteers said from the doorway.

I felt a surge of adrenaline as we walked to the elevator.

I was silent, and mentally checked my notes as we descended 20-something floors.

The doors opened in the hotel lobby, which was packed with fans. Some convention staffers walked ahead of the four of us, as flashbulbs popped and fingers pointed. I was somewhere near the middle of the pack and felt incredibly out of place.

I heard pieces of conversation as we walked across the lobby: ". . . Picard! . . . Data! . . . Wil Wheaton? . . . on stage now! Hurry!"

This continued for the remainder of our walk across the lobby. It's always easier for me to be in front of people when they're obscured by footlights, and this walk provided no such barrier. I smiled and waved to a few people, but kept my eyes mostly down, until we turned a corner and headed down a hallway to the ballroom.

The four of us crowded the doorway, and looked into the room. Robert Beltran stood on a stage in front of about 300 hundred excited *Star Trek* fans. Our escort waved at him, and he nodded. We walked toward the stage, and he lifted his microphone to speak.

"Ladies and Gentlemen, please welcome, from *The Next Generation*, Patrick Stewart, Jonathan Frakes, Brent Spiner, and Wil Wheaton!"

We took the stage as our names were called, and the audience applauded ferociously.

My heart raced in my chest and pounded in my ears. I was scared, excited, and overwhelmed.

"I can't fucking believe that I'm on fucking stage with these fucking guys! Holy fucking crap!" I thought.

"Watch the potty mouth, mister!" my mom's voice said.

I spent the next hour in a complete daze, and I can recall very little about what happened. It's interesting (and a little anti-climactic, I know) that I can recall my backstage conversations so clearly, but the actual "performance" is a blur . . . that's the way it always is with me, though. When I do well in a show, I never can recall exactly what happened, because I'm too busy reacting to the audience or the other performers to watch myself. When I tank (like my talk did in Vegas, for example), I can recall every word, every step, and every painful silence with photographic precision.

What I *do* recall, however, is how much fun I had, how happy I was to be on stage with my friends again, and how wonderful it felt to be on the same "level" as them.

I can recall all of us teasing each other, and saying to the audience, "Hey, which one of us doesn't belong up here?" in reference to myself.

We spent about 30 minutes just talking and reminiscing, before someone (Patrick, I think) suggested that we take questions from the crowd.

"Well, time to sit down and fade into the background," I thought.

I was certain that, with The Big Three present, people wouldn't want to ask me about anything . . . but lots of them did. Most of the questions I fielded were about my website, which was still in its infancy. Though my stats showed a few thousand readers a week, I was still having a hard time accepting that anyone actually visited WWdN on a regular basis. To be honest, I was a little embarrassed that so many people were asking me questions, when Patrick, Brent, and Jonathan were right there . . . but it felt good.

All that improv warm up in the car paid off too. When we were done, I had made the audience, myself, and (most importantly) my peers, crack up several times.

Our time onstage flew by, and before I knew it, the hour was up. The audience cheered for us, and I allowed myself to bask in their approval before I walked off stage.

Jonathan had to leave early, because he was taking his daughter rollerblading™, so I walked back to the green room with Patrick and Brent. I felt far less self conscious than I had just an hour earlier, but it still floored me when Patrick turned to me at the elevator and said, "Wil, I had no idea you were so funny!" He looked to Brent and said, "Can you believe how funny he is?"

"You've got the funny, Milt," Brent said to me, using the nickname he'd called me when we were shooting *TNG*.

"Thanks, you guys. It was . . . well, it was really fun. I'm so happy that I got to be part of this with you."

Patrick put his hand on my shoulder, and leaned close to me. "Wil, I must tell you, it's simply wonderful to see you. I was so happy when I heard you were coming today, because I thought you'd just vanished over the years."

I didn't know what to say. He was right. I had vanished, and I would probably vanish again. The undeniable fact was, and is, that I feel ashamed when I have to face anyone from *TNG*. I still regret my teenage idiocy—the big film career I was hoping for when I left never materialized and probably never will. Whenever I face anyone from *Star Trek*, I can't help but replay all the mistakes I've made, and I nearly choke on regret.

"Well, I did vanish," I said, "but I can't even begin to tell you how wonderful it is to see you today."

I thought about exchanging phone numbers with them before they left, but I lost my nerve.

When the day was over, I felt like I was part of the *Star Trek* family again . . . even if I was the Black Sheep. The timing was perfect, too, because an off-handed remark I'd made while taping *Weakest Link* was about to put me back into a Starfleet uniform for the first time in over 10 years.

13 NOVEMBER 2001
Tonight At Last I Am Coming Home

When I played *Weakest Link*, I was placed right next to LeVar. We were talking during the commercials and I said to him that I really missed them. He said to me that I should be in the movie, especially since it's going to be the last *TNG* movie. I told him that I would love to be in it, but I thought that Berman and company really didn't like me. He seemed surprised and he told me that he was going to call Rick the next morning and suggest to him that I be in the movie, at least as a cameo. I thought that would be really cool and told him so.

Last week, on Friday, my agent called me to let me know that there was an offer from Paramount to reprise the role of Wesley Crusher in *Star Trek X*. We just needed to work out the details.

So we spent some time negotiating it and—get this— Rick Berman told my agent that he was "very pleased" that I was going to be in the movie!

I am really excited about this for three reasons:

I am going to get to work with my friends again.

Wesley Crusher will have some real closure, finally.

For the last five years, at least, everywhere I go, fans ask me if I'm going to be in a movie, and what happened to Wesley. I can honestly say that I'm doing this for the fans, because it will be so damn cool to see all of us together again.

WHEEE!

I wasn't under any illusions that this small role would have a significant impact on my career, but I didn't care. The wish I'd made in September, on the bridge of the *Enterprise* in Vegas, had come true. I would get to go back to *Star Trek* and appreciate everything that I should have appreciated back when I was a teenager. I got my second chance.

I didn't work on the movie until the beginning of December, but I counted down the days until production like a kid waiting for Christmas. On December 2, the script finally arrived by messenger. I signed for it with trembling hands and tore the envelope open before the front door was closed. I ran into my office, shut the door, and began to read.

Page 1.

Holy shit. That's awesome.

Page 4.

Holy, Holy, Holy shit.

Page 28.

Oh wow. That's cool!

Page 38a.

That's funny.

Page 73.

Okay, that was sort of stupid, but I'm sure they'll fix that.

Page 82.

This is far and away the best Next Generation *movie.*

Page 97.

Okay, this is the best Trek movie since Wrath of Khan!

Page 99.

Gasp.

Page 105.

What the—?

Page 114.

Oh god. This really is the last Next Generation *movie.*

I closed the script, and gently set it down on my desk. *The Next Generation* was really over. Sure, they left a tiny window open, but *TNG* as I knew it, with the cast that I loved, was done. If this realization had come to me . . . well, any time before

Vegas, really, I wouldn't have given it a second thought, but as I sat there in my office, the sounds and smells of the holiday season creeping in under the door, it hit me *hard*. I vowed to take nothing for granted when I worked on the movie.

I had my final costume fitting the next day, and the day after that, I found myself at the Melrose Avenue guard shack, half-an-hour early for my 8:30 a.m. call time.

"ID, please," the guard said.

I pulled my driver's license out of my wallet, and gave it to him.

"And where are you going today . . ." he looked at my license. "Wil?"

"I'm working on *Star Trek*," I said.

"*Enterprise* or *Nemesis*?"

The Next Generation.

"Nemesis," I said. "I play Wesley Crusher."

He looked up at me. "Oh my god. You *are* Wesley Crusher. You look so . . ."

Washed up?

". . . grown up."

"Yeah," I said "It's been a long time."

"Do you know where to park?"

"Yeah. But I don't know where our dressing rooms are."

But I do! I do know where our dressing rooms are! They're trailers on the street in front of Stages 8 and 9. Mine is filled with Warhammer 40K figures and GURPS books. It's right next to Brent's trailer. It's 1989, and I'm back. I'm back home.

"Okay," he said, and gave me directions to an area on the lot where I'd never been before.

I parked my car and picked up my backpack. Inside was my script, a note pad, and a few tapes: *Only A Lad, Music For The Masses,* and *Squeeze: Singles 45 and Under* . . . all of them music I listened to when I was working on the series. I remember, when

I put them in my backpack, that I thought to myself, *"Maybe I can sit in my trailer, listen to 'Never Let Me Down,' and imagine that I'm back."*

I locked up my car, and walked toward the dressing rooms. Other than the addition of a back lot, Paramount hadn't changed in any substantial way since I was on the show, and my thoughts drifted as I walked down those familiar streets on autopilot.

That's where I met Eddie Murphy when I was 16 . . . Hey! I crashed a golf cart there when I was 15 . . . There's the mail room . . . There's Stage 6, where the bridge set started out . . . I almost got up the courage to kiss that girl at the Christmas party on that stage in . . . there's the stage where Shatner told me, "I'd never let a kid *come onto my bridge" . . . this street feels exactly the way it did when I worked here . . . here's where my trailer used to be . . .*

I stopped, and tears filled my eyes—tears of joy: *It's so good to be here,* mingled with tears of sadness and regret: *why didn't this happen years ago?*

Because I wasn't ready for it to happen. I walked a few more steps and looked into the foyer that led into Stages 8 and 9. Enterprise *lives there now. At least they kept the stage in the family.*

A few minutes later, my cell phone rang.

"Hello?"

It was my wife. "Are you at Paramount?"

"Yeah! Anne . . . it's so cool—"

"Wait. I just checked our messages, and they pushed your call to later."

"Uh-oh. How much later?"

"11:30."

I looked at my watch: it was only 8. *What the hell am I going to do for three hours?*

"D'oh!" I said. "Well, I guess I need to find something to do."

"How are you feeling?" she said.

"Excited," I said. "And sad."

"That makes sense. Have a good day, and call me when you can. I have to get the kids to school."

"Okay. I love you."

"I love you too. Don't forget to relax and enjoy yourself!"

I laughed. "I'm pretty sure I have that covered. Bye."

It was so familiar to stand there in front of the stage . . . I closed my eyes, and tried to put myself back in 1989.

No dice. Turns out I'm only a Time Traveller on Star Trek. *Maybe I'll go eat breakfast.*

I walked to the commissary and ordered a bowl of Irish oatmeal, two pieces of dry wheat toast with marmalade, and a large orange juice. It goes without saying that this was my usual, right?

I took my time and read my script while I ate. I had only three lines, and I'd learned them long ago . . . but it seemed like the right thing to do.

"Thank you, Captain. It's good to be back."

"Oh, the Titan is going to be a great ship! The warp core matrix is—" Goddamn technobabble. *What the hell is it?*

I laughed. Ten years ago, I would have hated the technobabble, but now . . . it was cool.

Time passed quickly, and around 11, I walked across the lot again, eager to report to duty. I mean, eager to report to work. Yeah, work.

A woman I didn't recognize spoke into a walkie talkie when I approached. "Wil Wheaton is here," she said. "Copy that."

She introduced herself to me as one of the assistant directors and walked me to my dressing room.

"I'll come back and get you when there's an available chair in the makeup trailer."

"Okay," I said. "I'll be here."

She left me, and I changed into my spacesuit. I put on a black undershirt, my pants, then my boots. I was wearing a formal Starfleet uniform, and the jacket portion stayed on the set until we were actually ready to shoot, so I put on a fleece jacket—similar to the one I had when I was on the series—and was very happy when I realized that I wouldn't have to wear an embarrassing fake muscle suit like the one I wore when I was a teenager.

I sat down and looked around. The trailer was bigger than the ones we had when we worked on the series. I guess it was a fringe benefit of the bigger budget. Thankfully, there was a tape player. I put on side one of *Music For The Masses* and remembered playing it in the makeup trailer when I was a kid. I remembered Jonathan laughing about the name "Depeche Mode," and Gates, who was fluent in French, telling me that it meant "Fast Fashion." I remembered how much Gates liked Oingo Boingo, and how great it felt to make that connection when I was 14.

There was a knock on the door, and the assistant director was back. "There's a chair available for you, Wil," she said.

"I'm on my way."

I took a deep breath. *I will not take a single thing for granted today.* Dave Gahan sang, "Never want to come down, never want to put my feet back down on the ground . . ." as I walked out.

All makeup trailers are essentially the same: as many as five, but usually three chairs face a wall of mirrors. It's always painfully bright, and though it's painted white and could feel like an operating room, it's usually the warmest, most welcoming spot on the entire production. Actors often congregate in the makeup trailer, and there is usually music and coffee, and sometimes, on a Friday afternoon, cocktails.

It wasn't the same trailer from the series, but the *feeling* was the same: the smell of freshly brewed coffee hung in the air, and jazz music played on the radio. There was Michael Westmore, gluing Worf's forehead onto Michael Dorn. There was Brent, getting his hands painted gold, and there's an empty chair waiting for me.

It was everything I could to do not burst into tears. I was *home.*

As I stood in the doorway, Brent said, "Milt! Milt Wheaton!"

"Is that the Teen Idol?" Michael Dorn said.

"Yeah, but he's not a teenager anymore," said Michael West-more. "He's got two kids."

"Two kids?!" Michael Dorn said.

"Stepkids," I said, as I stepped into the trailer and sat down in the chair.

That was cool. The Kid has kids. I mean, stepkids.

June Westmore (yeah, pretty much everyone who does makeup on *Star Trek*—well, in the whole industry, really—is a Westmore in some capacity) who did my makeup for years on *Next Generation*, began to turn me back into Wesley Crusher. While she created his flawless skin, I talked with Michael and Brent. Marina briefly came into the trailer, kissed my cheek, and went back out.

"So how are you doing?" June said.

Are you kidding me? This is a dream come true. I'm so happy to be back!

"Are you kidding me? This is a dream come true. I'm so happy to be back!" I said.

"Everyone's happy to be back together," she said.

Everyone . . . that includes me.

"Yeah. This rules."

She finished my makeup, and I moved down one chair to get my hair done.

"Do I have to wear Wesley's helmet hairdo?" I said.

"I don't think so," the hair designer said. "I really like this sort of messy thing you've got going on." She turned to Michael Westmore. "What do you think, Michael?"

"I think he looks great like that. Just make sure you put side-burns on him."

Sideburns?!

"Oh my god! That's right! I'm a Starfleet officer now, so I get sideburns!" I said, in spite of myself.

"Didn't you wear them before?" he said.

I shook my head. "I was a teenager, remember? No sideburns."

"You sure you've never had them?"

"Yeah. Believe me, that's something I'd remember."

"Well, then I want to put them on you."

COOL!

"Okay." I waited while he finished turning Michael Dorn into Worf, then sat in his chair.

We talked about family, kids, and *Trek* while he put my sideburns on. When they were trimmed into neat little points, he stood back and admired them.

"Those are some good looking sideburns," he said.

I smiled. "Yeah, they really are."

There was a knock at the trailer door, and a production assistant poked his head in. "They're ready for rehearsal," he said. "There's a van to take you all across the lot to the stage."

When I walked out of the trailer, I saw the entire cast, waiting to go to the set.

My family.

I slowly walked over to them. Except for Marina, who would be wearing a wedding gown, everyone was dressed, like me, in half a spacesuit.

"Hi guys," I said, when I arrived.

There were hugs and kisses and more hugs, proclamations about how great I looked, and how good it was to see me.

This choking back tears thing is getting pretty old.

"Hey, I'm going to walk to the stage," Jonathan said. "Anyone want to join me?"

"Sure," LeVar and I said.

Everyone else piled into the van, and the three of us made small talk as we walked across Paramount's back lot. As we passed Stages 8 and 9, I snuck sideways glances at the guys, but I couldn't tell if they experienced any of the nostalgia I felt. We went past this place called The Mill that made all the spaceship hulls and oddly shaped landscape features that *Star Trek* always needed to custom order from the studio, and we walked past Stage 16, which stood in for just about every planet we ever visited. It was hot in the summer, cold in the winter, and always filled with a haze of mineral oil–based atmospheric smoke, so we all used to half-jokingly call it "Planet Hell."

"Good thing we're not on Planet Hell," I said.

"We'll be there in a few weeks," Jonathan said.

"I can't say I'm sorry I won't be joining you," I said. *I wish that were true.*

We all laughed. God, it felt good to be there with them.

We were filming on the "television" side of the lot, on a stage that we never used during the series. Actually, I think *Solid Gold* may have been filmed on that stage at one time, but don't quote me on that.

Yet another assistant director (how many of them do they need on this picture?) met us at the stage door.

"We're still waiting on Stuart [The Director], so you guys can grab a coffee or something from craft services if you like. It should only be a minute."

"Cool. I think I'll get a soda," I said.

I really just wanted to take in the stage on my own. I've always loved the "magic" of making movies, and I still get a kick out of walking past hanging backdrops that look like cityscapes and climbing over fake rocks. On my way to craft services, which is just a fancy name for "the snack table," I passed a bunch of director's chairs—one for each cast member—near a huge bank of monitors. I looked for my name, but didn't see it.

I guess I'm "Guest Cast" today. Oh well, you can't win them all.

I reached into a cooler, and pulled out a soda. When I stood back up, Rick Berman was standing in front of me.

"Hi, Wil," he said.

"Hi, Rick."

"Can I talk to you for a moment?"

Oh shit.

"Yeah. Of course."

He took a few steps away from me and indicated that I should follow. He stopped behind one of those backdrops and waited.

"Wil," he said, "I hear that you think I hate you."

My heart pounded so violently in my chest, I thought I was going to fall over and die right there. There were bright flashes of light at the edges of my vision, and everything I heard took on this strange, metallic echo.

"Uhh . . ."

He put his hand on my shoulder. "Wil, I have never hated you."

So that whole ignoring me twice at major Star Trek *events was . . . tough love?*

"Really?" I said.

"Really," he said. "I am so happy that you're here, because this movie is all about family, and you are a big part of our family."

Okay. For today, I'm going to believe that.

"Thank you, Rick. I don't even know how to tell you how happy I am to be here."

"I think you just did," he said with a smile. "Have fun today."

From across the stage, the First Assistant Director called out, "We are ready for a first team rehearsal!"

Production assistants, DGA trainees and other assistant directors talked into their walkies: "First Team . . . Ready . . . To the set . . . I have Patrick and Jonathan . . . Stuart is here . . ."

"I have Wil Wheaton," said a voice behind me. "They're ready for you, Wil."

"I better get to the set, before the executive producer finds out I'm goofing off back here," I said to Rick.

"Good idea," he said.

I walked into the set, a ball of nervous excitement. I identified who the First AD was and introduced myself to him. He was polite, but disinterested. I found the director and introduced myself to him. He was also disinterested, but not polite about it at all. The entire time I worked on the movie, the only unpleasant experiences I had were the result of this guy, who was really kind of a dick.

We blocked the first scene, where Picard delivers a toast to Riker and Troi, Data does a song and dance, and the entire crew of the *Enterprise* celebrates their wedding.

I was pretty much reeling from my strange-yet-positive encounter with Rick, and my unexpected-yet-negative one with the director, so I don't recall much from that rehearsal, other than someone suggesting that I be seated at the head table on a stage with the rest of the cast, rather than down at a table on the floor.*

We rehearsed a few times, while the director worked out a few technical details. When he was satisfied, the first assistant director told us they needed about 30 minutes to get the shot set up.

"First Team is released to makeup and wardrobe," he said into his walkie.

I was camera-ready except for the top part of my spacesuit. I wouldn't put that on until right before we rolled, anyway, so I spent my 30 minutes walking around the stage. It was quite a difference from when I was a teenager: when we'd break during series production, I'd race back to my dressing room as fast as I could, so I could paint miniatures, or talk on the phone, or do

---

* If I hadn't been moved to that table, I would have been entirely cut out of the movie. As it is, you can still see me in the wide-screen version if you have a DVD player with a really good freeze-frame.

any of the countless other things I felt like I was missing out on because I was working . . . but that was then and this was now.

I will not take a single moment for granted today.

I decided to have a look at the other side of the set. On my way, a young, good-looking guy stopped me.

"Wil Wheaton?"

"Yeah."

"It's a real pleasure to meet you!" He extended his hand. "I'm John Logan, and I wrote the script."

"Wow! The pleasure is mine, man!" I shook his hand. "I think this is the best *Trek* movie since *Wrath of Khan*, and certainly the best *TNG* movie."

He grinned sheepishly. "Gosh, thanks. I'm glad you liked it."

"Oh yeah. And thank you for working me into the story."

"I am so happy that I could do it! I just wish it could have happened months ago, so I could give you more to do."

"I wanted to ask you about that . . . why is Wesley back in Starfleet?"

"Well, I couldn't get into specifics without writing a three-page scene, so I figured if I had Picard say, 'Hello, Wesley. It's good to see you back in uniform,' we could leave it up to the audience, you know? Maybe he's back in uniform because he's back from the Academy, or maybe because he's not being a Traveller anymore."

"The fans are going to ask me, you know," I said.

He laughed. "Believe me, I know. If this does well, and they let me write a sequel, I'll do my best to get more Wesley in it."

Okay. I'll let myself believe that for today, also.

"Cool! Can he get the girl, too?"

"I'll have to check Ashley Judd's availability."

We both cracked up pretty hard.

"I have to go talk to Brent," he said. "It's really nice to meet you, though, and I'll see you around the set today."

"Nice to meet you, too."

Wow. He's as excited to be here as I am. That's cool.

I walked around the stage a little more and ran into Whoopi Goldberg, who was there to reprise the role of Guinan, the Ten Forward bartender. She greeted me with a huge smile and a long hug.

"You are lookin' good, Wheaton," she said.

"You too, Shuttlehead."

Whoopi always thought the hats they put her in looked like shuttlecraft, and she called herself "Shuttlehead." I guess the name stuck, because we were still laughing about it 10 years later.

Before we could catch up, a production assistant tapped me on the shoulder.

"We're about two minutes away," he said. "Would you get into the rest of your wardrobe?"

"Sure." I said.

Wardrobe was set up in an alcove I hadn't noticed, off to one side of the stage. We had a lot of background actors in various Starfleet and civilian uniforms, so the room was buzzing with people when I walked in.

From behind a rack of costumes, I heard a very familiar voice. "Teen Idol!"

It was Mandy, who was my costumer when I worked on the series.

"Oh my god, Mandy! It's so great to see you!"

I will spare you, my faithful reader, the contents of yet another conversation wherein I am told how grown-up I look, I remind the teller that I've also aged over the past 15 years, and I do my best to keep my emotions under control.

"Are you ready to put the spacesuit back on?" she said.

Am I ready. Heh. I guess you could say that.

"Yes. Yes I am." I took off my fleece jacket, and Mandy pushed the tunic over my outstretched arms. I turned around, she zipped up the back, and fastened two hooks at the neck. She spun me around to face her, and made sure everything was in its right place.

"Looks good," she said. "God, it's so strange to see you in this uniform."

"You're telling me!" I said.

"First Team to the set!" the First AD announced.

"That's me," I said.

I walked into the set and did my best to play it cool while the rest of the cast walked in. Everyone was so happy to be there, almost like it was a real wedding. I found out later that some of the actors had been up in the desert for some location filming, but this was the first day the entire cast was together since the start of production, which explained the celebratory mood and festive atmosphere that permeated the entire place.

We all took our seats at the head table, and the background actors assembled around the rest of the set. Then Marina walked in, dressed in a beautiful wedding gown. I'm not sure if it was truly spontaneous, but everyone broke into applause as she walked across the dance floor and took her seat.

"Oh, you all just stop it!" she said, but I could tell that she enjoyed it. Hell, I think we all enjoyed it.

When we got down to filming, it was exactly like I remembered, minus the stupid teenage angst. There was laughter, and teasing, and a genuine affection among the cast members. I had no dialogue, so I spent the next few hours simply reacting to the scene: I laughed when Brent was funny, I sighed when Marina was beautiful, and I was quietly impressed when Patrick spoke. I'm sure I managed to get some acting in there, too. The scene was very complicated, so the day moved quite slowly, and we didn't finish it until our dinner break.

After dinner, I was off-camera for a few hours, but I stayed on the stage the entire time, sitting in the "Guest Cast" chair next to Rick Berman, watching the scene unfold on the bank of monitors.

"This is so cool," I said.

Rick just nodded his head.

I wonder if he realizes how important this is—not just to me, but to the fans, too? I wonder if anyone on this stage cares about this like I do?

Finally, long after midnight, it was time to shoot my scene. All the other actors were sent home, except for Patrick and Gates. I remembered how much I hated it when my scene would be the last of the day and recalled all the times I completely phoned it in for those shots.

Not tonight. I will not take a single thing for granted today.

The word had come down from the studio that they were "Pulling the Plug" at 1:30. "Pulling the Plug" means that production comes to a halt at a certain time, no matter what we're doing. It's pretty serious stuff—I've been on sets where the director has kept the camera rolling between takes, to prevent the studio from stopping the scene before he gets what he wants.

Suddenly, I had to stop drinking in the joy of each moment and focus on my job as an actor. I quickly ran over the scene in my head, and practiced hitting my mark a few times.

When the camera rolled, Wesley Crusher sprung to life: his unabashed enthusiasm for complex warp field dynamics and a double-refracting warp core matrix with twin intermix chambers combined with my overwhelming joy at being back in uniform. We smiled his goofy smile. I'm not sure where I ended, and he began, when we said, "Thank you, sir. It's great to be back."

"CUT!" the director shouted from monitor land.

I looked up. *Did I do something wrong?* Apparently not. It was something with the camera. We reset and did take two.

"Hello, Wesley, it's—"

"CUT!"

Another camera problem. This time it was severe enough to bring the director out from behind the monitors. He had several . . . words . . . for the camera crew, and we went again, but cut before any of us had a chance to speak.

It went on like this for several takes. *This is the reality of film-making. This is the job. Remember this? You're a professional actor, on a movie set.* Star Trek *isn't real, you geek.*

Eventually, the blocking, the acting, and the camera work all came together.

"Cut! Print!"

The First AD called out, "Okay, everyone, that is a wrap! Take your turnarounds, and we'll see you all tomorrow! Thank you for a great day!"

This is the way Wesley Crusher ends. Not with a bang, but a whimper.

I walked back to my trailer across the empty and silent Paramount lot, taking care to avoid the street in front of Stages 8 and 9. I changed out of my costume and hung it up.* I signed out with the DGA trainee, and listened to *Only A Lad* on the way home.

The house was asleep when I walked in, and even after the 18-hour day, adrenaline flowed through me like a magnesium fire. I grabbed a Guinness (hey, I earned it) and did some quick blogging.

06 DECEMBER 2001
A Sort of Homecoming

It's 1:15 in the morning. The crew is tired. I am tired. Most of the cast has been released, and it's only me, Patrick, and Gates left, along with about 30 background actors. It's the last shot of the night, and we're finally doing my scene.

We block it, rehearse it once, and then we shoot it. It's a pretty complicated shot, camera-wise, and I can tell that the director is getting frustrated with the constant re-takes, and

---

* I learned from a costumer when I was very young that professional actors always hung up their costumes at the end of the day. To this day, when someone is a pain in the ass on the set, I will say to a costumer, "He doesn't hang up his costume, does he?" So far, I haven't been wrong.

we all know that the studio will not let us go past 1:30, so there's a touch of urgency in the air.

Late on a Wednesday night. Long hours. Most of the cast has been released, because they've got a long day tomorrow.

It's like I never left, and I love it.

There's much, much more, but I have to go back to the studio in a couple hours, and I've got other work to do, so I'll write more tomorrow.

I never did write more, tomorrow or ever. Actually, if I can steal from *Stand By Me* and paraphrase just a little bit, *I haven't written about it at all until just now.* Thank you for your indulgence.

I fell into bed shortly after that, and 10 hours later, I was back on the set.

The day is a blurred composite of images, and no matter how hard I try, I can't get my brain to separate them into individual memories. All I can clearly recall is how I spent the day spiraling around the Yin and Yang of joy and sorrow, until the director called cut on the final take.

"Thank you, everyone!" the First AD called out. "That is a company wrap for today, and picture wrap for Wil Wheaton!"

There was some polite applause from the crew, who really didn't know me, and some very genuine applause from Patrick and Gates, the only cast members who were still on the stage. They walked over, and embraced me. We knew that this was the *real* Journey's End for me and Wesley Crusher, but we didn't talk about it.

This is all about family, and I'm a big part of this family.

"I'm going to walk back," Patrick said to me. "Would you like to walk together?"

"I'd like that a lot," I said.

It was late, but not nearly as late as it had been the night before, and it was very cold as we walked through the "New York Street" area of the back lot.

"Remember when they built this for *Bronx Zoo*?" I said. "I used to come over here and pretend it was real."

Patrick slowed, then stopped. A huge arc light towered over us. Apple boxes sat on the curb, cables ran into the façade of a deli, and someone had left a styrofoam cup half filled with coffee on the window ledge.

"When I first came here to audition for *Next Generation*," he said, "I didn't know if I'd ever get a chance to be on a back lot again, so I left the casting office and spent nearly an hour's time walking round here."

He began to walk again.

"That's so weird," I said. "I mean . . . here you are, 15 years later."

He smiled. "I know. I remember worrying that the security department would catch me, and I'd end up in a great deal of trouble!"

We laughed together.

"I've lost count of the number of times I had run ins with the security department," I said. "Most of them involved dangerously speeding around the lot in a 'borrowed' golf cart or playing music too loudly in my dressing room.

"I wish I'd been able to hang out with you guys when we were doing this every day," I said.

"Oh, my dear, you missed out on a great deal of fun!" his voice became excited. "The late Friday nights when we'd close down Nicodell's* were great!"

"Can I tell you something?" I said.

"Of course," he said.

---

* A restaurant that used to be on Melrose, with a back door that opened right onto the Paramount lot. It was bulldozed for "progress" in the 1990s.

"I really blew it when I was here before. I should have treasured the experience that I had working with you guys, and I didn't. I'm really sorry that I was such a dick when I was a teenager."

He stopped again, and put his hand on my shoulder. "Wil, my dear, you *were* a teenager. We all understood."

"Really?"

"Yes. And when we worked together, I always related to you as an actor, first, and you were a lovely actor. You know, I wasn't thrilled about working with a child, but working with you was a great pleasure."

What do you say to that? How do you respond, when it comes from the man who was, for all intents and purposes, a father figure, mentor, role model, and hero? If you're me, you say, "I'm so sad that this is over for me."

"So am I," he said. We began to walk again. As we turned the corner and neared Stages 8 and 9, I saw someone come out of the stage.

"Hey! That's Brad Yacobian!" I said.

"It is!" Patrick said. "Hello! Brad!"

Brad started as a First AD on *Next Generation* and has worked on all the incarnations of *Star Trek* since then. He was working as the coproducer and unit production manager on *Enterprise*.

"Hey you guys," he said. "Are you just wrapping?"

"Oh yes. It's Thursday, you know." Patrick said. Brad smiled a knowing smile, and I laughed. See, production usually starts out with early calls on Monday, but the Screen Actor's Guild requires a 12-hour break for the actors between their release and the next day's call time. So if we start at 8 but don't wrap until 10, we won't start until 10 the next day, and so on. This doesn't happen very often, because it's very expensive for the studios. If a show doesn't start until the afternoon on Thursday, it usually means that the director is incompetent, the schedule is very complicated, or a little of both.

"Director or schedule?" Brad said.

"Schedule," Patrick said. He pronounced it with a soft "ch" sound, like "shelf." I suppressed a giggle.

"Who's working tonight?" I asked, hoping the answer would be "Jolene Blalock, and she wants to see you without your pants in her trailer right now."

Brad looked at his call sheet. "Let's see . . . Scott is still here—"

"Is he in his trailer?" Patrick asked.

"I think so. You want to say hello?" Brad said.

Oh my god. I'm going to stand with Patrick while he talks to Scott Bakula!

"I'd like to, yes."

Brad walked us to Scott's trailer. It was in the same place where Patrick's trailer was so many years ago.

That's a little weird.

He rapped twice on the door, and from behind it, a muffled voice emerged. "Yeah?"

"Scott, it's Brad. I have someone here who wants to say hello."

I thought back to all the times I heard this when I was on the other side of that door, and felt a little uncomfortable. The door opened, and there was Scott Bakula, in that cool *Enterprise* jumpsuit.

"Hey, Patrick! How are you?" he said.

Oh . . . they know each other. Interesting.

"I'm well," he said. "Scott, this is Wil Wheaton, he plays Wesley Crusher."

Plays Wesley, not played Wesley. That was cool.

He extended his hand and I shook it.

"It's really nice to meet you," I said. "How are you guys doing?"

"It's Thursday night," he said with a tired grin.

"Some things never change, I guess, " I said.

We all laughed.

"Listen, Scott," Patrick said. "I've been on and off the lot for several weeks now, and I should have come over much sooner to say hello to you."

"Thank you," Scott said. "I've seen you pass by several times, but I've always been too busy to say hello myself."

They talked for several minutes about the things that you talk about, I guess, when you're the captain of the *Enterprise*. I remember Patrick said, "You're doing a wonderful job," and I realized that he was having the conversation with Scott that Shatner should have had with him in 1987. He was passing the torch to—well, to the next generation.

I looked at Brad, and before either one of us could say anything, his walkie said, "We're ready for First Team on the bridge." How many times had I stood in this exact spot and heard those exact words over the years?

"Gotta go to work," he said. "I'm so glad you stopped by. I'll come over and visit you . . . are you on 16?"

"Shortly," Patrick said. "We're on 29 until tomorrow, then location."

Scott shook my hand. "It was nice to meet you."

"You too."

"Have a good night, you guys," Brad said, as they walked into the stage. "I have Scott, and we're walking . . ."

I turned to Patrick. "That was very cool, man."

Patrick just nodded.

We arrived back at the dressing rooms. My trailer was farther away than his, so I said, "I guess this is goodbye."

"Not goodbye," he said. "Farewell."

We embraced. "Have a wonderful shoot. If I'm on the lot, I'll be sure to stop by."

"Please do." He walked into his trailer.

An assistant director walked over to me. "Michael Westmore is in the makeup trailer, if you'd like to have him take your sideburns off."

"Okay," I said, "Thank you."

Jonathan and LeVar were in the trailer, having their makeup removed, when I walked in. I took a seat in the chair between them and waited.

"You back with us tomorrow, W?" Jonathan said.

I shook my head. "Nope. This is it."

"You were only here for two days?" LeVar said.

"Yeah," I said.

"It feels like it should be longer," Jonathan said. "Much longer."

The prodigal son had come home.

Months later, I heard that Jonathan had directed a movie that my stepkids really wanted to see, called *Clockstoppers*. I had no problem calling his office and asking for some passes to see the film.

21 FEBRUARY 2002
Still Cool

Okay. It's 1988 and a little show called *Star Trek: The Next Generation* is in its second season. It's struggling a little bit, experiencing the typical sophomore slump of any new series and a writer's strike is not helping very much.

We are all working late one night, probably shooting blue screen on the bridge, so we all wrap at the same time (a rarity). I excitedly walk to the parking garage with Jonathan Frakes, who I am already looking up to.

We're walking back to our cars and we're talking about something, I can't quite remember what, but I really feel like Jonathan is treating me as an equal. He's not treating me like

I'm a kid. It really makes me feel good and I say to him, "You know, Jonathan, I can tell, just from talking to you, that when you were younger? You used to be cool."

He laughs and I think to myself that I've cemented my position with him as cool contemporary, rather than lame-ass kid.

Then he says, "What do you mean, used to be?!"

I realized what I'd said, and how it didn't match up with what was in my head, which was, "*Gee, man. You are so cool now, as an adult, I think that you were a really cool guy who I would have liked to have hung out with when you were my age.*"

He knew what I meant, I could tell, and he really tortured me about that for years. Every time I see him nowadays, he turns to a person nearby and he says, "You know, Wheaton here told me that I used to be cool." We laugh about it and I make the appropriate apologies and explanations, while Jonathan makes faces and gestures indicating that I am full of shit.

Now, when I was working on Trek, I always wanted to be:

- As good an actor as Patrick
- As funny as Brent
- As cool as Jonathan

I'm still working on those things, but Jonathan just recently showed me how cool he still is.

Jonathan directed this new movie, called *Clockstoppers*. It's a movie geared toward kids, but it seems smart enough for their parents to sit through it without dreaming up ways of eviscerating the writer responsible for robbing them of 90 minutes of their weekend, which sets it well apart from most "family" films.

Ryan and Nolan have been talking about how they can't wait to see this movie and I mentioned to them last week that I was friends with the director and I had heard that it was going to be really cool and I was pretty sure that I could get us into a screening.

I called up Jonathan's office and asked if I could get some tickets to a screening, so I could take the kids and be a hero to them. Jonathan's assistant said that it would be no problem and I'd hear from someone at Nickelodeon about the screening.

The next day, the phone rings and it's totally Jonathan himself, calling me back, telling me how happy he is that I want to take my stepkids to see his movie and that he's really happy to get me into the screening on Saturday.

See, the thing is, Jonathan is what we in Hollywood call A Big Deal™ and usually people who become A Big Deal™ don't usually talk to people who aren't also A Big Deal™.

But Jonathan is not only A Big Deal™, he's also A Really Great Guy™ and he didn't need to call me back, personally. Actually, I really didn't expect him to.

But he did and that proves that he is now and always has been, cool. Despite my fumbled proclamations as a 16-year-old dorkus.

A few months later, Jonathan called me in for an episode of *The Twilight Zone* that he was directing. I was excited to be called in, but the whole experience was made even more meaningful because Jonathan called me at home himself, to tell me that he was having his casting people phone my agent. He really was Still Cool™.

14 MARCH 2002

Submitted for your consideration, one actor

Night before last, I got home very late from work.

When I checked my messages, there was one from Jonathan Frakes, who said that he was casting a show and there was "a wonderful acting opportunity for Wil Wheaton in it."

I can't tell you how excited I was. To have one of my friends call me, at home, to tell me that they're casting something and they wanted to put me in it . . . well, it was awesome.

Now, my excitement is tempered, because the last time I was promised a role in a movie by a friend, I got a whole bunch of nothing, but there's something about Jonathan. He wouldn't call me if he didn't really think I could handle this role.

So yesterday, at 12:30 p.m., I get a call that they want to see me at 2 p.m. for Jonathan's project: *The Twilight Zone!*

That's right, they're doing it again! I love *The Twilight Zone* the most. When I was a kid it scared the shit out of me, but in a good way. The first thing I ever wrote was an adaptation of one of the scariest episodes, when I was like 11.

So I get the call at 12:30, the scenes for the audition arrive via fax at 12:45, and I have 30 minutes to prepare 16 pages.

Somehow, I manage to get a handle on this character, a task made much easier by the high quality of the writing. It's specific and clear, so I get an understanding of who this guy is immediately and I'm able to add my own shading and color to him really quickly.

When you look at a script, it usually tells you what the writer wants, what he's going for. All the actors coming in should know that, and should be able to meet the demands of the material. In my experience, sitting on both sides of the table during auditions, the thing that makes the difference among all the actors who come in to read is that shading and color; that little extra understanding, or that ability to recall something from your real life is what's going to make a difference and get you the role.

Of course, 30 minutes is not exactly the best amount of time to create this complex character, but what's great for me about not having all the extra time is I am forced to trust my instincts, which are almost always right on, but usually end up getting over-analyzed. I can be a little too smart for my own good.

So I am thinking of all this stuff, all the various colors I can add to this character, and the experiences I've had in my own life that I can draw upon, while I'm driving over to the audition, which is in the middle of downtown LA, at a place called "LA Center Studios." I've never been there before, but the place is really cool and creepy at the same time. It feels like the set of a '70s post-apocalypse movie. The floors are all marble and linoleum, the walls are all wood with these strange metal accents and the whole place is only about 20% occupied, so it really feels like, well, The Twilight Zone.

I get there, park my car in the mostly abandoned garage and try to find the office where I'm reading. That post-apocalypse feeling is reinforced when I walk up three flights of turned-off escalators, which are lit by fluorescent lights and covered with dust. I mean, I really did expect to come around a corner and see Charlton Heston screaming, "Soylent Green is people! It's people!"

I finally got to the room where I was supposed to do my reading and I saw Jonathan, who gave me a huge smile and a warm bear hug, and told me how happy he was to see me. He always has this twinkle in his eye, you know? It says, "I can't believe I'm doing this! I'm totally getting away with it! Woo! This is so much fun!"

The casting director tells me that they only want me to read the first and last scenes, which is great because I can spend my 15 minutes waiting just focusing on those scenes, while they set up the room for auditions.

So that's what I do: I work on those two scenes and go in. Jonathan thanks me for coming and introduces me to the other producers. He says, "Wil and I know each other, you know."

"Yeah, I knew him back when he was cool," I say.

"See? He tells the same story," he says to one of the producers.

"Well, your story checks out," the producer says to me.

"That's a relief. I thought that the five-year photographic record wouldn't be enough," I reply.

We all laugh, and he tells me to begin when I'm ready.

Now, here's something that I love about being an actor: I was just joking around, and now I get to totally switch gears and play a guy who starts out honest and earnest, yet becomes corrupted by power. The two scenes show the beginning and ending of that transformation. I love that I can go from joking around to becoming this character in a matter of seconds.

I do the first scene and I can see Jonathan out of the corner of my eye, and I can tell that he's really into what I'm doing. It fills me with confidence, and I totally relax into this character. He tells me that it was a great job, and asks me to read the second scene. He gives me some direction and tells me a bit about this character; stuff I already have figured out, but it really makes me feel confident, knowing that what they want is what I've already prepared.

I read the scene and he asks me if I wouldn't mind doing a third scene. This is a good sign, because he wouldn't ask for it if he wasn't happy with what I'd already done.

But I've had all of 30 minutes with the material and I really haven't prepared this scene at all . . . I mean, I read it once, looked at it again when I was waiting, but I am not nearly as confident with it as I am with the others . . . but I do it anyway and it feels really good.

I have really good instincts as an actor. I know when I totally suck and I know when I've done a good job. To use a baseball metaphor: I know when I've hit it out, when I bounce back to the mound and when I go down swinging. With the first scene, I hit it deep to center. With the second scene, I hit it out. I really need to get a stand-up double on this third scene, now. So I read it, and that's exactly what I do. If I'd had some more time with it, I would have gotten a triple, for sure, but I'll take the double, and hope that Sammy drives me in.

I finish, and put down my script. Jonathan says to the producers, "He is such a great actor."

He turns to me and says, "You are such a wonderful actor. You still have it, W."

Of course, it would be great to get this job, because I'd like to work with him and I think the marketing opportunity for the studio is huge: launch the new *Twilight Zone* with two guys from *Star Trek*!

But even if I don't book the job, I will have Jonathan's kindness and warmth to hold on to. It will be good balance for all the times I read for people who treat me like shit, and, as longtime readers know, it's all about The Balance.

I had a very good audition, had fun seeing my friend, and left feeling like someone I'd looked up to for several years was proud of me. The truth was, I knew that I wasn't going to get the job when I walked into the hallway, because all of the other actors (including Casey Siemaszeko, who played Vern's older brother Billy in *Stand By Me*) were at least 10 years older than me. I honestly didn't care, though. I was just happy to have done a good job.

EIGHT

April's Fool

"**CREATIVITY IS THE ABSENCE OF FEAR,**" a friend of mine liked to say. After Vegas, *Weakest Link*, The Galaxy Ball, and my return "home" on the set of *Nemesis*, a lot of the fear that Prove To Everyone That Quitting *Star Trek* Wasn't A Mistake and The Voice of Self Doubt relied upon to survive was gone. My creativity blossomed as a result. When I wrote in my weblog, I produced entries that were genuinely funny and entertaining . . . to me at least.

10 MARCH 2002
Make it burn!

As I write this, Anne is behind me, doing some workout video tape, and I can only hear the breathless voice of the girl who is leading the workout saying, "Oh yeah, oh yeah, doesn't that feel good? Don't stop, you're almost there. *pant* *pant*"

If I didn't know any better, I'd think she was watching "Debbie Does 7-Minute Abs."

But seriously folks, try the fish, and be sure to stick around for the comedy and magic stylings of Johnny Funnypants! I hear the late show gets a little naughty.

I was overflowing with creative energy, and on April 1st, I pulled a notorious April Fool's joke.

01 APRIL 2002
Good News, Bad News

Good morning, everyone and happy April! I hope everyone had a nice weekend. Okay, let's get straight to business. Here's the bad news: the entire site has crashed and we can't figure out why. I don't know when the crash happened, or why, because I was offline all weekend, but I'm working on it. I suppose that if you can read this, it means things are working again, which will bring us to our second bad news: I tried to upgrade to Movable Type 2.0 on Friday and it broke. Goddammit! I swear, I am fucking cursed. I know what went wrong and I'm going to start pleading with the authors for some help. They seem like cool people, so hopefully they will be willing to give me a hand. *sigh*

On to the good news! Oh, this is such amazingly good news and it's been so hard to keep this to myself, but there have been contract talks and all sorts of negotiations and all that . . . but I can finally make the big big announcement.

The official announcement will be made on Thursday, but I've been given permission by Paramount's hired goons to make the announcement today.

In four weeks, I will be joining the cast of *Enterprise* in a recurring role!

The details are still being worked out, but basically what they plan to do is have Wesley use his Time Traveler abilities to move through space and time to the NX-01. He'll be more like the dark, troubled Wesley of "The First Duty" and "Final Mission" and less like the gee-whiz Wesley of days gone by.

Here's a little history: *Nemesis* is testing very well and Paramount is extremely excited that this lame little website has generated such a huge following. I guess some people started a letter-writing campaign without my knowledge and Paramount listened. I spent most of last week on conference calls with Rick and Brannon, as well as some of the brass at Paramount, working out the details, making sure that Wesley will not be saving the NX-01 all the time.

grin

I'll be in 8 of 22 episodes for the two seasons, with an option to renegotiate at the end of the second season. I'm only recurring to allow me the freedom to participate in other shows, and pursue other projects.

I'm so freakin' excited, I don't even know what else to say. I can't believe that I'm going to be working on *Star Trek* again and I can't believe that I'm going to be working on Stages 8 and 9 again.

I have to go to a fitting right now. I'll write more when I have more details. I hope everyone has a great day!!

The Internet bought it completely. My announcement was posted on the mega sites Slashdot and Fark (who were in on the joke), and the "news" was carried by many sci-fi newswires (who were not). I had very carefully crafted the news, working it out over the course of several of days, adding in difficult-to-verify yet plausible details, like the testing status of *Nemesis* (they didn't even have a rough cut at the time) and talking with the producers about the nature of Wesley's character upon his return.

Minutes after I'd posted the prank, the e-mails began to pour in. Hundreds of Trekkies joined the regular readers of my website in expressing the excitement I would have felt had it been real. The genuine happiness and kindness, pouring in from people all over the world, was the opposite of the reaction I expected. As the happy e-mails piled up, I began to feel like I was misleading these people and taking advantage of their good will. By the afternoon, I felt awful and decided to set the record straight.

APRIL FOOL'S!

Well, most of you have figured it out by now, but the truth is . . .

. . . I'm not gonna be on *Enterprise*. Even as a computer voice, or within the secret, dirty, late-night thoughts of Capt. Archer.

I hope everyone takes this in good humor. Lots of people sent really kind and sweet congratulatory messages and I actually feel pretty badly for fooling such nice people. All the idiots who thought it was a really good idea to fill my inbox with "Wesley is gonna ruin *Enterprise*" crap should get a life and direct any further comments to /dev/null.

To be honest I was surprised at how many people were wishing me well; I was expecting the Kill Wesley Crowd to come out instead.

I think the greatest highlight of the day came when my mom called Anne while I was out.

The conversation went something like this:

Mom: Do you have something to tell me?

Anne: Uh, no.

Mom: Do you have some big news about Wil?

Anne: Oh, that. Uh, what day is today?

Mom: It's Monday!

Anne: Right. And the date is . . .?

Mom: It's April Fir- OH! Damn you!

Heh. I guess my dad was all pissed off, stomping around my parent's house because I didn't tell them myself and he "had to read it on Wil's fucking website!"

Thanks go to the Frodo Crew™ who helped me take this scheme from stupid idea to stupid fruition: Spudnuts, jbay, JSc, Roughy, Bobby The Mat and Greeny. Also to /. and FARK, for getting on board.

All those people really *did* want me to succeed, and they really *were* happy for me. The joy that I thought I would have felt, had I been given a chance to do *Star Trek* again, became real and undeniable when I realized that I had redefined myself with my weblog. Some people would still see me as That Washed Up Guy Who Used To Be An Actor When He Was A Kid, but many more people, including myself, saw me as That Guy With The Cool Weblog Who Is Just A Geek Like The Rest Of Us.

It was a good time to have this realization, because my acting career, which hadn't really gone anywhere for years, was about to crash right into a brick wall.

NINE

Alone Again, or . . .

ON APRIL 5TH, 2002, as Anne and I were packing for a Spring Break trip to Lake Tahoe with Ryan and Nolan for a much-needed change of scenery, I received a phone call from my manager. It was the end of pilot season—a period at the beginning of each year when studios cast for their new fall television shows. Most actors, myself included, hope to get a job on a pilot each year, because it means financial security and a chance to be on the next *Friends* or *West Wing*. During pilot season, most actors have several auditions each week, and it's a hectic but exciting time. The pilot season that had just ended was the fourth in a row where I'd had fewer than 10 auditions, all of them failures.

"Is your fax machine on?" my manager said.

"Yeah."

"Good. I'm sending you two appointment sheets for next week."

"Oh crap," I said. "I can't go. It's Spring break for the kids, and Anne and I are taking them up to Lake Tahoe."

"When do you leave?"

"In about 20 minutes. When are the auditions?"

"You've got an independent film on Tuesday, and at least one, possibly two pilots on Wednesday. Callbacks will be Thursday or Friday."

"What do you think I should do?"

"I can't make that decision for you. Talk it over with Anne and call me right back."

I hung up the phone.

"I know how you feel about your family, but this is our last shot at pilot season," said a familiar voice.

"This is stupid, Prove To Everyone," I replied. *"You and I both know I'm not going to book these jobs, and we're all looking forward to this vacation. We're packing up the car, for fuck's sake."*

"What the fuck is wrong with you?! You've had ONE audition in months, and you're going to pass on THREE OF THEM in one week? Do you want to be an actor or not?!"

"I'm not so sure I do."

"Oh, you think you're going to be a big writer because you write a stupid weblog?" we were joined by The Voice of Self Doubt.

"I thought you guys were gone," I said.

"We were just waiting for you to call on us again. You know that fear you feel right now? That fear that you may be letting a golden opportunity slip through your fingers, and you'll regret it for the rest of your life? We felt it too." Prove To Everyone was right. The Fear hadn't completely gone away. I'd just managed to keep it hidden for a few months.

"If you blow off this opportunity, you will live the rest of your life as That Washed Up Has Been Who Used To Be An Actor When He Was A Kid," he said.

I stammered something about April Fool's and how I'd redefined myself.

"That's bullshit. Anyone can write a bunch of drivel on the Internet," said The Voice of Self Doubt.

"No, Wil's right. If he passes on these auditions, he can always sign autographs at a Star Trek convention for a few more years until he digs himself out of debt," Prove To Everyone said. *"And there's always Celebrity Boxing to get that career going again."*

I walked out to the car and told Anne that I had to stay home.

A few minutes later, we called the kids over to the dining room table.

"You guys, I just got a call from Chris," I said, "and I have two auditions next week."

"Did you tell him that we're going on vacation?" Nolan said.

I couldn't look him in the eye. "I told him that we had that planned, but I have to stay here and go on these auditions."

"Why?! We're getting ready to leave!" Ryan said.

I looked to Anne. Her eyes were welling up, but she said nothing.

"I'm really sorry, you guys. I haven't had any good opportunities for work in months, and I have to take these chances when they come along."

It was silent in our house. A car drove by outside. Nolan said, "Well, can you drive up and meet us?"

I shook my head. "It's eight hours there and back, Nolan. If I get a callback, I'd just have to turn right around and come home."

"This sucks," he said.

I looked at Anne again. She looked away.

"I know how much we're all looking forward to this trip," I said, "but I just can't go. Once you're there, you won't miss me at all."

We all knew that wasn't true. We were having enormous problems with Anne's ex-husband, and our family desperately needed to get away from him. I really didn't want to stay home. I wanted to go with them, and play Auto Bingo and I Spy on the drive up. I wanted to play with the kids in the melting snow and roast marshmallows over the cabin's wood-burning stove.

Silence hung over the four of us, until Anne quietly said, "Why don't you two go and get your backpacks, and take them to the car."

The boys went into the back of the house, and I looked at my wife.

"I'm sorry," I said.

"I know." She wiped tears out of her eyes and left me alone at the table.

"You did the right thing," Prove To Everyone said.

"Fuck you," I said.

I sadly bid them farewell and watched them drive up our street. I stood at the end of our driveway long after they'd passed out of sight. When I walked into our silent and empty house, I sat at our dining room table, and wondered if I'd made the right decision.

---

05 APRIL 2002

Alone Again, Or . . .

The Big Plan for this weekend was to go up north with Anne and the kids, because it's their Spring Break, starting today.

We get the rental minivan (ugh) loaded up and ready to go, and I get a call from my manager: I have two auditions on Monday, both pilots, and I have an audition on Tuesday, for an indie. I'm also supposed to test for at least one, possibly two pilots on Wednesday.

So all of my stuff comes out of the rental beast and I go from spending the weekend with my family to spending it alone, preparing for these three auditions.

Holy crap, how things can change in an instant.

It's not a bad thing, missing the vacation, because I continue to make it down to the last handful of actors on all my auditions, (except for the call I had last week, where I got to spend all of 25 minutes with the material and the producers were taking calls on their cell phones and leaving the effing room while I was doing my audition) and the more I have the better my odds are . . . but I'd be lying if I said I wasn't going to miss them.

It's weird to be in my empty house, alone, without even Ferris to keep me company.

It's just me and the cats, just like the old bachelor days . . . except I am under pain of death to "keep the fucking house clean" from my old lady.

It should be interesting to see how I do on these three auditions, since I'll have three whole days to prepare a character and memorize the scenes, without any distractions.

What a huge, steaming pile of bullshit! *"It's not a bad thing?"* Who did I think I was fooling? Though I was desperately trying to believe that I had made the right decision, I wasn't even fooling myself. The only saving grace was the minute possibility that I could book one of these jobs. If I did, I would be able to convince myself that I'd made an acceptable sacrifice.

When we actors fight for roles (and unless you're a Big Hot Superstar, it's *always* a fight), we only control about 10% of the factors that will ultimately get us the job: our preparation and how we look. The rest of the process is completely out of our hands and includes elements such as:

- Casting Director prejudices—how excited about *me* is this casting director? This is about 60% of the fight.

- Studio pressure—do they want a big name for this part? This is about 20% of the fight.

- Nepotism—is one of Jimmy Kimmel's cousins available? Surprisingly, this is only about 5%.

- Chemistry—how do I fit in with the rest of the cast? This, too, is about 5%, but isn't even a factor until the very end of the process.

Since I had so much at stake, I did everything to ensure that I gave the best auditions possible. I spent lonely and silent hours in my house, creating unnecessarily complex character histories. When I finished, I memorized my lines. When my lines were memorized, I memorized the other character's lines. When that was finished, I tried different hairstyles and costumes. When I went into those auditions, I wanted to leave as little to chance as possible.

The first audition was a complete disaster.

It was at 2:30 in the afternoon, so I slept late, and then spent the morning reviewing my character notes and audition script, which actors call "sides." The second audition was to happen later in the day, and I wouldn't have time to return home between the two to change, so I carefully hung a different wardrobe in the back of my car before I left the house around 1:45, for Walt Disney Studios in Burbank.

When I was a kid, I always liked going to Disney. As far as studios go, it's actually pretty boring: no back lot like Universal or Warners, and no front lot like Fox, but standing at the corner of Mickey Mouse Avenue and Dopey Drive is pretty magical when you're a kid. Hell, it's pretty magical when you're an adult!

I showed my ID to the security guard and waited while they searched my car. There had been some nebulous threat against movie studios, and they were all really manic about security. Driving onto the lot at Warners was like going into an embassy, complete with concrete barriers and guys with guns, but Disney was a bit more relaxed. As long as there wasn't a box in the trunk that said "THIS IS A BOMB" in big red letters, you'd be fine.

I parked my car and checked my watch: 2:25. I looked at myself in my rearview mirror and said, "You're a good actor. Go kick their ass." It's something that I do before every audition. It started out as a practical way to steady my nerves, but over the years, it's turned into a superstitious ritual.

I walked across the parking lot, past several actors on their way out who looked exactly like me. *Was one of these "The Guy," or did I still have a chance to be "The Guy?"* Those thoughts, spoken by The Voice Of Self Doubt, lead to unemployment, so I pushed him out of my head.

I went out of my way to pass through the intersection of Mickey Mouse Avenue and Dopey Drive, and arrived at the audition one minute late. The room was empty except for a water cooler and a few chairs. A sign-in sheet sat on one of them. I picked it up, and wrote in my name, SAG number, character name, agent, and time I arrived. I looked up the list to see if there were any familiar names ahead of me, but I didn't see anyone I recognized. All the names were crossed out, and someone named David was ahead of me.

I looked around for David.

Was David the guy who was going to take my job away from me? Maybe I'd go Tonya Harding on him before he got to go in.

"Hey, David! Nice to meet you! I'm Wil. Did you see this interesting thing on the window ledge?" Shove. *"Oops. Sorry about that. Let me just cross your name off the list here . . ."*

David was nowhere to be found, so I sat down and waited.

And waited.

And waited.

At 10 minutes past 3, I heard the bell chime on the elevator down the hallway. Of course! David was downstairs, plotting my destruction. I heard footsteps coming down the hallway, and glanced at the open window that was next to me. When I looked back, Sean Astin walked into the room.

My heart leapt. Sean is one of my favorite people in the world, and we really hit it off when we worked on *Toy Soldiers* together. In the months of publicity tours that followed, we became good friends, but as his career took off and mine tanked, I fell out of touch with him. All my murderous thoughts about the still-unseen David went out of my head.

"Is that Sean Astin?" I said with a huge smile.

"You look just like Wil Wheaton," he said.

I jumped out of my chair, and we embraced.

"I am so happy to see you," I said.

He picked up the sign-in sheet. "How have you been?"

Shitty.

"I've been better, but I'm great now," I said.

"I'm sorry I couldn't come to your wedding," he said. "We were in New Zealand."

"Yeah, your assistant told us—what was that? Three years ago? Holy shit. That's a long time."

He nodded.

"Was it fun?" I said. *Fellowship of the Ring* had only been out for a few months, but it was well on its way to being a phenomenon.

"A lot of work, but also a lot of fun," he said.

I wanted to drop my sides, forget the audition, and spend the rest of the afternoon in a coffee shop, catching up.

"Hey, what are y—"

The door opened, and the casting director walked out, chatting amiably with a fairly well-known actor. *Why wasn't his name on the sign-in sheet?*

". . . so we'll talk to you soon!" he said.

The well-known actor shook his hand and left. The Casting Director looked right through me and said, "Hello, Sean! Thank you for coming in!"

Sean smiled, and I did my best impression of the invisible man while they shook hands.

The Casting Director looked down at the sign-in sheet and called out, "David? Is David here?"

"Dave's not here, man!" I thought, and stifled a giggle.

I looked around the empty room. Unless he was hiding behind the water cooler, David wasn't here. "Have you seen David?" The Casting Director said to Sean.

"No. But I think Wil is next," Sean said.

The Casting Director looked at me like I had just appeared in a puff of smoke.

"Just a second," he said, and walked to the hallway door. "David?!" he called out.

"Yes?" Came the distant reply.

"We're ready for you."

I guess he was sitting around the corner, or maybe down on the stairs, but the mysterious David walked into the room, and handed his picture and resume to the Casting Director, who turned to me and said, "You're next."

"Okay. Thank you," I said.

The Casting Director's voice took on an incredibly obsequious tone as the door shut behind him. "This is David, everyone . . ."

I looked at Sean.

"Tell me again why we do this?" I said.

"Because we love The Process," he said.

"Oh yes. The Process."

We both shook our heads, and I picked up my sides. There's a very delicate balance between over-preparation and under-preparation, that's best compared to a pitcher coming out of the bullpen: as an actor, I can't over throw before I get into the game, but I can't be warming up on the mound, either. Over the years, I've found this balance by reviewing my sides and notes when the guy ahead of me goes into the room. That way I have about 3–5 minutes (depending on the length of the scenes, of course) to warm up, and I usually go into the room ready to blow my fastball past them or stun them with the knuckler.

Of course, this doesn't work when the guy ahead of me stays in the room for over 20 minutes.

After 10 minutes or so had passed, I turned to Sean. "Do you want to trade numbers and maybe get together to catch up sometime soon?"

He reached into his pocket for a pen. "I'd love that," he said.

I tore the bottom off a blueish scrap of note paper that had directions to my second audition on it and handed it to him.

"I'll give you my cell and my home numbers," he said.

He wrote them down and handed it back to me. I tore off a smaller corner, and wrote my home number down. "I don't have a cell right now," I said with some embarrassment.

"Got it," he said.

I folded that scrap of paper in half, and put it into the breast pocket of the sport coat I was wearing for the audition. In the back of my mind, I wondered if I'd actually get the nerve up to call him.*

I sat back down, and looked at my sides again, but I didn't read them. I was dangerously close to over-preparation territory.

Another 10 minutes passed before the door finally opened.

"David, you were *wonderful*," the Casting Director said as they passed us. "Stay close to the phone."

David left, and the Casting Director picked up the sign-in sheet. He crossed off a name (presumably mine) and looked up.

"Wil?" He looked around the room.

"I'm ready," I said. Again, he looked at me like I had flown in through the window. *Is he doing this on purpose?*

---

* I'm writing this down on March 8, 2004. We're having a fantastic heat wave in Los Angeles and all my doors and windows are open. Led Zeppelin I plays "Your Time Is Gonna Come" on my CD player. I just walked to my closet and reached into the pocket of that sport coat, which I haven't put on since I had that audition. Sean's number was still there. I still haven't gotten up the nerve to call him.

I handed him my picture and resume, as I stood up.

"Break a leg," Sean said.

"Thanks," I said, and entered the same room I've been entering for 20 years: always too small or too big, harshly lit, and dominated by an enormous conference room–sized table, around which sit several studio executives, producers, writers, and casting assistants.

This particular room had something new, though: the infamous casting couch crowded the left side of the room; upon it sat five executives. Clustered around the ubiquitous table were another seven people. A casting assistant stood behind a camera, mounted on a tripod.

"This is Wil Wheaton," the Casting Director said.

I extended my hand to the executive who was nearest to me. She didn't take it, but chewed rather forcefully on her gum.

"Hello," I said, as I dropped my hand to my side.

Nobody said anything. One guy folded his hands in his lap, and looked at me expectantly.

"How are you guys doing today?" I said. *What the hell am I doing making small talk? Just shut up and do the audition!*

After a long pause, one of them said, "Fine. Thank you."

Another looked very bored as he turned my picture over and looked at my resume.

"Oh, you were in *Stand By Me*?" he said.

Have I been in anything else?

"Yeah," I said. "A long time ago."

One of the other executives coughed.

Over the years, I've developed a remarkable sixth sense for these things. When I walk into an audition, I can tell almost immediately how they feel about me. It's just like dating—within seconds, these people decide if they're going to take you on a nice date, or just fuck you and never call you back.

These people weren't interested in having dinner, that was for sure. An uncomfortable silence filled the room.

They hate me. What am I doing here?

"Okay, Wil. Go ahead and slate your name, then we'll begin," said the Casting Director.

Oh. This will be fun. Nothing like doing comedy for a room filled with people who hate me.

I turned to the camera, took a deep breath, and hoped that my years of acting experience would pay off: I was now acting like I didn't want to kill these people.

"Hi, my name is Wil Wheaton," I said.

"How tall are you, Wil?"

"Uh . . ." I held my hand up to the top of my head. "About this tall," I said.

Silence.

". . . which, of course, would be about 5'11"."

"Thank you."

In every audition, there is this moment similar to the time between the lights in a theater going down and the curtain coming up, or the time between the clapping of the slate and the director calling action. But in an audition, there are no lights, and there's no slate. It's just this awkward moment when everyone hits a mental "reset" button, and the actor begins. In this particular audition, the moment was made all the more uncomfortable by the oppressive silence in the room. I took a deep breath, and began the first of four scenes.

It was just awful. There was some forced laughter, almost like a half-hearted laugh track, but that was it. When the first scene was finished, I flipped over the top page of my sides and started the second scene.

"Jenny, I thought—" I said, before I was interrupted by one of the executives behind the table.

"Oh, we're just doing the first scene today," he said. "Thank you."

Boy, it took your hero David over 20 minutes to do "just the first scene today!" He must have been really slow. Or maybe you're just full of shit.

"Wait," I said. "I prepared *four* scenes. I spent three days preparing four scenes, and didn't go on vacation with my wife and stepkids so I could come in here and give you this audition. I've been working my ass off to give you this performance, and even though I can tell that you're not interested in me at all, I'm going to fucking do this, okay? I have a 25-year career behind me, including a performance in an Academy Award–nominated film, and that counts for something. So why don't you all just lighten the fuck up, and respect the fact that I came in here to do this stupid song and dance for your noncreative asses?!"

Well, that's not exactly true. I said something more like, "Oh. Well, thanks for seeing me," and I walked out of the room.

Sean looked up from his sides and asked me how it went.

"Not so good," I said, grimly. "I've set the bar nice and low for you."

"Sorry, man," he said.

"Meh. Whatever."

The office door opened. "Sean? We're ready for you."

"Hey, call me next week, okay?" Sean said.

"I will," I said. "Break a leg!"

"Thanks."

He walked into the room. "This is Sean Astin," the Casting Director said. A chorus of happy voices greeted him as the door closed.

I gave the best audition I could under the circumstances, but I was furious when I left, as much at myself as I was at them. I violently crumpled my sides into a ball, and slammed them into the first trash can I found. By the time I got to my car, I was seething. However, true to form, when I wrote about it, I did my best to focus on the positive, even calling these assholes, who I would have gleefully punched in the nuts if given the chance, "nice people."

---

09 APRIL 2002
Stay Gold, Pony Boy

There is no word yet on the auditions, but here is my personal recap:

The 2:30 wasn't as good as I had hoped. I went in after a guy who clearly did a great job (he was in there for close to 20 minutes), which is the absolute worst time an actor can go into a room . . . I could tell that he had given them exactly what they were looking for and I really felt like they just wanted me to hurry up and get out of the room. They were all really nice people, though . . . people I could totally work with. It was just bad timing for me.

A good thing though, was that I saw Sean Astin while I was there. Now, Sean is one of my absolute favorite people in the world. I've known him since forever and I respect him tremendously both as an actor and as a person. It's funny; every time I tease him about getting roles in *Lord of the Rings*, or *Goonies*, or any of the other kick-ass movies he's been in, he tells me, "Hey, you got *Stand By Me*. So we're even."

So, since I am always looking for the hidden positives in the increasingly shitty world of life as an actor, seeing Sean made that call worthwhile.

The 5:00 call went much better. It was also for a sitcom and it was over at Warner Brothers. It was tough for me to focus, because of the lousy experience I had just had at 2:30, but I was somehow able to leave that behind me and I did a pretty good job. There was only one other person in the room besides the casting director, which means that there is not a ton of laughter where there normally would be if you were in front of an audience. That can really throw someone who isn't experienced in these things, and I was really glad that I knew how to handle that. I think I'm a little bit too old for that part, but I guess they're seeing people of all different ages, so I think I'm still in the hunt on that one.

Thank you to everyone who sent me their good wishes. I especially enjoyed cat mojo.conf > /dev/Wil.

I copied that one onto the back of a calendar page and carried it in my pocket.

You know, the thing about both of these calls is, I did everything that I could possibly do to be prepared. I created characters, I learned the lines, I developed the relationships . . . I will never get used to the people on the other side of the table not putting as much effort into their side as I put into my side.

So, now the stupid waiting begins . . . I'll update when I hear something.

I waited for three days—without my wife, stepkids, or even my dog for company—for the call to come that I hadn't booked the jobs. When it did, I took a sardonic pleasure in the knowledge that, for once, I didn't come in second. I had bailed on my family at the last minute, and I hadn't even cracked the top 10.

12 APRIL 2002

I'm a Loner Dottie, A Rebel

I have a partial update from the auditions on Monday.

I've heard nothing from the second call. However, not surprisingly, the first call, where they really made me feel unwelcome, is going nowhere.

I talked with my manager about it and he got some feedback from them: they found people they really liked on Friday and I guess lots of actors left that room on Monday feeling shitty, like the producers didn't even want those actors to be there.

Well, duh. If they found people they really liked on Friday, why even bother to bring us in on Monday?! And why bother to bring in actors if they're going to make us feel like they don't even want us there?!

Now, I know I probably shouldn't say this, because in the entertainment industry, nobody is supposed to say obvious and truthful things, like Tom Cruise sucks, or James Cameron is an epic A-hole and Michael Bay is a complete hack, but here's some information from The Inside™:

This happens all the %$@!^ing time. Actors prepare their guts out for an audition, only to get there, wait an hour or longer (SAG says they're supposed to pay us like 30 bucks or something if we're there longer than an hour, but if an actor actually asks for that he will be blacklisted by that casting director, so nobody ever does) and go into a room where producers are on the phone, or looking through paperwork, or doing just about everything in the world except paying attention to the actor who is auditioning for them.

Most of the time, the person who is reading with you is so overworked, he or she doesn't take the time to learn what the scene is about and reads the other lines in the scene with a flat, monotone disinterest that throws off the best of us. I guess what most of them fail to realize is that the best acting is *reacting* and it's tough to react to complete and utter disinterest.

A notable exception to this rule is Tony Sepulveda, who casts at Warner Brothers. He is one of my absolute favorite casting directors to read for, because he ALWAYS makes me feel welcome and comfortable and he ALWAYS knows the material he's reading. The last time I read for him, he was totally off the script and even improvised with me. Tony is an incredibly busy man, yet he still manages to find the time to make actors feel welcome. It's a shame that there's only one of him.

You know, if I were a producer or director, I would want every actor who comes into my room to feel extremely comfortable. I would want to create an atmosphere where actors are free to feel vulnerable and take chances, where they are able to do their absolute best work. I would want actors to come before me and not worry about anything, at all, except showing me their take on the character.

Oh, I'm so living in a dream world. That is just not how it is. Four out of five times, I go into an audition and the people I'm reading for don't even stand up and thank me for coming in. Most of the time, I'm lucky if anyone other than the casting director even says hello, or shows a remote interest in my being there. I have experienced people taking calls on their cell phones and talking during my audition, taking calls on their cell phones and leaving the room while I'm doing my audition, reading the newspaper, reading their schedule for the rest of the day, talking to another person in the room . . . it goes on and on.

Good acting comes from an actor who is not afraid to stand there naked in front of a room and bare their soul to the camera. You'd think that the uncreative philistines who run this bullshit industry would give a shit about that and try to create an atmosphere where actors can relax and do their best work.

But here's the truth: these days, most of the people sitting in that room know that their show is going to *maybe* make it three episodes before the equally insecure and untalented people at the network cancel it before it can find an audience —and put reruns of some shitty reality show in its place. And because they know this, they are scared to death and they don't trust their instincts and they project all their insecurities onto the actors who are in front of them.

You know, the audition process for *Win Ben Stein's Money* was the most fun I have had in YEARS, and that was entirely because Andrew Golder and the entire group over there told me, from the very beginning, "We want you to feel comfortable and relaxed. We want you to feel free to make mistakes and not worry about looking bad, because when you can do your best work, it makes us look good." It made me feel like I was playing before the home crowd in The Big Game™.

So the challenge for me is to somehow get over this terrible environment that pervades auditions these days. I have to be able to walk into a room and not give a shit about them, because they certainly don't give a shit about me. But that's extremely hard! I do care about them. I have put time, energy, and effort into creating this character for them and I *want* to please them! It's really tough to do my best, when I feel like the people in the room don't care whether I'm there or not.

Now maybe I'm insane, but wouldn't it be better, and easier, and more cost-effective, for the studios to put actors at ease and make us feel like they do, in fact, give a shit about us being there? If they'd do that, actors would be able to do much better work, because they wouldn't feel nervous and overly scrutinized. Shows would be cast much more quickly and everyone would go home happy.

But, as I said, I am so living in a dream world.

Thought for today:

> *If imagination is not set to the task of building a creative life, it busies itself with weaving a web of inner fears and doubts, blame and excuse.*

—Laurence G. Boldt

Sour grapes, right? Sort of. The truth is, I'd put up with that sort of treatment for way too long, and I'd just had it. I'd rather not ever get hired for acting work again than continue to smile while being punched in the face.

The year before I wrote this blog, I'd been on the negotiating team for the Screen Actors Guild when we worked out our TV and Theatrical contract, and I was horrified to discover how our employers think of us: we're interchangeable, disposable, and not worthy of any respect. As an actor, I depended on those people to let me support my family and create the art that was such an important part of my life. Because we actors are so dependent on them, they can treat us like shit and we'll beg for more.

Well, I had a week to think about that, and I realized that I'd treated my family exactly the same way the Industry had treated me: I had totally disregarded their feelings and taken them for granted.

When Anne and the boys returned home, I knew what was important to me, I knew what I would fight for, and I knew where my priorities were. I met her in the driveway when they drove up and embraced her before she was even fully out of the car.

"I'm so sorry I didn't come with you," I said.

"I know," she said.

"Never again. I'm done with this bullshit."

Ryan and Nolan came out of the car, and made it a group hug.

"I love you guys so much. I'm so happy you're home," I said.

I vowed then, for better or for worse, that I would never let my career come before my family again.

TEN

"You're Gonna Be a Great Writer Someday, Gordie"

WHEN I WAS 14 and doing publicity for *Stand By Me*, I was often asked by interviewers if I was a writer like my character. This question usually went along with such deeply insightful queries as, "What's your favorite color?" and "Do you have a girlfriend?" ("Purple" and "Samantha Fox* hasn't returned my calls" were the respective answers.)

So many people asked me if I was a writer, I began to think that I *should* be a writer. But I wasn't a writer, right? I was an actor. By the time I was 14, I'd been a professional actor for over half my life, and I took it for granted that I would continue to be a professional actor for the rest of it. I can even recall this stupid career test I had to take in 10th grade, where a woman asked me, "What profession would you like to pursue as an adult?"

"Acting," I said.

She noted this on my permanent record, and said, "Okay . . . now what's your realistic short-term goal?"

"Acting," I said.

---

* I know, I know. But it was 1986 and she had big boobs.

"Okay . . . and how do you plan to earn money until you go to college?"

"Acting," I said.

The rest of the class period was pretty much *"Who's On First,"* with "Acting" filling in at third base.

The truth is, I always enjoyed creative writing in school, and English was always my best subject. But the thought of pursuing it as a career never entered my mind until—well, until about six months after *Dancing Barefoot* was published.

As a matter of fact, after the *Stand By Me* publicity cycle ended, the idea of me being a writer didn't come up again until 10 years later, when I ran into my 7th grade English teacher while I was visiting my parents in my hometown of La Crescenta, CA.

She was walking out of the grocery store while I was on my way in, and she nearly ran me over with her cart.

"Mrs. Westerholm!" I said. She was one of my favorite teachers, and I was very happy to see her.

"Wil Wheaton? How are you?!" she said.

My career is in the toilet and shows no signs of ever improving. Yeah. I don't want to have that conversation.

"I'm doing great!" I lied. "I've been having lots of auditions, and I'm getting closer and closer to a good job all the time."

She frowned. "You're still acting?"

I swallowed, and hoped I sounded more convincing to her than I did to myself. "Uh-huh."

"Why aren't you writing?"

I was taken aback by her question, and I was quiet for a second.

I'm acting because it's what I've done my entire life . . . and it's the only thing I know how to do.

"I don't know. Because acting is what I do, I guess."

She shook her head, and I was right back in seventh grade, getting an after-school talking to.

"You were always such a wonderful writer, Wil," she said, wagging her finger at me. "We all thought that you'd end up as a screenwriter or novelist."

Something started to slowly turn in the back of my mind.

"Yeah, I always enjoyed it."

"Remember your *Land of the Zombies* story? All the students loved that."

I smiled and nodded. As a creative writing assignment around Halloween in 1985, all the seventh graders wrote horror stories. I was inspired by *Dawn of the Dead, D&D*, and a family trip to San Francisco, so I wrote a story about a man and his wife who flee from the terror of zombies who were slowly taking over the country after escaping from an army research base. My heroes discovered that water can force the zombie-causing chemicals out of the living dead, so they end up on Alcatraz Island, which I had decided was the only safe place left in America.* I remember the story ended with something like:

Alcatraz was once a federal prison for killers. Now it's the prison that's saving our lives. We even sleep in the Birdman's old cell.

As the sun set over the Golden Gate Bridge, I looked out onto America: once, the land of the free. Now, the land of the zombies.

It's not Hemingway, but it's pretty good for a 12-year-old. It was voted scariest *and* goriest story by the seventh *and* eighth graders. I proudly photocopied it and sent it to all my relatives, who were all horrified and told my parents that I should get professional help.

"Well, I hope you end up writing someday," she said. "You definitely have writing talent."

---

* It made sense when I was 12.

"Thank you." I said. "Can I help you put your bags in your car?"

"Oh! I'm not that old," she said with a chuckle. "Please tell your parents I said hello."

"I will." I walked into the store.

I heard her voice frequently for the next few years, though the only writing I ever did was infrequently scrawled in a leather-covered journal that was a gift from one of my friends—my first offline blog, I guess.

A few years later, I was talking with my mom, after finding out that I hadn't gotten yet another acting job.

"You seem really unhappy, Willow," she said.

"I am. I'm really tired of putting all this effort and energy into these auditions, only to be treated like crap by everyone in the room," I said. "Oh, and the not-ever-getting-hired thing is getting pretty old, too."

I sighed.

"I'm so much happier when I write stories for my stupid website and stuff . . ."

"Wil, it sure does seem like The Universe is trying to tell you something," she said.

"What do you mean?" I asked.

"When you're trying to be an actor, you're struggling against a head wind dragging an open parachute behind you. When you're writing, the wind is at your back and everything conspires to ensure you're successful."

There was a long silence while I thought about this.

"You're supposed to be a writer, Wil."

While I had a lifetime of acting experience, my writing experience was severely limited. The idea of trying to start an entirely new career in my late 20s was terrifying.

Well, I hope you end up writing someday. You definitely have writing talent.

How in the world would I be able to compete with established authors?

"You were always such a wonderful writer, Wil."

What if I sucked? What if I thought something was good, but it was actually garbage?

"We all thought that you'd end up as a screenwriter or novelist."

"I don't know, Mom."

"I do," she said.

I was doing okay recounting the boring things that happened in my life, but could I actually tell a story that had a beginning, middle, and end?

It turns out that I could.

08 MAY 2002
The Trade

When I was a kid, I traded my Death Star for a Land Speeder and five bucks.

The kid who talked me into the trade wasn't really a friend by choice. He was the son of some of my mom and dad's friends and we'd play together at his house while our parents listened to Fleetwood Mac in the den with the door closed, giggling about stuff that just didn't make sense to me, at all.

So we were like prisoners of war, forced to share a cell together, knowing that once the war was over, we'd never talk again.

I was aware of this situation, even at 8, so I was naturally skeptical of anything he offered me. He was already 10, in Double Digits, so I knew that I should be a little wary of him.

The offer came to me one afternoon in his back yard, next to his parent's swimming pool. I'd brought over my Death Star and some Star Wars figures so we'd have something to do. There was no way I was going to endure a repeat of the last time I'd been there, where my only entertainment was watching him organize and gloat over his collection of exotic matchbooks.

So we were sitting by the pool, which was doubling for the shore of an exotic new planet where the Death Star had been relocated. He drove up his Land Speeder and as he began to help his passengers out, I casually admired it.

He immediately offered a trade, but I declined. There was no way I was about to give up my Death Star for a Land Speeder that didn't even have any obvious guns.

He expressed some shock at my reluctance, showing off its exciting retractable wheels and exquisitely detailed dash-board sticker.

Although I was intrigued, I resisted. I really liked my Death Star. It had a cool Trash Compactor Monster.

He then let me in on a secret that only the 10-year-olds knew: Death Stars were lame. Land Speeders were cool.

This was news to me and gave me pause for consideration. Did I really want to keep this Death Star, knowing that it was lame? How many of the Big Kids were laughing at me while they raced their own Land Speeders around, as I sat with my Death Star, wheel- and-stickerless?

While I wondered about this, he repeated his very generous offer: he would trade me the Land Speeder for the Death Star. He didn't need to worry about what the other kids thought, he told me, because he also had an X-Wing Fighter and Darth Vader's TIE-Fighter. This combination, he went on, was even cooler than a Land Speeder, so he was all right.

While I considered this new information, he made me an offer I couldn't refuse.

He would give me five bucks to sweeten the deal.

Five bucks?!

I didn't need to hear another word.

I made the trade, willingly handing over the deed to my Death Star without so much as a handshake. He gave me the

Land Speeder, followed by five bucks from the front pocket of his Rough Riders. Shortly after that, my parents came out of the house, telling me that it was time to go home, after a stop on the way to pick up many bags of potato chips and pretzels.

Now, I know this seems like a shitty trade, because it was, but at the time, five bucks was as good as a million and that Land Speeder did have wheels, man! WHEELS!

With those wheels, I thought, I could ferry four of my Star Wars figures across my kitchen floor with just one push!

One push was all it would take for Princess Leia and Luke Skywalker escape the dangerous prison The Empire had built from Tupperware cups and a Styrofoam drink cooler in the shadow of my parent's refrigerator! They could be accompanied on their journey to the safety of the Rebel base, which was cleverly hidden from the Empire beneath the breakfast table, by C3PO and R2-D2, who would be attached to the back of their seats via amazing foot-peg technology! This vehicle was all that stood between the Rebel Alliance and victory! I couldn't believe that I had even considered for a moment not trading my very uncool Death Star for this magnificent chariot.

The entire drive home, I sat on the back seat of the 1971 VW Bus, paying no attention to the cool strains of the Grateful Dead playing out of the 8-track while my parents did something on the back side of a frisbee. My mind was focused on the coming prison escape and ensuing battle, where I just knew the Empire would enlist the help of GI Joe and He-Man. Good thing Luke and company had this new Land Speeder to get them out of danger!

Sadly, once I was home and on the kitchen floor, the reality of the trade did not meet the grand build-up it had been given by my young imagination. That single push did not send my heroes to quick safety. Rather, it sent them forward about six inches and to the left, coming to an anticlimactic rest against the front of the dishwasher. Only the constant presence of my grimy eight-year-old fist would give them adequate propulsion away from danger. And the foot-peg technology was quickly replaced by the more reliable Scotch-tape-and-rubber-band technology. The novelty of rolling that Land Speeder around the floor quickly wore off and I really missed my Death Star. It had a cool Trash Compactor Monster.

Fortunately, all was not lost: I had that five bucks. Five bucks to spend any way I wanted. I was rich, man. Filthy rich. Filthy. Stinking. Rich. Like Mister Drummond, or Ricky on Silver Spoons. That fabulous wealth made me a god among the kids on my block.

For weeks I sat in my bedroom, atop my Chewbacca bed-spread, holding that $5 bill in my hands, just looking at it, admiring it, memorizing its serial number, and wondering how many exciting places it had visited since its birth in the San Franciso mint in 1979. I spent countless hours basking in the glow of unimaginable wealth while the now-forgotten Land Speeder gathered dust in the back of my closet, behind Mister Machine and a partially completed model of the USS Arizona.

I capriciously thought of ways to spread my new found wealth among the other kids in our group . . . a pack of Wacky Packs stickers for Scott Anderson, some Toffifay for Joey Carnes, maybe even an invitation to Kent Purser to play doubles on Galaxian, my treat.

I decided to be very generous with my new wealth. I would be an eight-year-old philanthropist. Maybe I'd set up a foundation for the kids around the corner, who always wore the same clothes and smelled funny.

Maybe I'd stand outside the doors of Sunland Discount Variety, offering low-interest loans to kids wanting to play Gyruss or Star Castle.

I even thought about opening a savings account at the local Crocker Bank, where I'd get my own passbook and a set of Crocker Spaniels as a thank-you gift.

Ultimately, though, like any normal 8-year-old, I kept it for myself and there was a brief but shining moment in the summer of 1980, when I was allowed to ride my bike all the way to Hober's Pharmacy, stopping at every intersection along the way. Oh, sure, I told my parents that it was to watch for cars, but in reality, it was to check the front pocket of my two-tone OP shorts to ensure that my $5 bill, which I'd folded into a tight little square and tucked into my Velcro wallet, hadn't somehow escaped my possession. I took that five bucks and bought myself Wacky Packs, a Slush Puppy and enough surgical tubing to make several water weenies. I even had enough left over after playing Bagman, Donkey Kong and Asteroids Deluxe to take a chance on the intimidating wall of buttons that was Stargate. It was one of the grandest days of my young life and helped soften the disappointment that came when my friend Stephen proclaimed that my Land Speeder wasn't "rad," but "sucked."

I recently went back to Sunland, hoping to pick up a Slush Puppy and maybe see one or two of the phantoms of my youth haunting those stores, but they were nowhere to be found. I ended up getting a Mello Yello–flavored Slurpee from 7-11 and heading back home, where I spent some time looking for that Land Speeder in my garage.

I don't know why, but I still have it. There's an inscription on the bottom which proclaims "THIS IS WIL'S LaNdSPEEdR! kEpP YOU hANdS OFF OF It OR ELSE!!"

I took it out of the box and dusted it off. I held it in my hands for the first time in 20 years and suddenly that trade didn't seem like such a bad idea, after all.

I have a message for Darth Vader: you can build your Prison
Fortress on my kitchen floor, but the Rebel Alliance has a new
escape pod on the way and you'd better "kEpP YOU hANDS
OFF OF It OR ELSE!!"

That story started out when a friend of mine made a passing reference to Wacky Packages in an e-mail, and my brief millionaire
summer flashed through my mind in Cinemascope. I started to
compose my reply, and after about two paragraphs, I realized that
I was telling a story . . . with a beginning, middle, and end. I
wondered to myself, *"How would David Sedaris write this?"* and I
then wrote in my best *Me Talk Pretty One Day* impression. It was
the step across the rubicon that I had needed to take for months,
if not years. After a lifetime of bringing other people's words to
life, I did it with my own: my memories, my thoughts, and my
images were brought to life by *me*. It felt wonderful.

My mom called me that afternoon, told me she had read my
story, and said, "I need to tell you two things. We didn't listen to
the Grateful Dead. It was Fleetwood Mac."

I laughed and asked her what the other thing was.

"I told you that you were a writer," she said. "I am so proud
of you."

"Thanks, mom."

"When are you going to write a book?"

"Uhh . . . I don't know. There's a big difference between
writing a book and writing a blog," I said.

"Why?" she said. Then, before I could answer, she added,
"You should do it. I bet you'll surprise yourself."

After I wrote *The Trade*, I looked for those Cinemascope
memories everywhere I went. I wanted to stop Prove To
Everyone That I Can Write More Than Just One Story About
Something That Happened When I Was A Kid from growing

into a monster like his big brother, but another memory didn't surface for two months. When it did, though, it was worth the wait.

05 JULY 2002
Fireworks

When I was growing up, we always spent Fourth of July with my father's aunt and uncle, at their fabulous house in Toluca Lake.

It was always a grand affair and I looked forward to spending each Independence Day listening to Sousa marches, swimming in their enormous pool and watching a fireworks show on the back patio.

This fireworks display was always exciting because we were in the middle of L.A. County, where even the most banal of fireworks—the glow worms—are highly illegal and carried severe fines and the threat of imprisonment, should we be discovered by L.A.'s finest. The excitement of watching the beautiful cascade of sparks and color pouring out of a Happy Flower With Report was enhanced by the knowledge that we were doing something forbidden and subversive.

Yes, even as a child I was already on my way to being a dangerous subversive. Feel free to talk to any of my middle-school teachers if you doubt me.

Each year, the older children, usually teenagers and college-aged, would be chosen to light the fireworks and create the display for the rest of the family.

I was Chosen in 1987, three weeks before my fifteenth birthday.

The younger cousins, with whom I'd sat for so many years, would now watch me the way we'd watched Tommy, Bobby, Richard and Crazy Cousin Bruce, who always brought highly illegal firecrackers up from Mexico.

I was going to be a man in the eyes of my family.

This particular 4th of July was also memorable because it was the first 4th that was celebrated post-*Stand By Me* and at the time I had become something of a mini-celebrity around the family. Uncles who had never talked to me before were asking me to sign autographs for people at work, older cousins who had bullied me for years were proclaiming me "cool," and I was the recipient of a lot of unexpected attention.

I was initially excited to get all this newfound attention, because I'd always wanted to impress my dad's family and make my dad proud, but deep down I felt like it was all a sham. I was the same awkward kid I'd always been and they were treating me differently because of celebrity, which I had already realized was fleeting and bullshit.

Looking back on it now, I think the invitation to light fireworks may have had less to do with my age than it had to do with my growing fame . . . but I didn't care. Fame is fleeting . . . but it can get a guy some cool stuff from time to time, you know? I allowed myself to believe that it was just a coincidence.

The day passed as it always did. There were sack races, basket ball games and water balloon tosses, all of which I participated in, but with a certain impatience. These yearly events were always fun, to be sure, but they were standing directly between me and the glorious excitement of pyrotechnic bliss.

Finally, the sun began to set. Lawn chairs were arranged around the patio, wet swimsuits were traded for warm, dry clothes, and I bid my brother and sister farewell as I joined my fellow firework lighters near the corner of the house. I walked casually, like someone who had done this hundreds of times before.

As the sun sank lower and lower, sparklers were passed out to everyone, even the younger children. I politely declined, my mind absolutely focused on the coming display. I wanted to make a big impression on the family. I was going to start out with something amazing, which would really grab their attention. I'd start with some groundflowers, then a Piccolo Pete and a sparkling cone. From then on, I'd just improvise with the older cousins, following their lead as we worked together to weave a spectacular tapestry of burning phosphor and gunpowder for five generations of family.

Dusk arrived, the family was seated, and the great display began. Some of the veteran fireworks lighters went first, setting off some cascading fountains and a pinwheel. The assembled audience cheered and gasped its collective approval, and it was my turn.

I steeled myself and walked to the center of the large patio, casually kicking aside the still-hot remains of just-fired fountains. Casually, like someone who had done this hundreds of times before.

My hands trembled slightly, as I picked up three ground flowers that I'd wound together. My thumb struck flint and released flaming butane. I lit the fuse and became a man. The sparkling fire raced toward the ignition point and rather than following the directions to "LIGHT FUSE, PUT ON GROUND AND GET AWAY," I did something incredibly stupid: I casually tossed the now-flaming bundle of pyrotechnics on the ground. Casually, like someone who'd done this hundreds of times before.

The bundle of flowers rolled quickly across the patio, toward my captive and appreciative audience.

Two of the flowers ignited and began their magical dance of colorful fire on the cement, while the third continued to roll, coming to rest in the grass beneath the chair of a particularly old and close-to-death great-great-great aunt.

The colored flame that was creating such a beautiful and harmless display on the patio was spraying directly at this particular matriarch, the jet of flame licking obscenely at the bottom of the chair.

The world was instantly reduced to a few sounds: my own heartbeat in my ears, the screams of the children seated near my great-great-great aunt, and the unmistakable zip of the now-dying flowers on the patio.

I don't know what happened, but somehow my great-great-great aunt, who'd managed to survive every war of the 20th century, managed to also survive this great mistake of mine. She was helped to her feet and she laughed.

Unfortunately, she was the only one who was laughing. One of my dad's cousins, who was well into his 20s and never attended family gatherings accompanied by the same date, sternly ripped the lighter from my hand and ordered me back to the lawn, to sit with the other children. Maybe I could try again next year, when I was "more responsible and not such a careless idiot."

I was crushed. My moment in the family spotlight was over before it had even begun and not even the glow of pseudocelebrity could save me.

I carefully avoided eye contact, as I walked slowly, humiliated and embarrassed, back to the lawn, where I tried not to cry. I know the rest of the show unfolded before me, but I don't remember it. All I could see was a mental replay of the bundle of ground flowers rolling across the patio. If that one rogue firework hadn't split off from its brothers, I thought, I would still be up there for the finale, which always featured numerous pinwheels and a Chinese lantern.

When the show was over, I was too embarrassed to apologize and I raced away before the patio lights could come on. I spent the rest of the evening in the front yard, waiting to go home.

The following year I was firmly within the grip of sullen teenage angst and spent most of the festivities with my face planted firmly in a book—*Foundation* or something, most likely—and I watched the fireworks show with the calculated disinterest of a 15-year-old.

That teenage angst held me in its grasp for the next few years and I even skipped a year or two, opting to attend some parties where there were girls who I looked at, but never had the courage to talk to.

By the time I had achieved escape velocity from my petulant teenage years, Aunt Betty and Uncle Dick had sold the house and 4th of July would never happen with them again.

The irony is not lost on me, that I wanted so badly to show them all how grown up I was, only to behave more childishly than ever the following years.

This 4th of July, I sat on the roof of my friend Darin's house with Anne and the boys and watched fireworks from the high school. Nolan held my hand and Ryan leaned against me as we watched the Chamber of Commerce create magic in the sky over La Crescenta.

I thought back to that day, 15 years ago and once again I saw the groundflower roll under that chair and try to ignite great-great-great aunt whatever her name was.

Then I looked down at Nolan's smiling face, illuminated in flashes of color.

"This is so cool, Wil!" he declared. "Thanks for bringing us to watch this."

"Just be glad you're on a roof and not in a lawn chair," I told him.

"Why?"

"Well . . ." I began to tell him the story, but we were distracted by a particularly spectacular aerial flower of light and sparks.

In that moment, I realized that no matter how hard I try, I will never get back that day in 1987, nor will I get to relive the sullen years afterward . . . but I do get to sit on the roof with my wife and her boys now and enjoy 4th of July as a stepdad . . . at least until the kids hit the sullen years themselves.

Then I'm going to sit them in lawn chairs and force them to watch me light groundflowers.

I wrote that while I was still in my bathrobe on the morning of July 5th. When I was done, I printed it out, and read it to my wife before I posted it.

"Do you like it?" I asked.

"Yeah. Is it true?"

"Anne, I'm not a good enough writer to make stuff up. Do you think other people will like it?"

She smiled. "Duh."

When *Fireworks* was posted on WIL WHEATON dot NET, hundreds of people commented or e-mailed their approval. Many of them suggested that I write a book, and I began to give the idea some serious consideration. I still didn't know what it would be about, but the seed, planted years earlier by Mrs. Westerholm, began to grow.

ACT IV

"I keep looking for a place to fit
Where I can speak my mind
I've been trying hard to find the people
That I won't leave behind."

—The Beach Boys
I Just Wasn't Made For These Times

"Mellow is the man who knows what he's been missing
Many many men can't see the open road. "

—Led Zeppelin
Over the Hills and Far Away

ELEVEN

The Wesley Dialogues

IT WAS LATE MAY, and Pasadena was in the middle of a heat wave. I sat at my dining room table, surrounded by bills. Many of them had PAST DUE stamped on them in threatening red letters. Others contained direct threats about my credit rating and veiled threats about my personal well-being. When the phone rang, I cringed. I had run out of excuses for creditors, and I was scared about losing my house.

Anne walked into the dining room and sat across from me.

"I am so tired of this," I said.

"Tired of what?" she said.

"Everything! I'm tired of court! I'm tired of lawyers! I'm tired of never getting cast in anything! I'm just tired of . . ." I picked up a fistful of bills. "THIS!"

I was humiliated. I was ashamed. I was frustrated. I was angry. How did I get here? How did I go from *Mr. Big TV and Movie Star* to *Mr. Dodging the Bill Collectors*?

"Maybe I shouldn't have quit *Star Trek*," I said. "You know, I quit to have this big fucking movie career, and that never happened. It's just been one shitty movie after another."

"You always say that when money gets tight, or you have a bad audition. You've got to stop worrying about a choice you made 15 years ago, because you can't change it." She took my hand in hers. "Maybe you could wr—"

"I'm not a good enough writer to write a book!" I said, "There's a world of difference between writing for my website and trying to write a book."

She sighed. "I don't know what to tell you. Maybe you could auction something on eBay again. That really helped out last time."

"I feel like such a fucking loser when I do that, Anne."

"How many other people are selling your autograph online?"

I shrugged. "I don't know. 10? 15, maybe?"

"Do you have a problem with that?"

"Of course not."

"Well, if someone's going to make money off your signature, why not you?"

"But I don't want to exploit the people who read my website."

"Please. Running an auction is not exploiting anyone. Charging memberships is exploiting people. You just need to get over yourself."

One of the things I adore about my wife is her ability to get right to the heart of my bullshit. I couldn't argue with her. The only thing that was preventing me from putting up auctions was pride. I made a little mental scale. On one side, I put my family. On the other, my ego.

It took me all of two minutes to make the decision.

"Okay," I said, "You're right. But I'm not going to put up another stupid headshot." I stood up. "I'm going to find something cool and do that instead."

21 MAY, 2002
Mirror, Mirror

I'm in my garage, digging through a box of stuff, trying to find my Awful Green Things From Outer Space game.

I'm on the cold concrete floor, looking through the open box. I move aside some books and find my game. As I lift it out of the box, it reveals this Cadet Wesley Crusher action figure, just sitting there in the bottom of the box.

I look at him, wondering whether I should just look away and pretend that I didn't see him, or take him out and say hello.

After an awkward silence, I pick him up and say, "Hey, how you doin'?"

He just stares back at me, silent and stoic from within his plastic cell.

I consider him for a moment and tell him, "You know, you look sort of cool in this uniform. You should have stuck around a bit longer, so you could have worn it more."

He gives no response and I pause a moment to admire his perfect hair. I run my hand through my own unwashed hair and my fingers get thick with yesterday's water wax. I wonder if his perfect hair still smells like Sebastian Shaper hairspray.

His eyes burn into mine, his blank stare mocking me and I can't take it any longer.

I put him back into the box and as I'm about to put an unopened box of 1990 Topps NHL trading cards on him he says, "Wait!"

I lift up the box of cards and he's looking up at me, his smug confidence replaced with sadness.

"Hey, I don't want to stay in this box any more. You gotta let me out." His green eyes implore me to release him.

"Sorry, Wesley, but if I take you off of that card, you're worthless."

"Well, at least let me come sit on a shelf in your house! This box is cold and dark and since you took out the Ren and Stimpy plush toys in December, there isn't even anyone to talk to!"

I think of the years he and I spent together. I think back to our falling out and I can't believe that someone I was so close to has become such a stranger.

I know what I must do.

"You're right, Wesley. You can't stay in this box any longer. It's just not right. I'm going to find you a new home. Someplace where you will have lots of other action figures to talk to and maybe even a collectible plate or two."

"You mean . . . you're going to put me on eBay?"

"Yep."

"No! You suck, Wheaton!"

"Shut up, Wesley."

When I started to write that entry, I thought, *"Hey, why make a boring announcement when you can turn it into a story?"* I also thought that Wesley would be sweet and polite, and would talk about how excited he was to have a new home—but I couldn't do it. It was too much fun to make him profane, and to reclaim the line, "Shut up, Wesley."

I checked the auction frequently over the next few days, and when I blogged about the auction's progress, I saw a chance to have another conversation. Cadet Crusher had to get some more things off his tiny plastic chest.

24 MAY 2002
Turnabout Intruder

It's late at night and the rest of my house is asleep. The only sound other than my typing is that soft comforting hum of the fan in my computer. The room is dark, except for the light falling off of my monitor.

He's sitting on my desk, just outside the monitor's soft glow, staring at me.

"Hey, Wesley, I've got some good news."

"You've had a change of heart and you're going to put me in a Jello mold with Counselor Troi and Princess Leah?"

"No. First of all, Princess Leah isn't even the right scale for you—"

"Who said anything about scale? I'm articulated!"

"Do you want to hear the good news, or not?"

He sighs the perturbed yet insecure sigh of an 18-year-old. He strains his little plastic body against the twisty-tie that is holding him to his cardboard backing.

"Yes."

"You're way more popular that I thought. People have bid nearly 300 dollars for you on eBay! You're a hit, Crusher! They love you!"

He stops straining and looks at me, incredulous.

"What?"

"Yeah! Take a look."

I pick him up and turn him to face the monitor.

"Hey, slow down, jackass. You're going to give me motion sickness."

I wonder if this is the correct doll. I wonder if I've picked up the Evil Wesley Crusher, instead. I spin him around again and look for the tell-tale goatee, but it's not there. I guess he's just cranky.

"Dude! Take it easy!"

"Sorry."

I slowly turn him back around and point him at the monitor. I click the URL and show him the bidding, which has climbed to nearly 300 dollars.

"See? Isn't that cool? All this time we thought people hated us, but they like us, Wesley! They really like us!"

He is silent for a moment and when he finally speaks, his voice is thick with emotion.

"Yeah. That's . . . well . . . that's really cool," he says and I swear I can feel the cardboard shudder a little bit in my hands.

"Hey, Wheaton,"

"Yeah?"

"Can you just put me down on the desk for a while? I've . . . . uh . . . I think I have something in my eye."

"Are you crying, Wesley?"

"Shut up, Wheaton."

————————————◇◇◇————————————

When I told Wesley, "All this time we thought people hated us, but they like us . . ." I could have said, "All this time, I hated you. I hated you so much, I started to hate myself. But it was time wasted. I've learned to like you, and the part of me that you represent." When he cried, the tears rolled off my face.

I had started out this auction as a means to an end: I just wanted to keep the water turned on in my house. I didn't know that it would become this enormous confrontation with one of my greatest personal demons, but when I wrote the final installment in the trilogy, I put Wesley in his place . . . and he put me in mine.

28 MAY 2002
The Big Goodbye

The time has come.

I've been putting it off over the weekend, attending my best friend's wedding, going geocaching with my stepson.

But it is time. Money has changed hands and I have an obligation to fulfill.

I pick him up from my desk and avoid eye contact as I carry him into the dining room.

I gingerly put him down on my dining room table and he looks like a patient about to undergo some sort of surgery. Strangely, I feel more like Doctor Giggles than Doctor Green.

He looks up at me and says, "Hey, Wheaton. What do you say you let me out of this box and take me for a spin in your Land Speeder?"

"Can't do it, Wesley. First, you're the wrong scale and second, you don't belong to me anymore."

He doesn't reply. He knows that I'm right.

I uncap a gold paint pen and get ready. The familiar burn of acetone and paint hits me in the face and a series of convention memories blurs through my mind, in hyper-real Hunter S. Thompson-o-vision: I sign a plate, a photo, a poster, field a question that I don't know the answer to, politely decline the offer of a hug from a sweaty woman in a "Spock Lives!" T-shirt. The memories race past and I watch them with a certain amount of detachment, a spectator to my own life.

Although the places and people changed, there was little difference from one hotel convention hall to the next: The same questions, the same jokes, the same inescapable smell . . . the memories engulf me with a frightening and surprising lucidity. I think that I've allowed these events to drift into the distance of memory, but they come back, immediate and insistent, as if no time has passed.

He looks at me, daring me to give voice to these thoughts.

I realize that we are very interwoven, whether we like it or not and as I open my mouth to speak, something I'd never thought of before comes into my mind: I can exist without him, but he could not, would not, does not exist without me.

Suddenly, I feel free.

I lift the pen up and touch it to the plastic and write what I've been asked to write:

Vincent -

I am sick of following rules and regulations!

-Wil Wheaton

It's done.

I sit back and regard him. He's obscured by my writing, which casts a latticework of shadows across his face and body. The symbolism of this moment is not lost on me.

"You know, that was a cool line," he says. "Remember how cool it was to stand up to Picard?"

"Yeah. It was fun being you back then," I tell him. "I watched Code of Honor last night though. Jesus, you were a dork, man."

"That wasn't me, dude. That was Wesley Crusher, the doctor's son. I'm Cadet Crusher, the bad-ass. Wesley was a dork. Cadet Crusher was cool. Need I remind you who waxed Robin Lefler's ass?"

"Why do you have to talk that way? People have a certain image of you, you know."

"Hey, they can kiss my shiny plastic ass. I have never been responsible for the things I say. I can only say what someone tells me to say. As a matter of fact, I'm not even talking now. You're putting all these words in my mouth."

"So my Tyler Durden is a five-inch action figure? That's just perfect. At least you can't force me into some sort of Project Mayhem."

"Oh, I can't?"

I can't tell through the gold paint pen, but I think he's sizing me up.

"You're such a pussy, Wheaton. We were cool when we wore this spacesuit and you know it. Fucking own that, boyo. If anyone has a problem with that, they can kiss my ass, your ass, their own ass, and then they can fuck all the way off, 12 different ways."

I'm a bit shocked to hear this come out of us.

"Uh, Wesley, you really can't talk like that."

"I just told you, it's not me. It's you, cock-knocker. Now put me in the box and find some other cool thing to auction. I think I saw a plate in the closet."

"Why didn't we ever talk like this before? I never realized that you were cool. Really. I mean, I hated you, man."

"Yeah, you and every other insecure teenage boy. Listen and listen good, because I'm not saying this again.

"You have always cared too fucking much what other people thought of us. Go read your stupid website and listen to your own advice. You'll be much happier. Now put me in the box and let's get this over with."

I look at him and a touch of sadness passes over me.

"Wesley, I have always been and I always will be—"

"Jesus H. Christ! I can't believe you were going to quote *Star Trek*. I am so embarrassed for you right now. Just close the fucking box and send me on my way."

I do it. I put him in the box, drop in some packing stuff and a few stickers.

We drive to the post office in silence.

I walk to the mailbox and open it.

I think about saying goodbye, but I know that Wesley won't be talking to me anymore.

I place the box on the edge and lift it up. The box falls into darkness.

I am Wil's freedom.

There's this great scene in *Lord of the Rings: The Two Towers* where we find out that as The One Ring slowly drove him mad, Smeagol created Gollum to help him survive. Once Smeagol has Frodo to look after him, he doesn't need Gollum any longer.

"Leave now, and never come back!" Smeagol tells Gollum, who hisses, spits, and fights like crazy to remain in control, until Smeagol ultimately finds the strength to drive him away.

That scene struck very close to home for me. My One Ring was Fame and Celebrity, and my Gollum was Prove To Everyone That Quitting *Star Trek* Wasn't A Mistake. When I wrote *The Wesley Dialogues,* I did prove to everyone that quitting *Star Trek* wasn't a mistake . . . but not in the way I expected. All the years I spent feeling trapped, like that action figure, in a little plastic box, unable to speak for myself or do anything *I* wanted to do, came to an end. I wasn't trying to achieve escape velocity from 15 years of frustration, angst, and regret—but that's exactly what happened.

"Leave now, and never come back!" I told Prove To Everyone as I wrote *The Big Goodbye. "I don't need you any more."*

"Quoting Lord of the Rings," he sneered. *"You're such a geek!"*

"It's Just a Geek," I said.

I haven't heard from him since.

TWELVE

All Good Things . . .

WHILE I WAS WORKING on *Nemesis,* I knew in the back of my mind that there was a good chance my scene would not make the final print of the film. It didn't add to the story at all, and I was the last person to be added to the cast. Because of those two factors, I wasn't too surprised when I started hearing the rumors that I'd been cut from the film and replaced with Ashley Judd, who was playing Robin "Mrs. Wesley Crusher" Lefler. The rumor about Ashley Judd turned out to be false and I understand that the credibility of the Internet as a source of honest and true information may never be restored. However, the rumor about my scene hitting the cutting room floor turned out to be true.

14 AUGUST 2002

Spare Us The Cutter

The call came while I was out, so I didn't get the message until days later.

"Hi," the young-sounding secretary said on my machine. "I have Rick Berman calling for Wil. Please return when you get the message."

I knew.

I knew before she was even done with the message, but I tried to fool myself for a few minutes anyway.

I looked at the clock: 8 p.m. They'd most likely be out, so I'd have to call tomorrow.

I told Anne that I had a message to call Rick's office and she knew right away also.

We'd thought about it for months, ever since I'd heard the rumors online. Of course, I tend to not put a whole lot of stock in what I read online . . . if I did I'd be overwhelmed with the sheer amount of hot teen bitches who want to get naked for me right now and I'd be rolling in Nigerian money.

But it made sense and I couldn't fight what I knew in my heart to be true.

I returned the call late the next day from my car on my way home from work. I was driving along a narrow tree-lined street in Pasadena that I sometimes take when the traffic is heavy on the freeway.

Children played on bikes and jumped rope in the growing shadows of the July afternoon. The street was stained a beautiful orange by the setting sun.

"This is Wil Wheaton returning," I told her.

She tells me to hold on and then he's on the phone.

"Hi kiddo. How are you?"

"I'm doing fine. You know I turn 30 on Monday?"

There is a pause.

"I can't believe we're all getting so old," he says.

"I know. I e-mailed Tommy [his son] awhile ago and he's in college now. If that made me feel old, I can't imagine what my turning 30 is doing to the rest of you guys."

We chuckle. This is probably just small talk, so it's not as severe when he tells me, but it feels good regardless. Familiar, familial.

"Listen, Wil. I have bad news."

Although I've suspected it for months and I have really known it since I heard the message the night before, my stomach tightens, my arms grow cold.

"We've had to cut your scene from the movie."

He pauses for breath and that moment is frozen, while I assess my feelings.

I almost laugh out loud at what I discover: I feel puzzled.

I feel puzzled, because the emotions I expected, the sadness, the anger, the indignation . . . aren't there.

I realize that he's waiting for me.

"Why'd you have to cut it?"

This doesn't make sense. I should be furious. I should be depressed. I should be hurt.

But I don't feel bad, at all.

"Well, it doesn't have anything to do with you," he begins.

I laugh silently. It never does. When I don't get a part, or a callback, or get cut from a movie, it never has anything to do with me. Like a sophomore romance. "It's not you. It's me. I've met Jimmy Kimmel's cousin and things just happened."

There is an unexpected sincerity to what he tells me: the movie is long. The first cut was almost three hours. The scene didn't contribute to the main story in any way, so it was the first one to go.

He tells me that they've cut 48 minutes from the movie.

I tell him that they've cut an entire episode out. We laugh.

There is another silence. He's waiting for me to respond.

I drive past some kids playing in an inflatable pool in their front yard. On the other side of the street, neighbors talk across a chain link fence. An older man sits on his porch reading a paper.

"Well Rick," I begin, "I completely understand. I've thought about this on and off for months and I knew that if the movie was long, this scene and maybe even this entire sequence, would have to go. It's just not germane to the spine of the story."

He tells me that they had to consider cutting the entire beginning of the movie. He tells me that he has to call one of the other actors who has suffered rather large cuts as well.

I stop at a four-way stop sign and let a woman and her little daughter cross the street on their way into a park filled with families, playing baseball and soccer in the waning light.

I look at them. The mother's hand carefully holding her daughter's.

I realize why I'm not upset and I tell him.

"Well, Rick, it's like this: I love *Star Trek* and, ultimately, I want what's best for *Star Trek* and the Trekkies. If the movie is too long, you've got to cut it and this scene is the first place I'd start if I were you.

"The great thing is, I got to spend two wonderful days being on *Star Trek* again, working with the people I love, wearing the uniform that I missed and I got to reconnect with you, the cast, and the fans. Nobody can take that away from me.

"And, it really means a lot to me that you called me yourself. I can't tell you how great that makes me feel."

It's true. He didn't need to call me himself. Most producers wouldn't.

"I'm so glad that you took the time to call me and that I didn't have to learn about this at the screening, or by reading it on the Internet."

He tells me again how sorry he is. He asks about my family and if I'm working on anything. I tell him they're great, that

Ryan's turning 13 and that I've been enjoying steady work as a writer since January.

We're back to small talk again, bookending the news.

I ask him how the movie looks.

He tells me that they're very happy with it. He thinks it's going to be very successful.

I'm feel happy and proud.

I've heard stories from people that everyone had lots of trouble with the director. I ask him if that's true.

He tells me that it was tough, because the director had his own vision. There were struggles, but ultimately they collaborated to make a great film.

I come to a stoplight, a bit out of place in this quiet residential neighborhood. A young married couple walks their golden retriever across the crosswalk.

We say our good-byes and he admonishes me to call him if I'm ever on the lot. He tells me that he'll never forgive me if I don't stop into his office when I'm there.

I tell him that I will and that I'll see him at the screening.

He wishes me well and we hang up the phone.

The light turns green and I sit there for a moment, reflecting on the conversation.

I think back to something I wrote in April while in a pit of despair: "I wonder if The Lesson is that, in order to succeed, I need to rely upon myself, trust myself, love myself and not put my happiness and sadness into the hands of others."

I meant everything that I said to him. It really doesn't matter to me if I'm actually in the movie or not and not in a bitter way at all.

I could focus on the disappointment, I suppose. I could feel sad.

Getting cut out of the movie certainly fits a pattern that's emerged in the past two years or so.

But I choose not to. I choose instead to focus on the positives, the things I can control. I did have two wonderful days with people I love and it was like I'd never left. I did get to reconnect with the fans and the franchise. Rick Berman, a person with whom I've not always had the best relationship, called me himself to tell me the news and I felt like it weighed heavily on him to deliver it.

Nobody can take that away from me and I'm not going to feel badly, at all.

Because I have a secret.

I have realized what's important in my life since April and they are at the end of my drive.

The dog-walking couple smile and wave to me.

The light changes.

Somewhere in Brooklyn, Wesley Crusher falls silent forever.

Okay, maybe I laid it on a little thick in the last line there, but I thought it was a nice dramatic finish, you know? I had shipped the Cadet Crusher action figure to Brooklyn, and Wesley *was* silent. *Nemesis* is the final *TNG* movie, my scene didn't even make one of the several collector's editions they released on DVD, and the only way to see me is if you freeze-frame the wide screen version. I'm cut out of the full-screen edition. Wesley Crusher will only live on in reruns. I will never get to bring him to life again, and that makes me a little sad. I'd like to try on his spacesuit and his oversized brain one last time and see how they fit now.

After I posted that entry, the comments and e-mails poured in. There were so many, it took me several days to catch up. Slashdot carried the story on the front page, and there were several hundred comments within hours, mostly from people who failed to get the point and attacked me for talking on my phone while driving. Fark linked to the story, along with several sci-fi news sites. I even did an interview with the BBC's *Radio Five.**

I was very moved by the support I received from the Trekkies and others, but the fact was, whether I actually made it into the final cut of the movie couldn't change the wonderful two days I'd spent with old friends. It wasn't going to affect my career in any real way, since it was just two lines, and I didn't take it personally. I didn't feel snubbed in any way, and I had a great conversation with Rick Berman. This would only be a bad thing if I allowed it to be a bad thing.

It was a major test for me: would I allow myself to wallow in indignant self pity? Would I take this as yet another rejection by The Powers That Be? No. I would not. There were too many things in my life to be happy about, and being at peace with *Star Trek* was one of them.

With all my conflicted feelings about *Star Trek* and Wesley Crusher resolved, I spent the next few weeks in a state of grace, and I was able to share a very difficult decision I'd recently made with my website readers.

Back in mid-May, I was asked to participate in an infomercial, selling 3D glasses for computer games. It was a Rubicon in my career. Would I cross it?

I discussed it at length with my wife, manager, and some trusted friends. Everyone agreed the decision was mine, and I agonized over it for a long time. I was committed to supporting my family in any way I could, but I was certain that this was a one-way bridge that I'd be crossing. If I accepted the offer, I'd also be accepting the end of my chances at ever being on the "A" list again.

---

* That interview on *Radio Five* led to me covering California's Recall Election in 2003. I'm still a BBC correspondent. Even though I only file reports once or twice a month, I'm intensely proud of my contributions to Auntie Beeb.

27 AUGUST 2002

Reflections — Artificial Sweetener

Sometimes we know in our bones what we really need to do, but we're afraid to do it.

Taking a chance, and stepping beyond the safety of the world we've always known is the only way to grow, though, and without risk there is no reward.

Thoughts like this have weighed heavily on me for the last year or so, as I look around and reassess my life.

This past year has involved more self-discovery and more change than any so far in my life. It's been tumultuous, scary, exhilarating, depressing, thrilling, joyful.

I've realized recently that I have changed dramatically since I started this website. When it began just over a year ago, I was very adrift, terrified that the Internet would tear me apart.

Well, it did and it turns out that was a great thing. The Internet kicked my ass and it forced me to find strength within myself and not to derive my sense of self-worth from the opinions of others.

This website has introduced me to amazing people, weird people, scary people. This website and many people who read it have also helped me figure out what is important to me in my life, what makes me happy.

I guess the feeling has been building for a long time and I knew it was there, but I wasn't willing to acknowledge it. It was—is—scary. It's a major change in my life, but I can't ignore it and to ignore it is to ignore myself and cheat myself out of what I think my real potential is.

Back in the middle of May, I was asked to do this commercial. Well, not just a commercial, more of an infomercial, really. My first reaction was, "No way. Infomercials are death to an actor's career."

But then I thought about the last few years of my life as an actor. The daily frustrations. Losing jobs for stupid, capricious, unfair reasons.

I looked back and saw that it really started when my friend Roger promised me a role in *Rules of Attraction*, then yanked it away from me without so much as a phone call or e-mail or anything. Then there was the roller coaster of *Win Ben Stein's Money* and missing family vacations so I could stay home and go on auditions that all ended up being a huge waste of my time.

Throughout this time, this painful, frustrating Trial, I began to write more and more. It's all here on WWdN. I can see my writing style change, as I find my voice and figure out what I want to say, and how I want to say it.

The e-mails changed, too. People stopped asking me to do interviews for them about *Star Trek* and started asking me if I'd contribute to their magazines, or weblogs, or books.

When this phone call came for the infomercial, I took a long walk and assessed my life.

The bottom line was: they were offering to pay me enough to support my family for the rest of this year. I wouldn't have to worry about bills anymore. I wouldn't have to view each audition as This One Big Chance That I Can't Screw Up.

Accepting it would mean some security for me and my family. It was also a really cool computer-oriented product (which I'll get to later, don't worry). It's not like I would be hawking *The Ab-Master 5000* or *Miracle Stain Transmogrifier X*!

It would also mean, to me at least, the end of any chance I had of ever being a really major actor again. That elusive chance to do a film as good as, or better than, *Stand By Me*, or a TV series as widely watched as *TNG* would finally fall away.

I thought of all these things, walking Ferris through my neighborhood.

It was a long walk.

I thought of Donald Crowhurst.

I thought about why actors—and by actors I mean working, struggling actors like myself, not Big Time Celebrities like I was 15 years ago—suffer the indignities of auditions and the whims of Hollywood.

I remembered something I said to a group of drama students just before their graduation, paraphrasing Patrick Stewart: "If you want to be a professional actor, you have to love the acting, the performing, the thrill of creating a character and giving it life. You have to love all of that more than you hate how unfair the industry is, more than the constant rejection— and it is constant—hurts. You must have a passion within you that makes it worthwhile to struggle for years while pretty boys and pretty girls take your parts away from you again and again and again."

I listened to my words, echoing off the linoleum floor of that high school auditorium and realized that those words, spoken long ago, were as much for me as they were for them.

I listened to my words and I realized: I don't have that passion any more. It simply isn't there.

I am no longer willing to miss a family vacation, or a birthday, or a recital, for an audition.

I am no longer willing to humiliate myself for some casting director who refuses to accept the fact that I'm pretty good with comedy.

I am no longer willing to ignore what I'm best at and what I love the most, because I've spent the bulk of my life trying to succeed at something else.

I walked back to my house, picked up the phone and accepted the offer.

It was tumultuous, scary, exhilarating, depressing, thrilling, joyful.

I would spend the next three weeks wondering if I'd made the right decision. I would question and doubt it over and over again.

Was it the right decision? I don't know.

Things have certainly changed for me, though. I have only had three auditions in the last three months. A year ago that would have killed me, but I'm really not bothered by it now.

I've made my family my top priority and decided to focus on what I love: downloading porn.

Just kidding.

I've decided to focus on what I really love, what is fulfilling, maybe even what I am meant to do, in the great cosmic sense: I am writing.

I write every day, and I see the faint outlines of something really cool. I occasionally catch glimpses of an ability, unrefined, long-ignored, coming to life.

Sometimes we know in our bones what we really need to do, but we're afraid to do it.

Taking a chance and stepping beyond the safety of the world we've always known is the only way to grow, though and without risk there is no reward.

Risk was always one of my favorite games.

It seems like such an easy choice, now, but as I stood at that crossroads, one road uncertain and the other clear, The Voice of Self Doubt wasn't about to stay silent. It screamed at me, *"You will prove right everyone who called you a washed-up, has-been loser!"*

Just a few months earlier, I would have listened to him and dismissed the offer immediately, but now I said, *"I've made a commitment to let the pursuit of fame go. I've grown up, and I'm doing what's best for my family."*

I was certain that doing this infomercial was the final nail in the coffin of my once-promising career. I mean, who goes from infomercial guy back to respectable career? I said *respectable*, so you can put your Steve Garvey away, buddy. If they'd asked me to hawk *The Ultimate Ab Machine 6000*, or *Even More Mega SeXXXy Girls Going Wild!!* or *The Super Amazing Hair Restoring Formula Number 29X That Doesn't Even Look Like Spray Paint!*, I would have declined without a second thought. But the X3D system that I was asked to sell was actually very cool. It really worked the way they claimed it would, so selling it wouldn't compromise my integrity in any way.

I struggled with many questions. Was I ready to admit defeat? Was I ready to admit that I'd given it my best shot, but I really *was* a washed up has-been? Was I willing to say out loud that I was . . . *That Guy*?

I was. I did.

The money I earned from the job gave me the financial security I needed to provide for my family. With that financial security, I was able to focus on my newfound passion to write. It was like I had a patron named X3D!

Accepting that I was *That Guy* was more liberating than painful, and it took the shame away from doing that infomercial. My career wasn't really over, it had just changed. I didn't worry about what critics said. I worried about feeding my family. I didn't worry about landing an acting job. I looked forward to writing. Like all the other things I'd agonized over, the process of making the decision took more time and energy—and was more painful and scary—than the result.

I was done trying to run out of the shadow of my youthful success, and I had accepted that I couldn't change the results of my teenage excess. I felt good. I felt free.

This resolution could not have come at a better time. In September of 2002, there was a huge *Star Trek* event right in my backyard, at the Pasadena Convention Center: a celebration of 15 years of *Star Trek: The Next Generation*. When I was invited months earlier, I'd accepted with some reluctance. But after Vegas, after *The Wesley Dialogues*, I wasn't reluctant at all. I was actually very excited to attend. I had cast off the baggage I'd been carrying for years. For the first time in over a decade, I was actually looking forward to speaking at a *Star Trek* convention!

28 AUGUST 2002
I See Another Hurdle Approaching

Yesterday, I wrote about the scary nature of facing the world outside of what I guess we'll call "your safety bubble."

At least that's what I was trying to write about.

Today, I am going to talk about why Creation cut me from their 15th Anniversary of *Star Trek: The Next Generation* convention and why I think it's a good thing.

To understand the events leading up to the cut, it's important to understand the realities of the *Star Trek* convention (and all sci-fi conventions, really): there was a time, long ago, when these cons existed by and for fans. They were places where fans could get together, safely dress up in costumes, debate the minutiae of scripts and generally geek out among friends without fear of The Jocks showing up.

Some folks realized that they could turn this phenomenon into a working business and for better or worse, Creation was born.

For years, I had a great relationship with Creation. When I was a kid, I attended the Fangoria Weekend of Horrors shows at the Ambassador Hotel. When I was on *TNG*, I appeared as a speaker at countless Creation conventions.

Then I had a not-so-great relationship with them for a while. I felt that they had become the 800-pound gorilla in the convention world. They were the only kid on the block who had that cool football that all the other kids wanted to play with. Without any real competition, they charged too much, and I felt that the fans were increasingly getting the shaft.

Not the cool Richard Roundtree Shaft, either, so you can just shut your mouth right now.

In retrospect, there were many factors contributing to what I would describe as the decline and fall of the convention experience and I think the guests need to be at the top of that list.

I never made very large speaking fees, even when I was A Big Deal™, but there were plenty of actors who did. It didn't bother me too much at the time, because I felt that the fans were mostly showing up to see these headlining actors and that meant Creation would earn a lot of money.

I always felt that the actors should share in that profit, until I became aware of the escalating costs to the fans and the declining quality of the convention experience.

It was like I'd stepped out of the ivory tower for the first time and seen the suffering in the streets. I didn't want any part of that world, and I didn't want to do any more conventions. However, I was heavily pressured by my agents and publicists, so I continued to go.

I felt obligated, and I hated it.

I withdrew when I was on stage, I didn't give it my all, and I even stopped signing autographs in person. I guess I was 16 or 17 at the time. What I really wanted to be doing was playing GURPS and goofing off on this new computer network called GEnie where I could talk to people all across the country in real time. Ohh! Nerdy!

After a few shows in this frame of mind, I quit entirely. Several years passed, and, other than a couple of cruises that I did mostly because I wanted to give my family a vacation, I only did one convention that I can recall, when I was about 20. It was in Kansas City, Missouri, and it was horrible. There were about 50 people there, all crammed into the back of this auditorium because they didn't want to pay for the "VIP" seats, so I was left talking to 50 people in a room intended for about 700, across 30 or so empty rows of seats.

I'm amazed that I didn't climb to the balcony and jump off right then and there. It was really hitting *Star Trek* Bottom™ for me, and I swore that I'd never do another convention again.

The convention world went on without me. My fellow cast members continued to regularly attend shows all over the world. I did one or two, including one in England, mostly because I love England and it was an opportunity to get over there on someone else's dime. I had a wonderful time while I was there, but it was an oasis in a desert of discontent. In my heart and in my ever-blackening soul, I hated conventions. So they were few and very, very far between, until I gradually stopped entirely.

Years passed and I grew up. Like a battered wife, I began to forget the bad things and only remember how exciting it was to see OJ run for 500 yards in a game, how he would smile at me from the end zone, how sharp he looked in those Bruno Magli shoes.

I agreed to attend a convention in Pasadena, where I did the interviews that are in *Trekkies*. I don't remember much beyond feeling like a complete loser for even being there and embarrassed that my girlfriend, who eventually became my wife, was seeing me like this.

The world turned and I eventually saw *Galaxy Quest.*

Seeing that movie reminded me about all the nice dinners I'd had with The Juice, how he always felt bad after he'd hit me, the fun trips we'd taken together and how nicely tailored his gloves were.

I made a call to Adam Malin at Creation. I told him that I'd seen *Galaxy Quest,* and that it reminded me how fun conventions could be. This was an entirely true statement. I told him that I'd be interested in doing some shows, if he'd have me. We had a very nice chat and he invited me in for a meeting.

I went and saw him the following week and we talked about what I was doing now, and how the convention world had changed. It was strange for me to be sitting in his corner office, on the top floor of a building in Glendale, looking out at the mountains where I used to live, telling him how grateful I was for the opportunity to talk with him about shows.

We agreed that I'd do some for him and they'd be in touch.

When we talked, I left out some information, like the fact that I hadn't worked on anything meaningful in years and I was really struggling as an actor. Anne and I had just gotten married, and we were under a mountain of debt.

I walked to my car, feeling dirty.

A month went by without any phone calls and I thought that I'd been involved in yet another meaningless meeting featuring yet another string of empty promises. I began to feel depressed.

While I waited for the call to come, I spoke with Dave Scott, who owns a company called Slanted Fedora Entertainment. Dave had been doing lots of conventions, and had a good reputation among the fans, and more important, among my *Star Trek* actor friends.* I told Dave that I hadn't done a convention in a long time and I was wondering if he would be interested in having me do one of his shows. He seemed interested and said he'd get back to me.

---

* Since I originally blogged this, Slanted Fedora's reputation has been tarnished by cancelled events, bounced checks, and poor fan relations. I've never had any problems with Dave or his company, but I've run into several fans who are pretty upset with him, and I know a few *Star Trek* actors who won't work with him.

Again, months passed. I did a few shitty, embarrassing, forgettable "pay the bills" movies and I began to wonder if maybe it was time to get into some other line of work.

Something that involved exotic language like "Soup du jour."

Before I could begin learning the art of up-selling wine, however, Dave called and invited me to a convention in Waterbury, Connecticut, in March of 2001. In addition to me, Brent Spiner, Gates McFadden and Denise Crosby would be attending. I was ecstatic. We agreed on a speaker's fee and I went to the show.

As an example of how long I'd been removed from *Trek*, I offer the following scene from March of 2001:

At the airport, I see Brent and Gates, standing in the departure terminal, waiting to board our plane.

My heart leaps and I walk toward them, beaming, with open arms.

They both look up at me, like I am Hannibal Lecter and begin to retreat.

They don't recognize me, at all, until I tell them who I am.

Yeah, I'd been out of the game for a while.

We did the convention and it was really great. I had a wonderful time, and I thought that everyone there enjoyed my talk. I didn't realize just how much they enjoyed it until I read a glowing review on Usenet.

A few months after I got home, the call from Creation came. I was invited, not as a speaker but as an autograph-signer, to the upcoming Grand Slam convention in Pasadena, California.

Not as a speaker, like the rest of the cast, but as an autograph-signer, like that guy who played Transporter Chief #7 in Episode 34.

This was a serious blow to my ego, especially after the success of the Slanted Fedora show, but I had swallowed my pride before, doing what I had to do in order to support my family.

Each time I'd done it, it had paid off in ways I didn't expect: when I went to ComicCon in 1999, I met Ben, who introduced me to Loren, without whom there would be no WWdN.

I'd also gone to the Hollywood Collector's Show, which is often referred to as "The Hollywood Has-Beens Show," where I realized that, no matter what anyone said, I really wasn't a has-been. I was just a guy who was really struggling, having had too much success too young.

Hey, at least I wasn't one of the Coreys, right? Yeah, that's what I'd try to tell myself.

However, at each of these events, as frustrated as I was, as much as it wounded my pride and bruised my ego, I knew that it was a much better alternative to, "Would you like to me to check your oil, sir?" I knew that I was very lucky, and I was grateful, if ashamed, for the opportunity to support my family.

So I accepted the offer to be a signer, rather than a speaker. I didn't get a speaking fee. I got what I could by charging a fee to sign pictures, posters, trading cards; sadly, no boobies.

Although, at one point during the day, a very pretty girl came over to me and I am not afraid to tell you, she was seriously putting the vibe onto your Uncle Willie. I mean, she was vibing me hard.

Check it out:

She walks up to me, hips swinging, lips pouting, eyes leering and says, "Do you have a girlfriend?"

"No," I tell her, expecting a replay of the Hooters incident. I look her right in the eye and after a dramatic, lusty pause, tell her, "I have a wife!"

BOOYAHBABY! OH YEAH! I await her chastened response.

"Oh," she says, coyly, putting a finger in the corner of her mouth and drawing her tongue seductively across the tip. "That's too bad."

And she walks away, hips swinging.

Swinging, man. The room falls silent as she walks out. A guy in a Red Dwarf *T-shirt drops a box of unopened Magic cards.*

I pick my jaw up off the floor.

Shortly after this convention, I was looking for posts about the con on Usenet and I saw that some dude had taken a picture of this girl, who was like a piece of steak in a piranha tank around all of us geeks.

The message said something like, "Look at this hot girl who was at the *Star Trek* convention!"

There was a reply, which said something like, "Look! Here's another picture of her!" It was that same girl, all alright, but she sure wasn't wearing the same Charlie's Angels T-shirt that she was wearing at the con . . . matter of fact, she wasn't wearing anything at all.

That's right, the full-on porn model totally hit on me, right there in front of everyone. Not that I would have hit it, being married and all that, but it sure did make my inner geek happy.

That convention ended up being really great. I was able to promote my ACME show and climb a little bit further out of debt. I did end up giving about a 20-minute talk in a very small room, which was intended to hold about 100 people, but was packed to standing with about 150 or so. The talk went fabulously well and Adam Malin sought me out himself to tell me that he was sorry for not putting me up on stage in The Big Room. He said that he didn't know how much the fans liked me, or how good I was on stage. He promised to have me speak at the Grand Slam Show in 2002.

At that show, I saw Dave Scott and he invited me to the Vegas convention that is chronicled in *Dancing Barefoot*, in the chapter "The Saga of SpongeBob Vegas Pants."

I was back in the game, baby and I was loving it. Cons were fun again. I'd been on the other side of the table, standing shoulder to shoulder with the fans, for a few years. I'd grown up. I'd spent time on stage in sketch comedy shows and improv shows. I understood what audiences wanted and I was learning how to connect with the Trekkies, how to identify with them. I felt like I was able to make up, in some small way, for the years I'd spent being an ass and I really liked it.

Then came 9/11. Then my great aunt died. Then the economy fell apart.

I had to cancel some cons, because of work and family commitments and cons had to be canceled because there simply weren't enough people willing to buy tickets.

The promised invite to Grand Slam 2002 never materialized, but I did attend again as an autograph-signer, this time without any damage to the ego. I saw it as an opportunity to promote WWdN and get closer to that magic Zero on the Home Equity Balance Sheet. I did speak in that same little theater, this time to about 14 people, because I was programmed opposite Ricardo Montalban, who was occupying The Big Stage.

The only cons I was able to attend were the Galaxy Ball and the CruiseTrek trip to Alaska.

I was also invited to attend the Creation Celebration of 15 Years of *Next Generation* and a Slanted Fedora convention in Las Vegas in early September.

My sketch comedy show was such a hit in Vegas, Creation asked me if I would bring my sketch comedy group to perform at the 15th Anniversary show.

I told them I'd love to, and they asked me about fees. I did some math in my head, figured out what it would cost for my group, reduced my personal speaking fee (bad economy, people losing jobs and 401(k)'s and all that) and gave them a figure. They said it sounded good and they'd be in touch.

They called back in early August, with a very different number. A low number. An insultingly low number.

I asked why the number was so low. I put my fees into perspective, alongside the fees commanded by some of the other *Trek* actors.

The terse answer came very quickly: "Well, we just don't think of you as a very big part of the *Trek* family."

Ouch.

They had a point, I guess. *TNG* ran for seven seasons. I did four as a regular, and a couple of episodes in the fifth year. I also guest-starred in the seventh season. There have been four *TNG* movies and I was almost in one of them.

Yeah, I guess I wasn't as big a part of the *Trek* family, from their point of view.

But I was an original cast member on *TNG*. This was a "Celebration of 15 years of *TNG*" convention. They'd just made several million dollars at a show in Las Vegas. Surely they could come up a bit, negotiate a little.

Not a chance. Take it or leave it, Wheaton.

I considered their offer and did some math. I thought about what it would cost for my comedy group. There are 11 of us and putting together a show is expensive. The people in my group are all professional writers and actors, and I have to pay them for their time. We have to pay for rehearsal space, costumes, and programs. I did the math and when it was all done, if I paid my comedy group what they deserve, I would earn a few hundred dollars. I was unwilling to make them work for less than they deserve. I told this to Creation.

They'd just made several million dollars at a show in Las Vegas. Surely they could negotiate a little.

I offered to do the show for the fee they were offering, but I wouldn't be able to provide the comedy group. In place of the comedy group, I'd bring some selections from my website—*The Trade, The Wesley Dialogues, Spare Us The Cutter*—and I'd read them on stage. It would fill the hour and it would give something really cool and unique to the fans. I read some things on CruiseTrek, and they loved it.

No dice, Wheaton. The offer is for your group. Not for you alone. Take it or leave it. You're not part of the family.

This put me in a very tough position. I wanted to be part of this show. I wanted to see the cast again. The fans, I thought, would really enjoy seeing me. The fans, I told them, have been reading my website in huge numbers. The fans, I told them, and I have really made a connection in the last year. I think it's going to suck if I'm not there. The fans are going to think it sucks if I'm not there. They'd just made several million dollars at a show in Las Vegas. Surely they could reconsider.

We've made our position clear, Wheaton. You're wasting our time. Take it or leave it.

Well, I had to leave it. I think that there is a certain value attached to having me at a convention, especially one that purports to celebrate 15 years of *The Next Generation* and while I was willing to adjust that value greatly, they'd just made several million dollars at a show in Las Vegas and I wasn't about to undervalue myself.

It sucks, I think, that I won't be there.

It sucks for me and I think it sucks for the fans.

Sure, there are fans that will be as angry at me as I am at baseball players right now and I can't fault them for that.

But I hope that there are fans who understand why I had to make the decision I made. They'd just made several million dollars at a show in Las Vegas. I tried to negotiate with them, but they had decided that I wasn't a member of the *Trek* family and it is their business. I respect that, though I may disagree with it.

When I hung up the phone with them, I felt awful.

I walked Ferris, which I often do when I'm upset, or stuck, or need to gain some perspective on things.

During that walk, I realized that in the long run this will be a good thing.

Yesterday, I wrote about the scary nature of facing the world outside of what I guess we'll call "your safety bubble."

Star Trek has always been my safety bubble and getting cut from this convention, along with getting cut from the movie, has pretty much burst that bubble.

As that bubble collapses and pools around me, I step out of its false sense of security.

I take another step into a brave new world, conquering myself until I see another hurdle approaching.

Though I tried to take a philosophical view of things, I was crushed, if you'll pardon the pun. I was more upset about being told that I "wasn't part of the family" than I was about being cut from *Nemesis*. Didn't Creation know that the Prodigal Son had returned? The feeling I'd endured so many times as an actor—the rejection and futility of even trying—slammed itself into my soul. Unlike a film role, this had nothing to do with my performance, or the way I looked, or nepotism. This was personal. It was directed squarely at me, and the pain of the rejection knocked me right off my feet.

My post was linked and reprinted on several *Star Trek* fan sites, newsgroups, and mailing lists. The comments and e-mails came, and they were furious! Most of them directed their ire at Creation, but some of them saw through my attempts at keeping my chin up and called me on it. I was hurt. I didn't want to step out of that safety bubble. I didn't want to enter a Brave New World. I wanted to walk back into the old safe world and view it with fresh eyes, without taking a single moment for granted, just like when I worked on *Nemesis*. I wanted to stand up there, and say "Thank you, *Star Trek*, for everything you've done for me. I'm glad we're cool again." *Star Trek* was a huge part of my life, and I'd wasted 10 years hating it. Now that I was finally able to appreciate it and had a chance to *enjoy myself* at a convention, it had been ripped away from me.

I never thought that it would be given back.

31 AUGUST 2002

Schism

"Individually we can get angry. Together we can and will, make a difference."

I wrote those words recently, hoping to rally and inspire people to action.

I was talking about the rapid erosion of our free speech and parody rights on the Internet, but that phrase applies to any movement, really.

One voice is easily ignored or silenced, but when other people add their voices to yours, you become a chorus not easily ignored.

It turns out that a lot of people got angry that I wouldn't be attending the 15th anniversary of *TNG* celebration next month. It turns out that those voices joined together in e-mails, phone calls, Internet postings, and faxes. It turns out that those voices became a chorus not easily ignored.

Thursday afternoon, I had a message on my machine from Adam Malin, president of Creation. He told me that he'd been "flooded" with e-mails, phone calls and faxes. He said he'd read the Internet postings, and he wanted to talk with me. He told me that he felt terrible, sick and was very upset that I felt the way that I did. He was apologetic and hoped I'd call him back so we could speak directly and, if nothing else, clear the air.

When I set the phone down in its cradle, I was surprised to feel my hands shaking.

I was, quite honestly, stunned. Shocked. A phone call from a lawyer I would have expected. An angry phone call, maybe, given the rage people were expressing on message boards at my own site and elsewhere. But a personal, cordial, apologetic call? I just didn't think it would happen.

I didn't have a chance to call him back until yesterday.

So lunch comes and I phoned him.

I apologized for not calling him back right away. Before I can say anything, he apologizes again for not talking to me directly and letting his underlings deal with me instead.

He tells me that he has never thought of me as "not part of the family."

I tell him that I have been given the impression from everyone at Creation, even the people with whom I am friends, that there are "levels," and it (rightly) goes: Captains, Data, everyone else . . . then there was me.

I tell him that I've felt marginalized and treated like my contributions to *Trek* weren't important to him, Creation, the fans, or Paramount.

He apologizes again, tells me again that he doesn't feel that way. Tells me that he wanted to make it right. He wants to have me at that convention.

I am stricken by how genuine he seems. I am beginning to feel bad for not going over the heads of his employees and speaking directly to him, myself.

I also notice something that is a new feeling to me, as far as *Star Trek* goes: I'm being treated like an adult. Treated with respect, spoken to forthrightly and candidly.

This may seem like an overstatement of the glaringly obvious, but even though I am 30 years old, I still feel like I'm "the kid" where *Trek* is concerned. Not feeling that way is something new to me and I'm not sure how to deal with it.

Adam tells me that he has heard great things about my sketch group. He's heard that they are fabulous and the fans really love the show we do. He tells me that he wants to hire them for the show, wants me to speak at the show and he really wants to make it work out.

I tell him that there isn't time to get the group together now and produce a quality show. He is really upset about that. He asks me if I'd be willing to get my group together for Grand Slam 2003.

I notice that we're having a cordial, comfortable conversation. It's like we've both been stung. Me by the posture taken during the previous negotiation and him by the vitriolic rebuke from the fans. He seems to genuinely feel bad that my feelings were so hurt and I get the palpable impression that he wants to make things right.

He asks me again if I'd be willing to do the show for a very reasonable fee, just a little bit below what I was asking for before negotiations broke down last month.

I am immediately torn.

I think about this thing that someone said in the comments yesterday: "If you turn your back on *Trek* one more time, I'm buying you a revolving door."

I think hard about that. It burns inside me.

I don't know what to do.

On the one hand, I want *Trek* behind me.

On the other hand, it will never be behind me no matter what, because, let's face it: *Trek* was and is HUGE. Bigger than me. Bigger than I will ever be in my (stalled and slowing) acting career.

After I'd gotten the first phone call from Adam, I talked it over with fellow EarnestBorg9* member Travis who is a very good friend of mine. Knows me very, very well.

Told him I'm having mixed feelings about it. I can think of reasons to do the show and reasons to not do the show.

He asked me why I didn't want to do it.

I gave him some reasons, pro and con.

He asked me if I was happy writing.

I told him I was.

He asked me if I liked being on stage.

I told him that I did.

He asked me why I could possibly not want to be on stage in front of people who want to like me and read my work to them. He reminded me of the sketch shows we've done together at conventions and how we have always felt great afterward.

He asks me again why I can't embrace *Star Trek* as something wonderful that I was part of and at the same time continue to move forward as an actor and writer.

I couldn't answer him.

Pride? Fear?

I don't fucking know.

The people on the Net have rallied around me about this. The fans have raged at Creation and Creation listened.

But there's that revolving door. I'm stuck in it, big time.

I think of this e-mail I got where a guy said he felt like I was trying to convince myself that it is okay to be booted from *Star Trek* things. He's right.

---

* EarnestBorg9 is the name of our sci-fi improv and sketch comedy group. We were originally called "Mind Meld," but we changed this after WILLIAM FUCKING SHATNER and Leonard Nimoy released a DVD with the same name.

I think of a comment where a guy criticizes me for being so angst-ridden about *Star Trek*, accuses me of being full of shit, and says he can see right through me.

He has a point too. I meant what I said about being cut from the film. But having the safety bubble burst? Well, I'm still standing in its remains, hoping I can find a way to refill it, just in case. Setting Wesley free, embracing a sense of freedom? I meant that, as well.

I feel like I have grown older and changed. But I feel unfulfilled, unsure and I know that the last few months of entries here have focused on that. Maybe I'm giving way too much weight to the comment of one random person who didn't even have the courage to put an e-mail address with the anonymous comment. For all I know I could be biting on the biggest troll ever.

But there is truth to what that anonymous poster said. I'm torn. I am caught in a revolving door and I don't know what will happen and I am filled with angst and that feeling is burning inside of me, keeping me awake at night, distracting me every minute of every day. It's burning in me so fiercely, so hot and insistent, that I have lost perspective. I can't make objective decisions and weigh the pros and cons effectively.

So I seek counsel from some very good friends of mine. Some people who I really trust and respect. I write to them what I've written above, with the following pros and cons:

Pros:

- Fans will be ecstatic that Creation listened, that the fans fought for me and won.
- Fans will be happy to see me in person.
- I'll earn money for my family and be able to perform what I love to do for an audience who *FINALLY* wants to like me.

Cons:

- That revolving door feeling and the fear of a massive backlash from . . . well, I'm not sure who, but backlash nevertheless.

It seems pretty slam-dunk, right? I should do the show and feel great about it. But it's not that easy for me. I am extremely conflicted, until I get the following responses:

This could not be easier, but that's really because I'm not you.

You think you'd be compromising or something if you went and changed your mind and went back to the show.

I don't. You're going to enjoy it. People like you.

You looked in the face of a thousand-million Internetters and said, "Hey, I'm a fucking human like you, I've been a dick, it's not right, this is what I did and this is what I think now. Sorry; won't happen again."

People like you, man. In fact, you're probably not even capitalizing off of all the Internet Momentum™ you've gained in the past year. Shit, Wil, people all over the place NOW LIKE YOU. Let's face it, you've only gotten limited access to those auditions, but how many magazines, newspapers, tv shows, etc. have you been on because you're a fucking computer geek-boy now? You want my point-blank, in-your-fucking-face opinion right now?

Go there in a big fucking "in your face, but I'm still just lil ol' Wil" way. Have the fucking time of your life—do it FOR YOU, not for the fans. These people want to see you—and even if they say something negative, just laugh it off like water on a duck and say, "Cool, but you know, you really don't know me" and know that you've won in that statement alone.

Another friend said:

Whatever you decide, right now, it's gotta be for you and not because X amount of people will judge you for doing it or not doing it.

If you feel it's right for you and will benefit your family and your writing and gain some recognition for you and you'll get to see some old Trek buddies again and that's what you want, then you gotta do that thing.

But don't do it if you now feel pressured by the fans to do it.

And don't NOT do it because you're afraid of what the fans will think.

Whatever you do, do it because you, you personally need to.

Because I think there comes a point where you have to acknowledge that This Thing You Did Back When is a part of you that's always going to be there. It's like Sue Olson (the actress who played Cindy Brady) once said—you have to accept that people will always think of you as that character, because only then can you really move on.

Once you accept that, the audience accepts you . . . and paradoxically, on your own terms.

See, this whole Turn Your Back On Trek thing, if you let that get to you . . . how do I put this?

If you don't do it because you have to Turn Your Back On Trek, well, then you're not really turning your back on Trek —you're still letting the Trek thing dictate what you do.

And, while we're putting our cards on the table, here, I think that you shouldn't look at not turning your back on Trek and finding your own voice as being mutually exclusive. As a former convention-goer, the Trek (or otherwise) speakers who I thought were the coolest were the ones who accepted that Trek was the reason they were there and why we were there, as opposed to the guys who seemed weirded out or perplexed that anyone gave a shit.

Not that you'd be that way—I'm talking about an initial attitude going in, not the handling of the experience from that point on.

As far as you feeling that you're reneging on what you said in your post . . . and here's some perspective:

The situation is different now.

It's not that they called you, snubbed you and you're going back anyway to eat shit for the peanuts.

It's that they contacted you, snubbed you initially, then realized they misjudged your appeal (and ability to bring in a LOT of new people) and finally were willing to meet you on terms you could accept.

I mean, it's great publicity for the website, and for you. You will have an ability to connect with the fans again—but this time it'll be a little different, because you're probably going to see more people you know you from the site—and Malin knows that."

Mixed in with all of this, I got an e-mail from a really nice woman who organized fans to share their outrage about this.

PLEASE do go, otherwise IMO Creation will win, as they can say you turned THEM down after they met your (original) terms or something like that. Then promote the hell out of the convention on your website. Perhaps if Creation and the others see how powerful you and your website is, they just MIGHT sit up and take notice and I'm not just talking about conventions here, but perhaps it might help you in other ways (as yet unseen) as well.

I'm calling for a campaign here to do right by you . . . 'cause I think it stinks. NO one messes with the Wil Wheaton, or they'll find that they have the "Posse" as you call us, to contend with and I suspect we are much MORE powerful together, than Creation realizes.

I'm doing this for you, cause I think you are a neat guy . . . but also mostly because, remember, I've been a Trekkie longer than you've been around (before you were born) and this is now really got me STEAMED how on their High Horse that Creation has gotten of late."

So. I think long and hard about these things and still I feel heavily conflicted.

I revisit those pros and cons and think to myself:

I'd love to have a chance to read some of my stuff for an audience who would really "get" it.

I'd love to go in front of fans who, for the first time ever, *want to like me.*

But that revolving door is spinning and I don't know how I can face the people who said "Good for you! Leave *Star Trek* behind you forever!"

Well, right now, the absolute truth is, as my friend said:

"If you don't do it because you have to Turn Your Back On Trek, well, then you're not really turning your back on Trek—you're still letting the Trek thing dictate what you do . . . you shouldn't look at not turning your back on Trek and finding your own voice as being mutually exclusive."

Well, I'm going to wrestle with that last one for a while, I think and WWdN readers can expect more angst in the months to come. Sorry, it's just part of the process. There are hundreds of great weblogs to read and lots of pretty trees to look at outside if you'd rather not read that stuff here.

Anyway, this is way too long already, so I think it's time to get back to the point:

Adam and I talk.

It is a good, long, honest, respectful talk.

We clear the air.

He tells me that his profit margin on the Vegas show was not several million dollars. He tells me that it was very, very slim, relative to his investment, which was nearly half a million dollars. I don't know if this is true or not, but it's not the most productive thing in the world to argue about it, so I don't.

He tells me that he didn't want me at the Grand Slam on stage because he wanted to hold off until the 15th show. He thought it would be cooler if he waited to have me come on then.

He tells me that he had no idea about my website or about how the fans felt about me now.

He asks me if I'd reconsider.

I reconsider. I replay all those e-mails in my head, I balance the pros and cons and I say to him,

"Adam. I am really conflicted about this. I feel like each time I do a *Star Trek* event, it's . . . well, it's not necessarily a step backward, but it certainly isn't a step forward, but I feel like I should listen to the voice of the fans. We should all listen to the voice of the fans, because that voice has been increasingly silenced over the last decade.

"I love to perform and I would like to give something back to the fans. I would love to attend the event and be part of the celebration, but I'd also like to share some of my writing with the fans. Would you be able to put me in an evening spot, so I can read some things that I've written?"

"Is it funny?" he asks me.

"It's funny, it's sad, it's bittersweet . . . it's really a reflection of the person I am and people seem to respond to it."

"Can I book your comedy group for Grand Slam in 2003?"

"Yes. I'd love to bring my guys out. We love to perform."

We talk about fees and agree on a very fair fee, which is right on par with the rest of the actors.

I will do a question-and-answer session at the convention and I will bring selections of my writing and read them for the audience during an evening program.

I ask him for one more thing. I tell him that I have more in common with the fans now than I do with the actors and I keep hearing how the fans are getting the in-person-autograph shaft these days.

I want him to put my autograph table in an area where I can sit for a few hours, so all the fans can get their stuff signed, so I can talk with people who are so inclined.

He tells me that he'd really like that. Many actors just won't do that and he thinks it would be great.

I feel very good about this conversation and I feel very excited to be part of this celebration.

Resolution? It's a long ways off. That's why they call it "angst."

But there is something wonderful buried in all of this:

I doubt I would have gotten this phone call if there hadn't been such a loud and immediate response from the fans.

You spoke up on my—you spoke up on *our* behalf and your voice was heard.

Think about that for a moment.

Your voice was heard. You made a difference. Creation is the 800-pound gorilla of conventions. They don't have to listen to anyone.

But they listened to you. They listened to us.

That, my friends, is huge. Everyone who is reading this gets to own part of that.

I strongly suggest that you take a moment and phone, write, fax, or e-mail Adam or Gary or whoever at Creation and thank them for hearing your voices.

And if you come to the 15th show, please, please, please seek me out and introduce yourself. I'd like to know you.

I went to the convention and it was wonderful. I spent three fun days, talking with Trekkies and WWdN fans alike. I met people who had never been to a *Star Trek* convention before and had specifically come out to meet me after reading my website.

When I took the stage for my talk, I said, "I was almost not here today. Because of you, I am. Thank you." There was thunderous applause. I have always had more in common with the fans than the franchise, and I felt like getting me on that stage was a victory for us all.

I had long and joyous conversations with every cast member who was there. Backstage, Patrick Stewart embraced me, as he always does, and lamented that we don't see each other very often. I told John Logan (the writer of *Nemesis*) that I was focusing on being a writer. He congratulated me and said, "Writing is a noble and respectable profession. It's a very adult job. I'm proud of you!"

Brent Spiner took me aside and told me how sorry he was that I'd been cut from the movie. He told me that he'd fought it as best as he could. I believed him. I told him what I wrote in my weblog, and he was surprised and happy that Rick called me himself. He told me how upset all the cast members were that I was cut, and he asked me if I'd be at the screening. I told him that I would.* He said, "You know, Wil, you should still be involved in all the press events."

He got this impish glint in his eye—the same glint that I lived for when I was sitting next to him on the bridge, even though I knew it was going to end up getting me in trouble when he made me crack up—and said, "I think you should sit there, answer as many questions as you can, even if you don't know the answers. I'll see you in Europe. It'll be fun."

Before I could play the "yes, and..." improv game with him, he was whisked away to go on stage, but not before he said, "Hey, you've got my number, right?"

"Yeah, I do."

"Use it when you need it, man. It's great to see you."

---

* Sadly, I wasn't invited to the cast and crew screening of the film. Though I was assured it was an oversight, I'm pretty sure it was yet another Code Red from The Powers That Be.

When Brent left I sat next to Gates McFadden, who played my mother on *TNG*. We laughed about how we were spending more time backstage at this convention than we spent on camera together in five years. She told me that I had become quite a handsome man.

I was an adult, among peers. I would never be The Kid again.

I had long talks with Gary Berman and Adam Malin, who own Creation. I learned about their history as sci-fi and horror fans. I got the distinct impression from Gary, who is often described (perhaps unfairly) as the "bad cop" of the two, that he was saddened by the impression across fandom that Creation Entertainment is only doing these shows to get rich. He pointed out several times, in many different ways, that he and Adam had been doing conventions since they were teenagers, and that they will always be fans in their hearts.

They both made me feel welcome, and embraced me as part of the family. I thanked them for having me, and told them that it is because of guys like them, the convention promoters, that I can maintain a connection to some of the happiest days of my life. On the last day of the convention, Adam took the stage and asked the assembled fans to indicate, by their applause, who they thought was the highlight of the convention. When he said my name, they went nuts. They screamed, they whistled, they stood on their chairs and pounded their feet. I was stunned and humbled. When Adam asked me if I'd witnessed that, I told him I had, and that it surprised me. He smiled, and told me that it had surprised him, too.

The convention was celebrating 15 years of *Star Trek: The Next Generation,* but what *I* was really celebrating was my return to the family—as an adult, no longer burdened by the stupid and arrogant things I'd done as a child.

I read selections from *Dancing Barefoot* and this book to a very appreciative audience who gave me a standing ovation when I finished. When I got home, I wrote, "I am really excited, guys. For the first time in ages I look forward to each day and I feel like I'm finally doing something, which really makes me happy."

I finally was.

Hooters 2: Electric Boogaloo

A FEW WEEKS BEFORE THIS BOOK went to press, I met my best friend Darin for lunch in Old Town. He wanted to celebrate the impending arrival of his daughter, and I wanted to celebrate finishing this book and *Dancing Barefoot's* success.

We met at the usual place, ahead of the lunchtime rush, so we could sit wherever we liked. We stood in the doorway, and Steve Miller blared above our heads that not only was he a joker, but he was a smoker *and* a midnight toker. He's a busy guy, that Steve Miller. We looked around, and chose the section with the hottest waitress in the joint.

As we took our seats, she came over to our table: a classically beautiful girl in her early 20s. Long, jet black hair, flawless skin, long legs. Hooters. Her name tag said "Jessica."

She sat on my lap and flirted with us as she took our order, all smiles and giggles. We ordered chili fries and anticipated a spirited game of "pull my finger" later on.

She stood up and left to put in our order. After a few steps, she stopped and turned around. She looked right at me and said, "You're Wil Wheaton, aren't you?"

"Oh for fuck's sake," I thought to myself. *"This can* not *be happening to me again."*

My throat went dry. My face flushed and my pulse quickened.

"Yeah," I croaked, bracing myself.

She screwed up her courage and slowly walked back to our table. She leaned close to me and rested her hand on my thigh, her full, pouting lips just inches from mine. A simple silver chain encircled her neck, her hazel eyes were ringed with gold, and she smelled like Springtime. Her ample cleavage seductively longed to bust out from beneath her thin cotton T-shirt as she said, breathlessly, "I love your website. You're a great writer."

The WWdN FAQ

THE FAQ IS BROKEN DOWN into the following categories:

- *Star Trek*
- *Stand By Me*
- Other Movies and Television
- The Site
- Other Questions

STAR TREK

Why'd you quit?

The following is reprinted from the best interview* I ever did:

Here's the absolute truth why I left *Star Trek*. I left *Star Trek* because it was seriously interfering with my career in feature films. I was in a situation where I was constantly having to pass on really good movie roles because I was on the series. I had a film career before *Star Trek*. People knew me before

---

* The interview was for the website Ain't It Cool News and can be found here: *http://www.aint-it-cool-news.com/display.cgi?id=6627*.

Star Trek. As a matter of fact, at Comic Con, a lot of people came up to me and said, "I started watching *Star Trek* because you were on it and I was fan of yours from *Stand By Me*. I stopped watching it after you left." I had a lot of people say that to me.

After something like this had happened a lot of times, I finally had the last straw: I had been cast by Milos Foreman to be in *Valmont*. I had gone through lots and lots of callbacks, I had met Milos personally a number of times, and he was really supportive of me and told me, "I want you in my movie." I was going to go to Paris, I was going to be in this movie and stuff, and we were going to shoot it during the hiatus. The shooting schedule for *Valmont* would have carried me over about a week into the regular season schedule into *Star Trek*. I would have had to sit out the first episode of the year, right. That's not a big deal, it's not like I'm the fuckin' Captain, you know. At that point, I was the guy who pushed buttons and said, "Yes, sir!" So, I said to the people on *Star Trek*, "I need to be written out of this particular episode, because I'm going to do this movie and my film career's going to take off." This is after Gene Roddenberry had died. Had Gene been alive, it would have been no problem at all, because Gene was that kind of guy. Gene would have said, "Great! Go ahead, you do what you need to do," because he was that kind of person. After Gene died, a very different type of person took over, and he said, "We can't write you out because the first episode of the season is all about you. It focuses entirely on your character and it's your story..." I said, "Well, this really sucks, but I'm under contract to you guys and if that's your call and if that's what you say I have to do, I have to do." I had to pass on the movie.

A couple of days before the season was ready to premiere, they wrote me out of the episode entirely. They were sending me a message. The message was, "We own you. Don't you ever try to do anything without us." That was the last straw for me. I called my agents and said, "They don't own me. It's time for me to leave this show. It's time for me to be gone." That's what really pushed me over the edge. It's not worth it anymore. That's why I left.

But Gene was alive then. You're a liar!

Many people have pointed this fact out to me, and you're right. Gene was alive. But he was in poor health, and wasn't heavily involved in the production of the show at that time. That's why I thought that he had already died when I did that interview. Hey, I make mistakes. Too bad I don't have FOX News to help me cover them up.

Will you be in any of the movies?

Well, I worked for two days on *Star Trek X* (*Star Trek OSX.1*, if you're a Mac user), but my scene was cut. Maybe it will be on the DVD.

I bought the DVD, and you're not on it! You're not even in the full-screen version!

Well what the hell are you doing buying a full-screen version of anything?

I am quite surprised that they didn't include my scene on the DVD, to be quite honest, and I have no idea why they didn't. It certainly lends some weight to the theory that TPTB really have it out for me, doesn't it?

What is your favorite episode?

My favorite episode to watch is "The Inner Light." Picard gets zapped by a beam of alien light. Although he's unconscious only for a few minutes on the *Enterprise*, he lives out an entire life on another planet.

My favorite episode that I worked on is "The First Duty," because it was one of the few times I got to work with actors my own age. Robbie McNeill, who was on *Voyager*, played opposite me in that episode, and we had hella fun. Hella hella hella. Robbie told me that he had been on a soap, and the producers had created this character arc for him where he was to work with this other actor most of the time. Apparently, they had so much fun and made each other laugh so much that the producers rewrote the entire character arc to made sure they'd never be in any scenes together for the rest of the series. It's because I liked Robbie so much that I can't crack on *Voyager* too hard, even though it sucks.

Did it bother you that the fans didn't like Wesley?

Yes, at the time, it really really did. Imagine being a teenager, trying to handle all the things a teenager has to deal with. Now multiply that times being on a HUGE TV show and having all these people hate you. It was tough.

Although, I recently realized something. At the time, I kept saying to people, "It's a TV show! Don't take it so seriously! It's just a character!" But at the same time, I really was taking it seriously, as well as personally. And it hurt. But I didn't handle myself with much grace, which I think echoes Wesley's situation: he had the intellectual capacity to be with these adults, but not the emotional capacity. It was the same for me, in real life. I've written some things about it in my weblog, and I write extensively about it in my forthcoming [this] book, *Just a Geek*.★

I hated Wesley!

Really? He always had such nice things to say about you.

★ This FAQ is taken directly from WIL WHEATON dot NET.

Is it true that you were really Ashley Judd's first onscreen kiss, and you ruined her for the rest of her life?

Yep. It is 100% true. Ashley Judd played Robin Lefler in the episode "The Game," and Uncle Willie went to bootytown. And by bootytown, I mean when the cameras stopped rolling, we were just two actors doing a scene. Only one of us had a boner.

Do you stay in touch with any of the cast members?

I wish I could say that we hang out all the time, but that's just not the case. I really, really like all of them, and the cast is the thing I miss the most about working on *Star Trek*. The thing is, when we all worked together on the show, I was a lame-ass teenager, and they were all cool adults in their 30s, so it's not like we had a lot of similar interests. Now that I'm a cool adult in my late 20s, they're all old and in their 40s, so they are *so* uncool. Just kidding. Truth is, when I am around them, I feel like I am a lame-ass teenager all over again, and I clam up. I once told Patrick how I felt so lame, because I felt like I didn't appreciate them when I was younger, and I wished that I had. Patrick put his hand on my shoulder and said, "My dear, I always related to you and thought of you as a fine actor." Patrick is very cool.

Was anyone a dick?

No. believe it or not, nobody was a dick. Everyone was very, very cool. When you're on a show like that, you spend about 10 hours a day, 5 days a week, together. Some shows will have a prima donna or 4, but we never did.

Oh, come on. You expect me to believe that?

Do you need a time out, mister? What did I just say?

Can I see you at any of those conventions?

You sure can. I am doing a few conventions every year, mostly on the West Coast, so I don't have to travel too far from home. You should check the conventions page (*http://www.wilwheaton.net/cons.php*) to find out if I'm coming to a hotel conference center near you any time soon!

What do you think of Enterprise?

I loved it when it started. However, I don't like the way it's gone at all, and I don't watch it any more.

Hey, I watched Weakest Link. What was that all about?

Heh. Well, see, *Weakest Link* is all about making people look bad and making Anne Robinson look good. I thought that I'd have fun with her by being even ruder and more offensive than she is. I thought the best way to accomplish this would be to play a condescending A-hole.

Mission. Accomplished. >:-)

So you aren't really an asshole?

Well, that depends on who you ask.

WTF is up with you and Roxanne Dawson?

Well, that was all a joke, too. I guess the producers decided to really make her look bad with the interview they chose. She is a really cool person, and everything between us is fine. But thanks for asking.

STAND BY ME

Were the leeches real?

They sure were. Can you imagine the shit Rob Reiner got for putting REAL LEECHES on 12-year-olds? I mean, I still have a scar from that scene, if you get my drift. He tried to run us over with the train and make sleeping bags out of our skin, too. Oh, and everything I wrote between the words

"They" and "too" is a lie. Please replace that with, "No, you dumb shit. Do you actually think they'd put real leeches on a bunch of kids? Why don't you just admit that you're a sick fuck who wants to hear me talk about my junk?" Thank you.

Was the train real?

Strangely enough, the train was fake. We never once, in the entire production, used a real train. Something about unions. Oh, and for the sake of this answer, please replace the word "fake" with "real and scary." You can pretend the line about unions doesn't exist, unless it made you laugh. If it made you laugh, I'd like you to send me a dollar. Comedy isn't cheap, you know.

Were you scared?

Even stranger than the fake trains (which were all made from cardboard and tin foil placed over a wooden chassis pushed by twelve midgets) was my abject fear of them. Particularly when we shot the running-across-the-trestle sequence. The stunt coordinator, Rick Barker, likes to tell this really funny story about how he put Jerry and me on the tracks and had the train about 50 feet behind us, traveling at something like 4 miles per hour. We were running towards a 500-mm lens, so it would look like the (fake) train was right up our asses. Well, when you're 12, and you're standing on a train track, and there is a train behind you, I don't care how slow it's going—if it's moving at all, it is scary as shit. So Rick has us on the tracks, making us wait to run. In the dailies, you can see Jerry and me, with tears running down our faces, turning off camera, saying "Can we go yet? Can we go yet?"

What a couple of wimps we were. Oh, and my stunt double for that sequence was a woman, because I was so skinny and whatnot. The rest of the cast (bastards) had a field day with that one.

How was it working with Rob Reiner?

It was awesome. I always say that Rob deserves all the credit for *Stand By Me* being the wonderful movie that it was. He really knew how to communicate with 4 12-year-olds (I have a hard enough time communicating with my *own* 12-year-old) and had the good sense to cast kids who were more or less exactly like their characters.

And here is something about Rob: he always made me feel like I deserved to be on that set. He never made me feel like I was a snot-faced kid (which I was), and he always treated me like an equal. I wish more directors were like Rob, and less like complete A-holes.

How was it working with River Phoenix?

River was really, really cool. At the time, I looked up to him because he was such a cool guy.

He was a wonderful actor and a wonderful person, and it really fucking sucks that nobody tried to stop him from becoming a complete junkie.

When I see the bullshit hacks who are passing for young, hot actors these days, I really miss River. Because he was a REAL actor, not a prepackaged bunch of hype and marketing.

How was it working with Corey Feldman?

Corey was a huge pain in the ass, but I don't think that was entirely his fault. Corey was a product of his environment. His parents were really into that whole "My kid is famous" thing When we shot *Stand By Me*, they didn't even stay in Oregon with him; they hired a woman that he didn't even know to be his guardian.

I think Corey was an angry kid who was in a lot of emotional pain. Rob Reiner confirmed that for me when I asked him, "Why did you hire Corey? He's such a pain in the ass!" Rob said, "Corey was the only actor we saw who had enough anger bottled up inside of him to play this role."

During that summer in Oregon, Corey (and River) began their love affair with the drugs. River's dead now, and Corey has been sober for something like 10 years. I understand that he's doing everything he can to get his career back on track.

Do you stay in touch with any of the other actors?

Not really. River is dead, Jerry is like a multimillionaire movie star, so we live in different worlds, and Corey is . . . well . . . Corey.

Why isn't there a commentary from you, Wil Wheaton, on the DVD?

Because Columbia/TriStar was afraid that I, Wil Wheaton, would bring the noise and testify! Because The Man couldn't stand to have me, Wil Wheaton, stand up and let the word ring out from the DVD box!

OTHER WORK

The Curse: what were you thinking?

Well, at the time, I was just a young'un and some really evil producers from a scary foreign country came to me and said, "We have this movie for you to be in, and we want to give you lots of money to be in it." And I didn't have the best advisors at the time, and nobody told me that this big pile of shit would be around forever. Consider it a very expensive lesson. At least I didn't get a tattoo.

THE SITE

What's with the quotes all over the place?

I like to quote things. The old site had more random quotes than this one does. Maybe I'll have a "name the quote" contest someday.

Do you really run this site on your own?

Yep. I am what you call a "Type-A control freak." You can view the source code if you doubt me. I figure that if this site is going to represent me, I should be run it.

Who hosts your site?

Logjamming. They are the coolest guys, ever.

Why'd you put a porn link on your site?! You're squeeky clean!

Because I wanted to upset you, mom.

What's with the autoresponse?

The autoresponse is no more, but people who e-mailed me used to get the following:

From: wil@www.wilwheaton.net Subject: Automated reply from wil@www.wilwheaton.net

Hey!

Don't you hate autoresponders, $GOOD_FRIEND?

I know that I do, and I would *never* dream of sending an autoresponse to anyone, not $MUTUAL_FRIEND, or $OTHER_MUTUAL_FRIEND, or even, $ENEMY.

You know, $THING_YOU_EMAILED_ABOUT really was ${fVAR=TRUE_FALSE)! It reminded me of $INTERESTING STORY.

Well, I have to get back to ${fVAR WORK_PLAY_SCHEMING}, $GOOD_FRIEND, so I'd better sign off.

$CLEVER_PERSONAL_CLOSING,

Wil

So are you going to reply to my e-mail or what?

Sadly, the answer to this question is most likely no. I really do read everything that is sent to me, but I just don't have the time anymore to personally reply to everyone who e-mails. I used to be able to keep up with it, but the time just isn't there anymore, between my commitments to work and my family.

OTHER QUESTIONS

Why don't you talk about Toy Soldiers *in this FAQ?*

When I wrote this FAQ originally, I didn't realize that so many people were interested in *Toy Soldiers*. I'll get around to writing all about it very soon.

Is it true that you're married?

Yep. My wife, Anne, and I have been married since 1999.

So you're not gay?

I am not gay. But thanks for asking.

Wait. I heard that you and...

Yeah, I heard that too. And since I read it on the Internet, it must be true, right?

So why don't you post lots of pictures of your stepkids on the site?

I prefer to keep them out of the limelight. That's why it's called WIL WHEATON dot NET, not WIL WHEATON AND HIS STEPKIDS dot NET. Seriously, I expect everyone to respect my limits and my stepkids' privacy.

I want to be an actor. Do you have any advice?

Yes, I do: study, study, study. Read the classic plays and see the great movies. And for the love of Bob, study with a great teacher! Get yourself into some sort of acting program or workshop. Just avoid anything that tells you they'll give you a free book by L. Ron Hubbard. It's a scheme to recruit you into Scientology.

I wrote you a letter, and you never answered, jackass.

Yeah, I'm really sorry about that. I have all the letters I've gotten over the past two years or so, and I'm gonna hire someone to help me out, so I can reply to them all.

Will you come over to my house and tell my brother to stop leaving the toilet seat up?

Yes. Just as soon as you tell your mom to stop calling me. I was drunk, and it was a one-time thing.

Selected Interviews

AS MY WEBSITE GAINED POPULARITY, I did several interviews. This appendix contains two of them. The first is from BBspot, a website that satirizes just about everything, particularly technological issues. The second is from Slashdot.org, a website that contains "News for Nerds, Stuff That Matters."

BBSPOT.COM

The original story, complete with hilarious pictures and links, can be found at *http://www.bbspot.com/Features/2001/10/11_questions_wil.html.*

11 QUESTIONS WITH WIL WHEATON

Real interviews with real people. Unlike the rest of BBspot, there's nothing made up here. I know it's a difficult transition, but I'm not fooling. We did e-mail these questions and these were the responses.

In the first of what will be a continuing series, Wil Wheaton of *Star Trek: The Next Generation*, *Stand By Me*, and *Python* fame subjects himself to 11 questions from BBspot. Enjoy!

BBspot (1): All the geeks want to know, what kind of computer system you have and what games do you play on it? Processor? OS? Details, please.

Wil: Oh boy. Well, all the geeks are going to rejoice when they hear that the box they use for target practice is probably superior to mine. My computer was built from zero by me and my friend. It's a Pentium 2, 128 megs of ram, uh . . . I have some kind of swell video card that does all those 3DFX things, and a crappy soundblaster sound card. My brother and I just crammed a bunch of big hard drives into the case and put in a new CD-ROM drive, so we're completely out of space inside. Tell you what, if I ever find Gordon Moore, I'm gonna kick him in the neck.

Put it this way: when it was built, it was hot, like Jolene Blalock. Now, it's more like Teri Hatcher: hot in it's day, but now it's just sad.

The games I play these days are *Diablo 2: Lord of Destruction*, *Unreal Tournament*, and *MAME*.

Oh, and I'm running Windows 2000, because I'm too lame for Linux. But some day . . . oh, some day I will learn Linux, and then, from Hell's dark heart I will stab at thee!*

BBspot (2): Did you learn anything important about being an actor when doing Stand By Me*, or did it just help you meet chicks?*

Wil: Meeting chicks? Dude. I was 13. If you had put a naked girl and a 720 degrees set to free play in front of me, I would have said, "Skate or die!" as I pushed her aside.

Come to think it, things haven't changed too much . . .

---

* This interview was done in 2001; I am using Linux now.

BBspot (3): Were you nervous working with OJ on the set of Hambone and Hillie?

Wil: There are very few times in my life that I am grateful to not be a blonde woman. Being around OJ was one of those times. Poor, poor OJ. He's been able to convince only 12 people in the whole world that he's not a murderer. Personally, I think Gary Condit is The Real Killer.

BBspot (4): Who would you like to see yourself pitted against in MTV's Celebrity Death Match *and why?*

Wil: Britney Spears. But we'd fight it out Pam Grier/Cleopatra Jones–style: in the first minute, I'd rip off her shirt, we'd scream "Bitch" at each other, and then we'd do it to sweet-ass 70s porn music. Hit me baby, one more time!

BBspot (5): Did you feel like your character suffered from an Oedipus complex in Star Trek: The Next Generation? *I mean, your mom was really hot, and your dad died under cloudy circumstances.*

Wil: When Wesley's dad died, Wesley was so traumatized, he had to spend many, many nights sleeping in Dr. Crusher's quarters . . . and the therapeutic sponge baths really helped with the grieving process. Oh, and the oral sex.

BBspot (6): Do you have a tactful way of telling Star Trek: The Next Generation *fans who can't separate Wesley from Wil to get a life? I mean, it WAS just a TV show . . .*

Wil: Yeah, it goes something like this: "Dude? What's your fucking problem?" Notice I didn't say "loser."

BBspot (7): You said you left Hollywood for five years because you "needed to get away from the Evils of Hollywood for a while." Now that you have returned, how are you dealing with the Evils?

Wil: Sometimes you have to take some time away from the Evils to really appreciate how much those Evils mean to you. We had a trial separation, and during that time, I realized that I was just suspicious of the Evils because of some intimacy issues I had, due to experiences as a child. The Evils came to see that we can't change each other, and we need to respect our differences, and celebrate them. We still have a stormy relationship, but the Evils and I watch Dr. Phil every week. Although I am beginning to suspect that The Evils and Dr. Phil speak to each other in some Evil-speak that only they and Oprah can understand.

BBspot (8): When the Titanic sunk and that Leo guy froze to death, did you secretly rejoice, or did you throw a Dead Leo party?

Wil: The captain of the Titanic was a Leo? I heard he was a Capricorn. Let that be a lesson to you about believing everything you read.

BBspot (9): How did you avoid becoming an E! True Hollywood Story like Corey Feldman or River Phoenix?

Wil: I think it has something to do with the lack of drugs in my life. Funny, being so uncool as a teenager kept me away from all that stuff. That's right kids, if you want to be cool, use lots of drugs. Oh, and then OD and die in front of the Viper Room. That's the COOLEST!

BBspot (10): How does it feel to have a site like this on the Net? Does it make you more popular with the girls or old men? Oh and can you hook me up with some better shots those are a little grainy, maybe put them in your online store? *

Wil: That site makes me feel like a camwhore without the wish list.

BBspot (11): Tell us why you're doing WilWheaton.net and about future plans for you and the site?

Wil: It's all part of my Bavarian Illuminatti–driven plot to rule the world. Now that you've read that, we're coming for you with our Orbital Mind Control Lasers.

---

* This question linked to a website containing pictures of me at about 14 years old, called "Wil Wheaton: Shirtless."

SLASHDOT.ORG

The original thread at Slashdot, complete with user comments as well as some of my own, can be found at *http://interviews.slashdot. org/article.pl?sid=01/10/29/173252.*

ASK WIL WHEATON ANYTHING

Wil Wheaton is our latest interview victim. Best known here as Wesley Crusher on *TNG*, Wil has a history doing movies both good (*Stand by Me*) and, uh, otherwise. His movie, *The Good Things*, just won the grand prize at the 27th Festival of American Cinema at Deuville. His current project is *Jane White Is Sick & Twisted*. A big thanks to Wil for taking the time to answer so many of our questions.

THOSE SILLY AUTOMATIC DOORS

By wikki on 07:36 AM October 15th, 2001: When you were on the set of TNG, did you ever find yourself running into the automatic doors when there was no one there to open them for you? How about at your house or other places? Was this a problem for any of the other cast members? Did you ever find yourself going to grocery stores and running in and out of the doors just to make you feel better?

This happened all the time. We'd get so used to those doors opening when we approached them that we'd keep going right into them if they didn't. It was very embarrassing when I'd be taking some friends on a tour of the sets, and I'd expect the doors to open, and they wouldn't. Sometimes it would happen during work, because the FX guys wouldn't get their cue, or someone would decide to enter a scene early. One time, Jonathan was in the turbolift on the bridge and decided that he'd come into the scene a little bit earlier than we'd rehearsed. So I'm sitting in my chair, Patrick is going on and on about the Prime Directive or something, and there is this loud CRASH! from the turbolift. We all turn around to look, and the doors slowly open (like the FX guy is scared to open the door), and Jonathan is on the floor. I think it was Michael Dorn who was in the turbolift with him, and he is standing over him, just pointing and laughing. We did a lot of that on *TNG*. The pointing and laughing, I mean.

Those doors do have a legacy that cascades into my current work. They were loud when they opened and closed, sort of like a sliding glass door. So the sound man would ask us to hold our dialogue until the doors were open or closed. Go watch *TNG* and watch for it. We rarely speak when doors are opening or closing on screen, because we'd have to re-record the dialogue later in ADR.* The thing is, even though I've been off the show for years, when I'm doing a movie today, I still don't talk when doors are opening or closing. Even if they're normal doors.

One time, I was at the grocery store, walking through the doors in a wistful attempt to recapture the magic, and I was attacked by some Girl Scouts. Apparently, they were trying to sell those damn cookies (which are Soylent Green, by the way—you heard it here, first), and I was scaring off the potential customers. Those Girl Scouts are very territorial, and they'll stab you in the neck if you don't watch it.

WHERE'S THE PARTIES, DUDE?

By imrdkl on 07:48 AM October 15th, 2001: Seriously, how much time do you spend reading techie sites like Slashdot and keeping up with the issues? I see lots of nice links and banners on your webpage that seem

---

* *ADR* stands for Automated Dialogue Replacement or Additional Dialogue Recording depending on who you ask. It's something actors do to replace dialogue when there are problems with production audio (like the doors, or an airplane, or a grip coughing offstage). It's also called "looping," because in the old days, editors would put together actual loops of film from the affected scenes and record the actors as they lipsynched themselves. It's not the easiest thing in the world, because we have to have perfect timing to match the movement of our mouths, and also perfect vocalization to match our performance. Just about every scene where we're walking down the corridors of the *Enterprise* was looped, because the floor always creaked under the weight of the camera dolly.

*to advocate. How would you "rate your geekness"? Is setting up your
own server really fun for you, or just another way to score babes? :-)*

Thanks, I enjoy a lot of your work.

Well, here's my geek code:

```
- - -BEGIN GEEK CODE BLOCK -   - -

Version: 3.12

GPA d - ( - -) s:- a- C++++ UL P>++ L+>++++ E -  W+++ N+ o- K-
w++++> -  - O -  M+ V -  PS++(+++) PE Y++ PGP++>+++ t++@($) 5 X+++
R++ tv -  b+++ DI+D++G++ e*>++++ h -  -  r+++ y+++

- - - END GEEK CODE BLOCK -  -  -
```

I've been reading /. (Slashdot) for a few years. It was my home
page for a while, even. I check in a few times a day, so I can keep
up on what's going on and complain that none of my submis-
sions are ever taken. The issues that I am most passionate about
are Privacy and YRO (Your Rights Online). Every chance I get,
I bug these guys to publish a quarterly YRO journal. Unfortunately, every chance has been once.

Setting up my own server is still beyond my abilities, but it is
something I will be able to do, someday. Often, when I'm in a
"down cycle," or whatever the buzzword is for not working for
months at a time, I think about getting a "fall back" job, so I
could have a regular day job if I ever needed it. Recently, I've
been thinking very seriously about pursuing a CCNA (Cisco
Certified Network Associate).

BORN A GEEK, OR DID ST PUSH YOU IN THAT DIRECTION?

*By anvilmark on 12:27 PM October 15th, 2001: Did you have a
technical inclination prior to ST:TNG? Did you become more/less interested in tech from your ST experience? If so, in what ways?*

Ever since I was a kid, I've been interested in science and engineering. Unfortunately, my complete inability to do simple
mathematics (when I got my SATs back, it said "3% of people
who take this will score higher than you" in the verbal section—

it said 95%"would score higher than me in math) really interferes with my ability to take my interests further than just a hobby. I built one of those crystal radio kits when I was 8 though . . . that was pretty cool. And I *did* assimilate lots of other computers to make mine.

I've been a voracious reader my whole life, reading mostly non-fiction books, up until I was about 13 or 14, when I read Ringworld . . . something about reading that book . . . it was like a switch was turned on inside my head, and I suddenly couldn't get enough of science fiction. I read all of Niven's books, then nearly everything Asimov had ever penned . . . *Ender's Game* . . . all of what are considered the classics, I guess. During that time, I developed this insatiable desire to understand the science behind the science fiction, so I read many of Asimov's nonfiction books, starting with his *Guide to Earth and Space*. I think that Asimov is truly one of the greatest authors of all time. For actors, his *Guide to Shakespeare* is required reading. Anyway, after reading some of his books, I read *The Mind's Sky*, *A Brief History of Time*, and, finally, *Hyperspace*. It was really cool to be reading about all that theory and acting it out at the same time. I wonder if any of the other actors got it when there'd be a graphic in engineering labeled "Kaluza-Klein Field."

I spent hundreds of hours, over the years hanging out with Rick Sternbach (in addition to all his great contributions to *Trek*, Rick also illustrated the cover of *Tales of Known Space*, and autographed my copy, which was cool) and Mike Okuda, in the art department, asking them all about what made the ship go (because I look for things . . . things to make me go . . .), and making sure that I was touching the buttons in the correct sequence to do whatever I was supposed to be doing. Once, in 10th or 11th grade, I had to write a research paper, and I got permission from my teacher to do it on the fictional technology of *Star Trek*, focusing on propulsion. This was before Mike and Denise had written their books, so I actually had to interview the

Techies on our show. (Oh, I guess they like to be called "Tech-ers." Sorry.) Anyway, I had to conduct interviews with them and buy some of the fan-authored books . . . but the final project was really cool, and I was forever able to explain to tour groups exactly what each thing in the engine room did.

Wow. I am realizing what a super geek I am. But that makes me cool, right? Right?

I've just remembered something that I haven't thought about in years. Sorry for the tangent. I know this is sort of off-topic, but you can't mod me down! *cackle* Ahh, the sweet, sweet elixir of corrupting power!

Once, I was at a Los Angeles–area convention—not as a guest, but as a convention attendee, complete with badge and geeky T-shirt. I'm thinking it was LosCon, but I'm not sure. It's not important. The important thing is, I tied an onion to my belt, which was the style at the time, and I walked into a room where there were lots of authors signing books. One of the authors there was Larry Niven. I just about gave birth. I had just finished reading *Ringworld* and *Ringworld Engineers*, and I was in the middle of *Tales of Known Space*. I had even bought a copy of *Ringworld* while I was at this con, I think as a gift or something, without knowing that Niven was there. So I ran up to him, and the exchange went something like this:

> *Me: Oh my god! You're Larry Niven!*
> *Him: Oh my god! You're Wil Wheaton!*
> *Me: I love your books so much! [Insert huge geek out here]*
> *Him: I love you on Star Trek! [Insert minor geek out here]*
> *Me: Really?!*
> *Him: Really?!*
> *Me: Yes!*
> *Him: Yes!*
> *Together: Can I have your autograph?!*

No kidding. That really happened, and it was just amazing. I will never forget that. Stuff like that happens sometimes, and I always love it when I meet someone who I admire, and they're just as excited to meet me. When I was working on *Flubber*, one of the other actors—I think it was Clancy Brown—came up to me on the first day and said, "Wil. I have to come out of the closet." I thought it was weird that he was coming out to me, but I said, "Okay . . . .?" And he says, "I am a huge *Star Trek* fan. I didn't want that to get in the way of our work."

I looked at him, and said, "Clancy, Robin Williams is a huge *Star Trek* fan, too. . . and THERE CAN BE ONLY ONE!"

And I cut off his head.

WESLEY CRUSHER JOKES

By DarkDust on 07:58 AM October 15th, 2001: As you mentioned on your FAQ page, the Wesley Crusher character from TNG was target of some not very complementary jokes. But are there any Wesley Crusher jokes that you liked ?

I can't recall any that I thought were very funny, actually. They are all pretty much just variations on the same theme, and I just don't find being sodomized by a Klingon to be the height of humor. Unless it's animated by Terry Gilliam.

There is a funny story that involves the whole "put Wesley in the airlock" phenomenon . . . I wrote about it at my site a few weeks ago, and I'll reprint it here:

It was my fanatical love of *The Prisoner** that allowed me to understand why anyone would want to wear a spacesuit and go to a convention. Because I used to have a lame little Number 6 pin, and I would wear it to game cons, back in the day.

---

* *The Prisoner* is a British cult TV show from the 1960s starring Patrick McGoohan. It is easily one of my favorite TV shows of all time. I was introduced to it right after I started working on *TNG*, and I fell in love with it. In fact, without *The Prisoner*, I wonder if I'd ever have been able to grok what it means for Trekkies to fully nerd out over *Star Trek*.

This reminds me of this one time I went to a huge game con, and some guy was selling "Put Wesley In The Airlock" buttons. I went up to his table, and he saw me coming and tried to hide them, but I got there too fast and took one. While I was looking at it, I could see the huge drops of sweat falling off his Hutt-like visage, and I asked him, "How much?" He told me $2.50, or something like that, so I bought it and wore it on my Batman T-shirt the rest of the day. That was cool.

ENTERPRISE

By abde on 08:00 AM October 15th, 2001: I liked your brief appearance in the Sprite commercial :) My question is, have you thought about sticking with the Star Trek *franchise? With* Enterprise, *the franchise is taking a new direction, in which the characters are more human and not ultra-competent Utopians. Have you considered trying for a part, recurring or otherwise?*

I've thought about it, sure. I even made calls to Berman and Co. back in the day, with some cool ideas, which were never developed.

I really like *Enterprise*. I watch it every week in the hopes of seeing more naked T'Pol. As much as I loved *TNG*, it did wear on me a bit that everyone was so damn perfect. I love that the new show has lots of conflict, and the crew seems to be in real danger each week. The cast is great, and, so far, they haven't completely ruined the continuity of the *Trek* universe. Also, the captain has a beagle. A beagle! And he talks to it! You have to love that.

However, I left *Trek* when I was 18 so I wouldn't be doing it for the rest of my career. Trying out for a regular role on the new show would be a step back, career-wise, and very unlikely, considering the treatment I've gotten at the hands of Berman and Company since I left. However, I would be open to guesting, and I'm really sad that I don't get to be in the movie. Especially if there's a wedding in the script. I think it'd give some nice closure to the character.

ARE YOU WORRIED ABOUT BEING TYPECAST?

By wrinkledshirt on 08:03 AM October 15th, 2001: Jason   Alex-
*ander once said in an interview that every single episode he did as George
on* Seinfeld *made it harder and harder for him to be marketable in show-
biz as any other sort of character. Given that most people know you as
Wesley Crusher, do you ever worry about it? If that's a problem, how
does an actor break out of it?*

When I was 18, I was beginning to have precisely those feelings
that Jason talks about. I did an interview with AICN, where I got
to talk about that. Success is a double-edged sword, you know?
On one side, it's simply amazing to be associated with such a successful show and play a character that so many people get to
know. On the other side, that association can utterly kill any
chance you have of having a career beyond that show.

I have no idea how an actor breaks out of that, because Hollywood works very hard to establish an actor as a "type" and then
leaves that actor in that "type" because they know that the audience will tune in to see it. Bob Saget is a perfect example. Holy
shit. He is one of the dirtiest, funniest, stand-up comedians I've
ever seen . . . but Hollywood just won't cast him in an "edgy"
role, because he's forever the guy from *Full House.*

Hollywood is all about insecurity. Studio heads know that
their jobs are only temporary, and they know that when they
make one mistake, they're gone. So they don't like to take
chances. They don't like to take an actor who is good in action
and put him in a comedy, because the audience may not buy it,
and the actor may not be able to handle the role.

I have a reputation in Hollywood as a very good dramatic
actor, and I think I've earned that, and I'm proud of it. What's
currently driving me crazy is this reluctance by the industry to let
me show them that I'm funny. It's maddening, because I've been
doing very funny sketch comedy at the ACME Comedy Theatre, and improv with the Liquid Radio Players and Los Angeles

Theatresports. I have a plan, though. I adapted one of my sketches into a screenplay, and if this thing I talk about in my next answer works out, I can just make it myself and take over the WORLD! </scheme>

NEWTEKAND THE VIDEO TOASTER

By suso on 08:11 AM October 15th, 2001: On your homepage, you mention that you once worked for NewTek during their development or initial release of the Video Toaster. I've always been curious to know how you got the job there and what you exactly did for them? Did you ever own an Amiga prior to working at NewTek?

I was invited to NewTek's XXXmas party when I was 19, and I was simply blown away by what they were doing out there.

For those not familiar, NewTek was the company that brought desktop video to the consumer market while also redefining the professional market. They made The Video Toaster, which was an amazing, affordable way to make television yourself that looked as good as the stuff the networks made, with nifty effects, graphics, and what was probably the coolest 3D program back then.

I firmly believe that the Video Toaster created the market for the iMovie and the other rash of desktop video solutions.

While I worked there, I was part of the research and development team, working mostly on the Video Toaster 4000. I also spent LOTS of time traveling around the country giving demos and stuff for the launch of the 4000 when it was finished.

The year and a half I spent at NewTek was one of the best in my life, as far as personal growth goes. I learned that I *can* make it in the Real World, but, more importantly, I learned that I am very unhappy if I'm not being an actor. I'm a pretty skeptical person, but I tell you this: I really believe that "do what you're supposed to do" stuff, and I learned, while I was there, that I am supposed to be an actor.

I had this plan when I worked for NewTek, and, unfortunately, I never got to complete it. It went something like this: I can write, and I can write well. I have TONS of creative ideas, that would make cool short films, but none of them would ever make money or be suitable for TV. In short, no network or studio would ever give me the money to make them. So I decided that I would make them myself, using a digital video camera and the Video Toaster. I'd give the movies to NewTek, and they could use them in marketing as an example of what the Toaster could do.

Good idea, right? We all thought so, and we were doing it, until NewTek fell apart, and the core group left to form Play Incorporated, in the mid-90s. It's actually a good thing that NewTek imploded, because it gave me this kick in the ass to get back to LA and rededicate myself to acting. However, a few years went by, and I was feeling like I had started this thing and never finished it, which was bugging me. So I called up Paul Montgomery, my friend who left NewTek and became the vision behind Play Inc. Paul thought it was a great idea, and we started working out the kinks. And there were some kinks, believe me. There were some people at Play who I just couldn't work with. Paul and I were in the process of working all that out when Paul had a heart attack and died, at age 31. Holy shit. Paul was the soul of NewTek and the soul of Play. With him gone, Play completely fell apart. I tried to keep going with our idea, because that's what I thought he'd want, but the person who took over Play was just impossible. He treated me so badly, and so dishonored Paul's memory, that I told him to shove it, and walked away. Shortly after Paul died, they ran Play into the ground, too. Completely sucked, because Play had amazing potential.

Thing is, I still want to make my own movies, and I still think that people like you and me can do it with great ease, using tools like the iMovie. Matter of fact, if anyone reading this knows people at Apple, have them get in touch with me. I'd still like to produce my own stuff, and I'm thinking iMovie is the way to go, now, as far as I can tell.

I never owned an Amiga before working at NewTek, but I loved them while I had them. They were always easy to use and stable as hell. Too bad Commodore never "got" the Amiga. Yet another example of Corporate America failing to see the forest through the trees.

USENET

By Herbmaster on 08:16 AM October 15th, 2001: When did you first hear of the classic Usenet group, alt.wesley.crusher.die.die.die, and what was your reaction?

I first became aware of it while visiting the HAL labs in Urbana, Illinois on the 12th of January, 1992. I really didn't care about it, at first, because by that time I had gotten used to people hating not only Wesley, but me. Over the years, though, all that negativity and the inability to separate me from a character I played has really wore on me. Since I launched my website, I now have a presence on the Internet, and a lot of that crap has come crashing back down on me. Honestly, you'd think that people would grow up and move on, seeing as it was so many years ago, but you'd be wrong. You know what's weird? It hurt, all that criticism. It hurt then, and it still hurts now. Sometimes it just makes me feel bad, and other times, it makes me mad. Once, after enduring a particularly vicious attack from someone, I wrote:

> *Thank you for blaming ME for the writing of a fictional character, on a fictional TV show. That makes complete sense, considering all the input the writers would take from a 15-year-old kid. Have you ever bothered to ask? Did it ever occur to you that I just said the lines I was given? Don't take it out on me. I'm just an actor, who did the best job he could with what he was given.*

*I don't care if you're The Guy From TV or if you're the kid from
math class. Being personally attacked by people who don't know a
thing about you hurts. It sucks. I wonder, do you spend a fifth of the
time you spend dumping on me doing something constructive with your
life? I certainly hope so. You people are just like the people in high
school who never took the time to get to know me and judged me before
I even showed up.*

*Aren't we mostly geeks here, online? Didn't we all, at one time or
another, get bullied by the cool kids? Don't any of you remember what
that felt like?*

So, yeah. That's how I reacted when I was hurt and mad. It's
strange to me that I'm 29 now, and people are still giving me shit
for a show that I did when I was 15. What's surprising to me,
still, is that I even care, and that the criticism still hurts. If I could
only live my life with my threshold at 4.

WIL'S JOB AT NEWTEK'S LIGHTWAVE

By peter303 on 08:17 AM October 15th, 2001: *You worked at the
animation software shop NewTek for a while. What did you do there?
Do you thing you'll get back into tech again someday?*

Well, I think I pretty much covered the NewTek stuff already,
but as far as tech goes, the farthest I can go with my technical skill
is what I've done with my website. I think I've come a long way
from my first überlame page that I built with Pagebuilder at
Geocities. The problem that I always run into is that my aspira-
tions constantly out pace my abilities. I have these dreams of
doing all sorts of amazingly cool PHP things at my site, but these
are months, maybe even a year off. Technology is moving so
quickly these days, if you stop to look around, you get left in the
dust, and it's pretty hard for me to keep up.

I have always loved technology, and when I can afford it, I will have all the cool tech toys that they sell at ThinkGeek. They will be mine. Oh yes. They will be mine.

HOLLYWOOD ACTIVISM

By Dunkirk on 08:23 AM October 15th, 2001: Wil, you have made comments to the effect of poo-poo'ing celebrity opinions about issues in general. Yet in your blogs, you spend a lot of time discussing politics, and you make no bones about which side of the isle you favor. As someone in the public spotlight—and especially as someone in the geek spotlight (being a celeb that has your own self-coded website)—do you consider it a duty of sorts to be an activist? Does being a celeb[rity] bring any more responsibility over the common, First Amendment–empowered citizen in voicing your opinion? Also, do you feel that you have qualities above and beyond other Hollywood celebrities that makes it important that you share your feelings?

Thanks,

dk

One of my defining characteristics is that I can't keep my mouth shut. I can't stand idly by, and if somebody has to say it, it may as well be me. I am extremely passionate about virtually everything, and that passion drives me to discuss, argue, and learn about issues that have an effect on my life. I'm sure that it would just be easier to stay quiet and live happily in McWorld, but I will not go gently into that good night.

I don't know if I have qualities above and beyond other celebrities that make it important to share my feelings. I don't know because I don't hang out with other celebrities, at all. But I do know that my passion is genuine, and I really do care about the issues I discuss. I don't know what the others do, but I carefully research issues before I get on one side of them. I evaluate both sides of an issue and apply my own filters, based on my knowledge and previous experiences. I draw a conclusion, I test the conclusion, I form an opinion, and then I post about it. I just write about the things that matter to me. I would be writing about this stuff, even if nobody came to my website to read about it. However, for better or for worse, in our culture we tend to give more attention to a celebrity than an equally educated non-celebrity. So if I can use my visibility to bring attention to the idiocy of the DMCA (Digital Millennium Copyright Act), or the things the MPAA (Motion Picture Association of America) and RIAA (Recording Industry Association of America) have been pulling the last two years, then I will do it, gladly. That falls under the heading of "Using the Power of Celebrity for Good." Of course, I'm sure it's fun to use it for Evil, but that opportunity hasn't presented itself to me yet.

I don't want people to listen to me because they think I'm a celebrity. I don't view myself as a "celebrity" at all. Matter of fact, one of the freakiest and most surprising things I've discovered since I launched my website is that way more people know my work than I ever imagined. So I guess that makes me a celebrity to some people, but not in my own mind, if that makes any sense.

RADIO FREE BURRITO

By webword on 08:42 AM October 15th, 2001: You seem to know a lot about music. How big is your collection? What are your favorite bands? What is Radio Free Burrito and what do you think of broadcasting live?

I am a total music weenie. I aspire to be like the guys in High Fidelity. Yeah, I'm that lame.

As I say on my music page, I think that you can learn a lot about a person through the music they listen to. The bands that I like—though they cross many genres—all have souls. What I mean by that is, all the bands I really like all say something with their music. It somehow affects me when I listen to it. The first time I listened to *Kid A*, for example, I had this visceral, emotional reaction to it, and I still get that when I hear it. When I hear the first "ping" of "Echoes",* I still get chills. I am so awed by the power of music to evoke emotion in people, and I admire the bands who take advantage of that power and use it for Good. Pop music is so packaged and over-produced, and so clearly exists only to make money, that it just offends me. That's using the power of music for Evil. Unless you're Huey Lewis and The News. Then you use music for The Power of Love.

I have a real fondness in my heart for the Emo bands and the indie rock. Some of my current listens are Radiohead, The Pixies, Tool, The Ataris, Coldplay, They Might Be Giants, Portishead, *NSYNC, (just seeing if you're skimming or really listening. har.), Pink Floyd, The Rushmore soundtrack, fairview, Alkaline Trio, Hot Water Music, and The Get Up Kids.

Tangent, here: I think The Ataris are like a musical Linux, sort of. They publish all the lyrics for their songs, as well as the guitar tabs, and make every single one of their songs available as an MP3 for free download. Yet they still make tons of money at MP3.com, and their records sell like crazy. I think it's a great analogy . . . you don't have to be closed source to be profitable.

Radio Free Burrito is my attempt to fulfill a childhood dream of being a DJ. I stream my MP3s through a Live365 server using shoutcast almost every day, and I do live broadcasts a few times a week, where I joke, do news "Letterman-style," run a chat room, and stuff like that. It's really fun, and I still get this giddy excitement when I check the station stats and see that there's 50 people listening. Broadcasting live is insanely fun and gives me another chance to reach an audience directly, on my terms, rather than for some producer or network. I have a whole

---

* "Echoes" takes up all of Side Two of Pink Floyd's 1971 record *Meddle*. (For those readers who are under 25, ask your parents what a "record" is. Living history is fun!)

page at my site devoted to the rfb, with a playlist and links to hi-fi and lo-fi streams. Come listen someday. You'll be glad you did! </shiteating grin>

My CD collection is HUGE. I think I have over 6,000 CDs in various places around my house and in the garage. I would have more, but when I moved out of my parent's house, my younger brother moved into my bedroom, and sold all of my Cure, Depeche, Bauhaus, Boingo, and other 80s alterna-rock at some used music store. I think he used the money to buy rugs. Not drugs, rugs. My brother has had a rug habit for years. Persians, throws, areas, even Berber carpets. Sad thing is, he can't admit he has a problem. He's probably at Carpeteria right now.

WESLEY VS. ADRIC

By wowbagger on 08:51 AM October 15th, 2001: Many   people have compared Wesley Crusher to Adric on Dr. Who. In both cases, the character was reviled because of the way the writers handled him. What are your thoughts on this? How would you recommend an actor handle this sort of situation in the future?

Okay, first let me put on my Asbestos suit.

Alright. I don't know who Adric is, so I can't address that.

duck

However, I can address the rest of your question. When I was on *TNG*, I had zero input into the character. The writers and producers never listened to me, and they shouldn't have. I was a teenager, and, contrary to what we all teenagers think at the time, teenagers know absolutely nothing. Of course, at the time, we as teenagers clearly know everything, so we get caught in an infinite loop of knowing everything and nothing at once, which should produce a wonderful, Zen-like existence, but never does . . . but I digress.

As an actor, I feel that it is my job to live up to the demands of the script and perform what the writers are asking me to do. I did my best to fulfill that obligation, but I think the writers missed a huge part of Wesley, and I think that's why so many people didn't like him.

Wesley and I were very similar at the time: we were both teenagers who were pretty smart and pretty skilled. Matter of fact, we were both smart enough and skilled enough to work alongside adults and hold our own with them professionally. At the same time, neither one of us had the grace, maturity, or wisdom to hold our own with them socially or emotionally, and that created lots of conflicts. By not exploring that side of Wesley, beyond "Just tell me to shut up, Wesley, and I will," the writers took a lot of his humanity away from him. It also didn't help that they gave me lines like, "We're from Starfleet! We don't lie!" and "You mean I'm drunk? I feel strange, but also good!"

The few episodes where Wesley was actually not a complete tool were, I think, "The First Duty," "Final Mission," and one or two others. Those were the ones where Wesley was actually a fully developed, flawed, interesting person. If they'd given me more stories like those, and written my character more like he was in those episodes, it may have made it easier for me to miss the film opportunities that were passing me by while I was saying "Aye, sir. Warp 4, sir."

GEEKESS OR VALLEY GIRL?

by Dyrandia on 08:54 AM October 15th, 2001: As a lifelong geekess whose first crush was on Wesley Crusher, here's a question I'd love answered by Wil Wheaton, as well as the general male Slashdot population. Which would Wesley Crusher, in character, prefer? An attractive, yet slightly braindead, clothes/hair/nails-oriented girl, or her equally attractive, intelligent geekess identical twin sister? Someone who can't carry on a conversation unless it involves who was seen where, with whom, and what each was wearing, or someone who can argue the pros and cons of which programming language suits a certain task best?

What about you as a person?

This is such a no-brainer. Geekess. Duh. Especially if she's a karma-whore. That is *so* sexy.

DEAR WIL

by sllort on 09:27 AM October 15th, 2001: Wil, you mention in a LA Times interview that you dumped Linux for Windows because "While I'm a champion of open source, I don't think Linux is there yet." Was there a specific bug in Linux that prompted you to dump it, or was it just the entire operating system?

Thanks!

When I said "Not ready for prime time," I was not putting down Linux. "Not ready for prime time" means to me that it's not ready for The Masses. That's not necessarily a bad thing. SNL wasn't ready for prime time back when it started, and it was superior to virtually everything else on TV. Now that it's been processed for The Masses, I think it sucks more often than not. Except Will Farrell. That man is a genius.

I had Linux installed, and I dual-booted for quite sometime, but I was never able to actually ★use★ it to do anything. I have given O'Reilly LOTS of my money over the years, attempting to learn how to run it, but it's always ★just★ eluded my grasp. I had the hardest time just getting it to do things like find my sound card or give me fonts in X-Windows when I was running Netscape that didn't make my eyes bleed. It also didn't help that when I did my install, it never seemed to tell me exactly what dependencies I needed, so lots of stuff didn't work correctly, and I could never figure out where things were supposed to go, which was frustrating to me. I rely on computers for too much in my life to make my primary OS one that doesn't run in idiot (also known as Wil Wheaton) mode.

I completely support the Open Source and Free Software movements. Let's just say that I hate The Borg as much as you do. I aspire to a complete removal of The Borg from my life, and

I would like nothing more than to be the number one ex-trek-actor Linux cheerleader, with the little suit and everything.

So have I just lost all of my cool points, or what?*

PATRICK STEWART'S BALD HEAD

By Genie1 on 09:40 AM October 15th, 2001: Have you (or any of the TNG cast) ever rubbed it for good luck?

Are you kidding me? We'd gather every Monday morning in the center of the bridge, cry havoc, and let slip the rubbing of Patrick's head. We always wanted to rub Shatner's bald head for luck, but he'd never take off his toupee. So we'd just rub his belly instead.

FAN FIXATED MOMENT?

By broody on 09:41 AM October 15th, 2001: While this may seem way off the wall, please give me a moment.

Kurt Russell, in the commentary to the Big Trouble in Little China *DVD, talks about how his trip down the elevator on the way to confront "the ultimate evil spirit" has generated more comments then any other. Fans are always quoting back lines from that scene, particularly in elevators.*

Here is the question: are there particular lines from one of your roles that fans repeat back to you? Which role do people most often identify you with when they see you in the real world? If you could change this defining moment to an alternate scene or line, what would it be and why?

People seem to think that it's really funny to ask me if I really have the biggest one in four counties. (I do, by the way. But the counties are all in the former Soviet Union, and none of them touch each other, for what it's worth.)

---

* About a year after this interview was conducted, I did switch to Linux (as mentioned earlier). In my home, I have two machines, currently running RedHat 9 and a hard drive install of Knoppix 3.4, which is based on Debian.

Something that I've noticed myself doing is quoting some of my own things, because sometimes it's just too funny not to. Once, I was working on a movie in Kansas. We were driving from the set to the house where we were all staying, and it was close to a 40-minute drive. Now, 40 minutes in a city is nothing. But 40 minutes along a rural highway seems like an eternity. So we're driving along, and I ask my friend if we're there yet, and he says no, so I say, "Jesus. By the time we get there, the kid won't even be dead anymore." There is this pause in the car, and one of the other actors says, "Dude. Did you just quote your own movie?" I answered in the affirmative, and he says, "That was very cool."

I find myself saying that things are "goochers" all the time, too. Does that make me lame?

I guess that the thing people say to me all the time is, "Were the leeches real?" They then turn to their frat guy friends and snicker, like they're the first person to ever say that to me. I wait for a second, so they think they've really cut me down, and I say, "Yeah. Ask your mom about my scar."

Finding new and preferably disgusting ways to degrade a friend's mother is always held in high regard.

INDUSTRY INSIDER?

By Stavr0 on 10:47 AM October 15th, 2001: Since you're part of Hollywood and somewhat of a geek (if you really are "CleverNick-Name"), here's the thing:

Would you be interested in becoming a (scifi/hollywoood/?) contributor to Slashdot (a la Jon Katz)? I'm sure you could get lots of exclusives from Paramount, actor friends etc. ...

...assuming ,of course, you're prepared to be a lightning rod for all the Katz-haters cum Wesley-haters ;-)

You know, I don't have a huge problem with Katz, and I don't really understand why some people do.

But, as we've discovered during our little chat today, I am exceedingly lame, so maybe there's part of the joke that I don't get.

Sure, I'd contribute, but I don't see what I could bring to the discussion that isn't already covered here, because nobody ever gives me exclusives, or inside info on anything, which is exactly the type of blinkard, Philistine, pig ignorance I've come to expect from that noncreative garbage. They sit there, on their spotty behinds, picking blackheads, with their bleeding Hollywood Insider secret handshakes . . . I always wanted to be a Hollywood Insider, but they wouldn't let me!

HOW DID YOU FEEL ABOUT BEING SLASHDOTTED?

By waffle zero on 10:51 AM October 15th, 2001: How did you feel about being Slashdotted? And did you expect this to happen?

Yeah, actually, we knew it was coming, and I got really nervous. I've endured some pretty horrible slings and arrows over the years, the most recent coming from MeFi and MemePool within 24 hours of my launch. This may sound totally lame to you, but I really cared what /.-ers thought about my site and about me, because when you get right down to it, I am just an insecure geek, hoping to someday sit with the cool kids. The guys who host me were a little nervous, because we knew that it would kill all the sites on the server. By the way, if you're a weblogger and want hosting for five bucks a month, you should check logjamming out. They're really cool guys.

I gotta say that the coolest thing so far was just being asked to do the interview, and all the positive feedback I've gotten from people who came to see my site. The whole reason I made my website is my wife is always telling me that I could shake the *Star Trek* thing, and the *Stand By Me* thing, if people would just get to know me. I've always been frustrated that people, inside the industry and out, have this one-dimensional preconception of me. Building and running my website has given me a chance to challenge that preconception, and hopefully change it.

This interview has been really fun to do, and I want to thank Chris for asking me, Rob for e-mailing me and telling me not to be afraid, and everyone who posted questions and comments.

Oh, and that guy who said, "Shut up, Wesley!" That was really funny. I've never heard that before.

FNORD.

Acknowledgments

WHENEVER I OPEN A CD from one of my friends' bands, I scan the acknowledgments, hoping to see my name stuck down there, near Zildjan, Fender, Patricia Ford, Brianna Banks, Jenna Jameson, and Sky Lopez. However, my name is never there. Sure, I supported them, went to their shows, and listened to their jam sessions. But there is only so much room for thanks, and including me would mean taking out someone else who deserved to be there.

I mention this, because I *really* hope that more porn stars will e-mail me so they can make it into the next book. I also offer this as an apology to all the people who I love, and who love me, who won't get thanked here. If I listed all of you, it would fill its own book. Having said that, there are a few people who were instrumental in seeing the book completed, and I would like to thank them now.

Mom and Dad, Jeremy, and Amy. You have been with me my entire life. Without you, there are no memories, and no stories to tell.

Anne, Ryan, and Nolan. You looked at my back for months while I wrote this, and endured my temper tantrums when I couldn't get words to string together just the way I wanted them. You are my life.

Gene Roddenberry. Thank you for letting me spend some time beneath the wing of The Great Bird Of The Galaxy.

Mrs. Westerholm. In 7th grade, you told me that I was a great writer who would publish a book someday. Thank you for encouraging me. We need more teachers like you.

Mrs. Lee. In 9th grade, you told me that I was a terrible writer who would never amount to anything, because I was a stupid actor. Kiss my ass, baby.

Marian Fife. You took me from 10th to 12th grade in the "real" Starfleet Academy. I credit you with my relentless drive to be the best I can be.

Brett McLaughlin. You knew when to push, when to back off, and have an uncanny knack for picking out the stuff that sucks from the stuff that doesn't suck.

Everyone at O'Reilly Media, but especially Sara, Kyle, Kathryn, Ellie, David, Mary, and, of course, Tim.

Loren Cox, Josh Sisk, and Ben Claassen. You guys encouraged me to build WIL WHEATON dot NET. Without your moral and technical support, the website would never have been more than an idea. The weblog that is the foundation of this book would not exist.

Chris Black and Hank Hedland. You've made such a difference in my career . . . if I ever get back on camera, it will be due in large part to your hard work and faithful counsel.

Travis Oates, M.D. Sweeney, Dan O'Connor, Tracy Burns, Susie Geiser, and Cynthia Szgeti. You all taught me how to trust my instincts and encouraged me to develop my comedic voice.

The cast of *Crouching Tiger, Hidden Sunday Show*. We found our funny together.

Sam Christiensen. When I (and Hollywood) had no idea who I was, you helped me discover my essences. Without you,

I'd never know that I'm passionate, uncompromising, wry, crackling, unfulfilled, honorable, and too smart for my own good.

Oingo Boingo and Cake provided the soundtrack for the first draft. Massive Attack, Portishead, Underworld, Blueman Group and Dirty Vegas provided the soundtrack for the first rewrite. U2, Led Zeppelin, Pink Floyd, The Beatles, The Getup Kids, Saves The Day, and The Pixies provided the soundtrack for the final draft.

John Kovolic. You are an amazing artist and creator, and I am so honored that you gave me drawings for this book. Just like Ben's illustrations in *Barefoot*, you've added an entirely new and wonderful level of humor and warmth to my story.

The Monkeyboxers and the Früdø crew: jbay, Roughy, Spudnuts, Greeny, Colin, MrsVeteran, JSc, Bobby the Mat, and bluesman. BINGO, fuckers! Rest in peace, Colin.

Drew Curtis and all the TotalFarkers. Thanks for providing just the right amount of distraction when I was in the homestretch.

Jen Frazier and all the GeekMonkeys at ThinkGeek.com. Thanks for hooking me up with all sorts of cool geek gear for the cover shoot. I swear that Guinness just compiles better when I drink it from a pint glass labeled #include <beer.h>

Maryelizabeth Hart at Mysterious Galaxy, Amber Berger at Powell's, Steve Jackson at Steve Jackson Games, and Warehouse 23 all stocked *Dancing Barefoot* when nobody was really sure if I could actually do this writing thing. Thank you for believing in me.

Everyone who has read, linked to, and contributed comments to WWdN over the last three years. You all encouraged me to write a book. Well, here it is!

Cory Doctorow, Dan Perkins and Rob Matsushita. Your advice and encouragement have made this book better and made me a better writer. Thank you.

Kathleen McGivney. I'm so glad we're friends. Thanks for your encouragement during the "this sucks and nobody's going to like it so let's just get drunk" hours. Your One Eyed Cat has a Cult!

I must also give very special thanks to my good friend Andrew Hackard. Andrew took time off from his real job at Steve Jackson Games to edit the first draft of this book. Andrew's red pen, knowledge of the rules of English grammar, and tireless support have made all the difference. Without Andrew's devotion and care, this book wouldn't have ever made it past the "hey, maybe I'll write a book" stage.

Finally, Nunu and Aunt Val. Somehow, I think playing "The Gong Show" in the kitchen at Topanga when I was three had something to do with all of this. I miss you. I love you.

Further Reading

OF COURSE, THE STORY that you've read here is just the beginning. A LOT has happened since I first wrote this, and there are lots of stories that I just couldn't include because of space and time, and spacetime (stupid laws of physics.) Some of the stories that I think are cool, but didn't make the cut, are in my first book, *Dancing Barefoot*, which is also conveniently available from O'Reilly Media.

You can also point your browser to *www.wilwheaton.net*, and you can read all the original weblog posts, including the original comments! Marvel at my terrible spelling! Gasp in horror as I mangle the English language with my "style!"

Colophon

The first draft of this book was written online, using Blogger, then Greymatter, and finally Movable Type. I took all that material and moved it into OpenOffice.org 1.0.1. Along the way, I used gEdit, Kwrite, and occasionally *vim* (sorry, but I couldn't find the text editor in *emacs*). The first rewrite was done in OpenOffice.org 1.0.2. Then I hosed the the *gdm* login manager on my Linux machine and moved everything to my iBook. The entire final draft was completed in Apple's TextEdit.

Mary Brady was the production editor and the copyeditor for *Just a Geek*. Philip Dangler was the proofreader. Darren Kelly and Claire Cloutier provided quality control.

Ellie Volckhausen designed the cover of this book and produced the cover layout with Adobe InDesign 2.0.2 using Adobe's Syntax font and Shy Font's Movie Poster.

David Futato designed the interior layout. This book was converted by Julie Hawks to FrameMaker 5.5.6. The text font is Adobe's Bembo; the heading font is Syntax; and the code font is LucasFont's TheSans Mono Condensed. The cartoons for each Act were drawn by John Kovalic, Director of Dork Tower (*http://www.kovalic.com/*).